D1083587

JOHN DEWEY

Lectures in China, 1919–1920

THE EAST-WEST CENTER—formally known as "The Center for Cultural and Technical Interchange Between East and West" —was established in Hawaii by the United States Congress in 1960. As a national educational institution in cooperation with the University of Hawaii, the Center's mandated goal is "to promote better relations and understanding between the United States and the nations of Asia and the Pacific through cooperative study, training, and research."

Each year about 2,000 men and women from the United States and some 40 countries and territories of Asia and the Pacific area work and study together with a multi-national East-West Center staff in wide-ranging programs dealing with problems of mutual East-West concern. Participants are supported by federal scholarships and grants, supplemented in some fields by contributions from Asian/Pacific governments and private foundations.

Center programs are conducted by the East-West Communication Institute, the East-West Culture Learning Institute, the East-West Food Institute, the East-West Population Institute, and the East-West Technology and Development Institute. Open Grants are awarded to provide scope for educational and research innovation, including a program in humanities and the arts.

East-West Center Books are published by The University Press of Hawaii to further the Center's aims and programs.

JOHN DEWEY

LECTURES IN CHINA, 1919-1920

TRANSLATED FROM THE CHINESE AND EDITED BY

ROBERT W. CLOPTON / TSUIN-CHEN OU

AN EAST-WEST CENTER BOOK
THE UNIVERSITY PRESS OF HAWAII

Honolulu

Library of Congress Catalog Card Number 72-84061

ISBN 0-8248-0212-8

Copyright © 1973 by The University Press of Hawaii

All rights reserved

Manufactured in the United States of America

Designed by Eileen Cufley Williams

CONTENTS

INTRODUCTION

A half century has passed since John Dewey left China in 1921, after a visit of twenty-six months. His brief stay was one of the most significant and influential events in recent Chinese cultural history, but the Chinese have been so familiar with Dewey's influence that they have not bothered to analyze it, nor even to write extensively about it. Americans, on the other hand, are largely unfamiliar with Dewey's impact on Chinese thought. In view of the reputation he established throughout the world, it is scarcely surprising that special attention to Dewey's Chinese sojourn should have been delayed. Yet there can be no doubt that China was the one foreign country on which Dewey exercised his greatest influence, particularly in the field of education.[1]

It was not until the early 1950s, when the Chinese Communist regime began to purge Dewey's Chinese disciples in an effort to extirpate all traces of his pragmatic philosophy from the Chinese intellectual scene, that the West began to be fully aware of Dewey's incalculable influence on modern China. In a public lecture delivered in 1959 (the centennial of Dewey's birth) at the Third East-West Philosophers' Conference at the University of Hawaii, Hu Shih, an eminent contemporary Chinese philosopher, pointed out the importance and significance for China of Dewey's sojourn in that country.[2] In 1960 the Harvard University Press published *The May Fourth Movement, Intellectual Revolution in Modern China*, by Chow Tse-tsung, a volume which devotes a great deal of attention to Dewey's lectures in China, and which provides what is probably the most complete and authoritative analysis of his influence yet to appear in English. Father Berry's 33-page paper appeared in the same year. Since the publication of Hu Shih's lecture, Chow's book, and Fr. Berry's essay, scholars in the United States have taken an increasing interest in Dewey's China visit, his lectures there and his influence on contemporary Chinese cultural trends, and have come to recognize that the lack of any version in English of the lectures which exerted such a decisive influence constitutes a glaring and regrettable lacuna in Dewey scholarship. This volume and the typescript translations listed in Appendix B are an effort to remedy this lacuna.

It may seem strange that lectures originally delivered in English (Dewey did not speak Chinese) have to be returned to English from their original translation into Chinese. Hu Shih indicated in his "Introductory Note" to the *Morning Post* (Peking) publication in book form of some of the lectures that "Dr. Dewey intends to revise and expand his original lecture notes for publication in book form. When his manuscript is complete, I hope to translate it into Chinese, so that both English and Chinese versions can be published at the same time."[3]

Unfortunately, this intention was not carried out. While Dewey did make careful notes for his lectures, these notes were not preserved.[4] Mrs. Dewey generously gave one of the translators of the present volume access to Dewey's papers, but a diligent search revealed no notes in any way related to the lectures delivered in China.

While Chow uses extensive excerpts which he himself translated from Dewey's China lectures, and summarizes others, there has been no publication in English of the lectures as Dewey delivered them, and in the form in which they exerted such great influence.

There is at least one interesting precedent for a literary work's having to be translated from the Chinese back into the language in which it was originally written. A Buddhist classic, *Mahayāna-śraddotpādaśatra* [The Awakening of Faith], attributed to Aśvaghosa, was translated from Sanskrit into Chinese, first by Paramārtha in A.D. 553. Subsequently the original Sanskrit text was lost in India. Hsüan-tsang (A.D. 596–664) translated the text from Chinese back into Sanskrit and sent it to India.[5]

The translator-editors hope that this introduction to the English version of Dewey's China lectures will provide readers with a modicum of background on his sojourn in China, which will enable them better to appreciate the lectures themselves and to understand Dewey's impact on Chinese thought.

Dewey's Sojourn in China (May 1, 1919–July 11, 1921)

In January 1919, John Dewey and his wife, Alice Chipman Dewey, started on what was originally intended as a pleasure tour of the Orient.[6] While in California, however, Dewey was prevailed upon to deliver a series of lectures at the Imperial University of Japan in Tokyo. The series of eight lectures which he delivered there in February and March, 1919, was rewritten and published the following year as *Reconstruction in Philosophy*.[7] While lecturing in Tokyo, the Deweys received a joint invitation from five Chinese academic institutions to lecture in Peking, Nanking, and other cities in China. This invitation was prompted by three of Dewey's former students: Hu Shih, professor at the National Peking University; P. W. Kuo, president of the National Nanking Teachers College; and Chiang Monlin, editor of *New Education* magazine.

The Deweys arrived in Shanghai on May 1. Immediately after his arrival, Dewey addressed the Kiangsu Education Association on "The Relation between Democracy and Education." After visiting Hangchow and Nanking, Dewey settled in Peking, devoting most of his first year in China to several series of public lectures delivered in Peking and other cities. His reception was so cordial and enthusiastic, and he became so fascinated with the rapid and drastic social, political, and educational developments of the country, that he allowed himself to be persuaded by his Chinese friends to prolong his stay for another year. During his second year he taught regular courses at National Peking University, National Peking Teachers College, and National Nanking Teachers College. He also lectured in most of the coastal cities, and visited at least eleven different provinces: Fengtien, Chihli, Shansi, Shantung, Kiangsu, Chekiang, Kiangsi, Hunan, Hupeh, Fukien, and Kwantung. In one of his speeches Dewey mentioned that he had visited twelve cities. Whether he visited others afterwards has not been determined.

Everywhere Dewey was warmly received by teachers, students, intellectuals, government and social leaders, and the general public. He liked to mingle with the people, and was once photographed holding a small boy in his arms. During his visit, Dewey's name was constantly associated with that of Bertrand Russell, who was lecturing in China at the same time. Both men were so widely known that no educated person in any large city was unacquainted with their names.

In 1920 the National Peking University conferred on Dewey a doctorate *honoris causa*. The Deweys wrote numerous letters about their experiences and observations in China to their daughter Evelyn, who preserved, edited, and published them. Dewey also wrote numerous articles for the *New Republic* and for *Asia,* most of which were reprinted in 1929 in *Characters and Events.*[8]

The Deweys left China on July 11, 1921, to return to the United States, where he resumed his teaching duties at Columbia University. Altogether they had spent two years, two months, and ten days in China.

Factors which Created a Favorable Climate
for Dewey's China Lectures

Before considering the lectures themselves, it should prove instructive to glance briefly at three circumstances which combined to make it possible for Dewey to have so pronounced an impact, as these are alluded to by Berry and Chow.[9]

Increasing contact with the rest of the world throughout the nineteenth century, at first commercial, then intellectual, as well as in armed conflict, had shattered China's long tradition of isolationism, and had undermined her stability. In common with the rest of the world, though later than the nations of the West, China was beginning to be subject to the growth of industrialism. Western ideas and ideals appealed to the Chinese intelligentsia, more and more of whom came to look upon their own traditions as outmoded and unsuited for participation in the modern world.

The Manchu dynasty had been overthrown in 1911, but the republic which replaced it was far from stable, and political unrest was the order of the day. Japan's twenty-one demands in 1915, and then the Shantung resolution of the Versailles Peace Conference in 1919, incited students and new intellectual leaders to promote an anti-Japanese campaign and a vast modernization movement to build a new China through intellectual and social reforms, stressing primarily Western ideas of science and democracy.

Y. C. Wang points out that Confucianism, as a system of values which for centuries had governed virtually all aspects of traditional Chinese life, had been increasingly discredited during the late nineteenth and early twentieth centuries by attacks of Chinese intellectuals who had been educated in Japan and the West.[10] Finally, between 1915 and 1919, a group of Chinese professors, some trained in Japan and some in the West, carried the revolution beyond the political border into the realm of values. They held Confucianism to be the basic evil that must be discarded so that China could achieve true modernization .

It is only recently that the nature and extent of Western influence on

China, and the rapidity with which it became dominant, particularly in intellectual and educational circles, has been analyzed and assessed.

Educationally, the most striking feature was perhaps the returned students' dominating position. From 1902 on, college professors in China were either foreigners or foreign-trained Chinese, and after 1922 all of the important teaching and administrative positions fell to men educated in the West. To be sure, this monopoly did not mean that such men could do as they wished, for they still had to cope with a variety of social forces. Nevertheless, in a comparative sense they were almost in control of the situation.[11]

Books by Western authors were translated and published in Chinese by the score. The works of Herbert Spencer, Thomas Huxley, and Charles Darwin enjoyed great popularity among intellectuals—a fact which Berry sees as predisposing them to a ready acceptance of Dewey's pragmatism. In any case, it is difficult to cavil with the conclusion that Dewey arrived in China in 1919 in "the most critical years of modern Chinese history. The more westernized elements in Peking were taking control. Confucius, and his greatest modern defender, K'ang Yu-wei, under the assault led by Ch'en Tu-hsiu and Hu Shih, had just retired from the scene."[12]

The intellectuals of China were indeed hungry for ideas, eager for suggestions for ways in which they could remake their society so that China could take her place within the family of nations. They wanted something "to fill the vacuum left by the discredited Confucianism."[13] Dewey brought them bold ideas and offered concrete and practical suggestions, and he found a receptive and sympathetic audience. Berry characterizes this as "the supreme moment of intellectual communication between China and America. . . . Emotionally and intellectually the Chinese were keyed to hear and to give serious consideration to the thoughts that he [Dewey] would present to them."[14]

Notwithstanding the enthusiasm of the Chinese intellectuals for Dewey's ideas, these ideas could not have had the profound effect on the country at large that they did, had it not been for a second extremely important development in the years immediately preceding his visit. With certain important exceptions, for hundreds of years most of the books, magazines, and even newspapers of China had been printed in the language of the classical tradition, *kuo-wen.* This language was so different from *Paihua,* the spoken language, that it could be read and understood only by a small educated minority.

Around the turn of the century *Paihua*

. . . began to be used by a few scholar reformers and foreign missionaries in publishing periodicals, newspapers, and other writings. Ch'en Tu-hsiu and Hu Shih joined this movement during their youth, in 1904 and 1906. In the last quarter of the nineteenth century a great number of novels in the vernacular tradition had been produced, though they were not recognized as literary works.[15]

One of the manifestations of the New Literature movement which started in 1916, and in which both Ch'en and Hu Shih were prominent leaders, was the rapid shift of the periodical press to the vernacular. The leaders of this movement thought that they were being optimistic when they conjectured that the full transformation might take a decade or more, but the movement succeeded beyond their wildest hopes. Within four years "the vernacular language was widely used in the majority of student publications. Almost all magazines, newspapers, and literary writings began to change to the new literary medium."[16] By the time of Dewey's arrival in China, *Paihua*

. . . had become the language of the schools, and the re-education of China was begun in earnest. Politics, language, thought, and education, all were to become democratic at the same time. One important result of this linguistic change was that communication between the scholars and the people was now more complete and more immediate than at any time in Chinese history.[17]

A third circumstance which combined with the two just mentioned to prepare the ground for rich fructification of Dewey's ideas was the May Fourth incident in Peking. Regarded by the authorities in the beginning as student riots (which they undertook to stamp out by mass arrests, until the students courted arrest in such numbers that the officials finally emptied the jails and apologized to the rioters!) this movement proved to be the initial stage of an intellectual and social revolution (subsequently often referred to as the New Culture movement) which was ultimately to assume a significance that dwarfed the political revolution in which the Emperor had been overthrown eight years earlier.

The May Fourth movement was both evidence of and stimulus to intellectual ferment. Within six months after the incident, more than 400 new periodicals, all in *Paihua,* appeared on the newsstands. Established journals which had not yet switched to *Paihua* were forced to do so in order to survive and retain their readership. Newspapers added special columns or supplementary magazines in order to print new literary works and discuss cultural and student movements. Book publication boomed, especially publication of Chinese translations of foreign works. Imports of paper for printing more than doubled.[18]

Commenting on this phenomenon, Dewey himself noted:

> It is significant that at this moment in the height of the revolt against corrupt and traitorous officials and also of the Japanese boycott, these topics were secondary in the students' journals. . . . Their burden was the need of educational change; attacks upon the family system; discussion of socialism; of democratic ideas; of all kinds of utopias.
>
> . . . There seems to be no country in the world where students are so unanimously and eagerly interested as in China in what is modern and new in thought, especially about social and economic matters, nor where the arguments which can be brought in favor of the established order and the status quo have so little weight—indeed, are so unuttered.[19]

Chow notes that academic and popular lectures became a vogue in China in 1919 and the years immediately following. Dewey was the first of a considerable number of prominent Western thinkers who were invited to visit China for the purpose of lecturing, and all of them were enthusiastically received. Not only were these lectures widely published in Chinese, both in periodicals and in books, but usually earlier works of the lecturers were translated into Chinese and published, sometimes in sizable editions. In the years following Dewey's lectures in China, more than a dozen of his books were translated into Chinese and published.

Thus the confluence of three streams of influence—increasing enthusiasm for the works of Western thinkers, the phenomenal rapidity and completeness of the shift from classical Chinese to *Paihua,* and the eruption of smoldering resentments in the May Fourth incident which triggered the New Culture movement—created a climate which favored Dewey, which insured him eager audiences, and which conduced to the tremendous influence which he was to wield on Chinese thought.

The Lectures

While in China Dewey delivered several major series of lectures on broadly conceived subjects. One series of sixteen lectures on "Social and Political Philosophy" is included in this volume. Other brief series and individual lectures which can be classified under the same heading are available in reprography. A second series of sixteen lectures under the title "A Philosophy of Education" is also included in this volume. Again, briefer series and individual lectures dealing with a wide range of educational topics are available in reprography. A series of fifteen lectures on

"Ethics," a series of eight on "Types of Thinking," one of six on "Three Contemporary Philosophers" (William James, Henri Bergson, and Bertrand Russell), all delivered in Peking, together with a series of lectures on the "History of Philosophy" (limited to Greek philosophy), and a series on "Experimental Logic," delivered in Nanking, can also be secured in reprography.[20]

Thus, all the major series of lectures which Dewey delivered in China are being made available in English, along with most of the individual lectures which he delivered before teachers' institutes, educational associations, and young people's clubs, and on other occasions.

Dewey's lectures were published in Chinese, many of them in the *Bulletin* of the Ministry of Education, as well as in many other sources—with the same lecture often appearing in several different periodicals and newspapers. A list of all known Chinese publication sources of Dewey's lectures has been compiled by Mr. Barry Keenan, to whom the authors express their thanks.[21] Unfortunately, thirty-four of the individual lectures appeared in newspapers and journals of which files are not available outside mainland China. Even so, and taking into account that two collections of Dewey's major series of lectures appeared in book form in Chinese, the present series of translations constitutes the only attempt that has been made to collect all the lectures and to group them by subject matter. There is no other such comprehensive collection, even in Chinese.

The first five series of Peking lectures were reprinted as a book, which went through fourteen printings of ten thousand copies each within the next two years, and which, according to Hu Shih, continued to be reprinted for three decades, until the Communists decreed discontinuance of publication.[22]

The Nanking lecture series on "A Philosophy of Education" differed in content and style from the identically titled series which Dewey delivered in Peking. The Nanking lectures, being addressed to students, are more technical and somewhat similar in content to his by-this-time famous "Democracy and Education."[23] The lectures, taken from the *Bulletin* of the Ministry of Education, were subsequently reprinted in book form by the Commercial Press, Shanghai, as an official publication of Nanking Teachers College, under the title *Dewey's Philosophy of Education*. Another version of the same lectures was recorded by Shen Chen-sheng, and published by the T'ai Tung Company, Shanghai. There is still a third publication based on Dewey's lectures on "A Philosophy of Education" in a postgraduate course he taught at the National Peking Teachers College in 1920–1921.[24] In this course Dewey used his *Democracy and Education* as a text. Ch'ang took his class notes in English, then translated them into Chinese, using Dewey's text as a guide. The book is therefore not as immediately faithful a translation of Dewey's actual lectures as are the others that have been referred to; on the other hand, Ch'ang did not represent it as an actual translation of *Democracy and Education.*

Hu Shih has described the process by which Dewey's lectures were translated and recorded:

> A number of Dewey's students were asked to interpret his lectures in the Chinese language. For example, I was his translator and interpreter for all his lectures in Peking and in the Provinces of Shantung and Shansi. For his several major series of lectures we also selected competent recorders for reporting every lecture in full for the daily newspapers and periodicals. . . . I have recently reread most of his lectures in Chinese translation after a lapse of 40 years, and could still feel the freshness and earnestness of the great thinker and teacher who always measured every word and every sentence in the classroom or before a large lecture audience.[25]

These same procedures were followed in Nanking, where the lectures were interpreted by Liu Po-ming (K. S. Liu), who had earned his Ph.D. degree at Northwestern University, and who was a professor of philosophy and a vice-president of Nanking Teachers College. Liu was also one of the founders and a coeditor of the *Critical Review.* The lectures were recorded by various outstanding students of the college.

Dewey's lectures and speeches in other cities were subjected to essentially the same process of delivery, interpretation, and recording. His Shanghai lectures, for example, on "The Relation between Democracy and Education," were interpreted by Chiang Monlin, who had studied under Dewey at Columbia, and whose translation was as reliable as those of Hu Shih and Liu Po-ming. While any translation from one language to another involves the danger that certain nuances will be lost in the process, the qualifications of the eminent scholars who translated Dewey's lectures into Chinese warrant the conclusion that both the flavor and the meaning of what Dewey actually said were carried over into the translations as accurately and authentically as possible. Several scholars who have read the manuscript of the retranslations into English have been kind enough to comment that even after this second translation, the style and language are reasonably representative of Dewey's own style during this period.

Dewey's Influence on Chinese Thought

An accurate assessment of Dewey's influence on China is impossible. In the first place, more time is needed to evaluate objectively the work and influence of a great thinker. We are still too close to, too familiar with, the man. Second, China has suffered from continuing unrest and has undergone tremendous change since Dewey's visit. It is difficult to evaluate a thinker's influence on such a rapidly changing scene. Third, Dewey's reputation as a philosopher and educator has suffered some diminution in certain quarters in recent years, a circumstance which only adds to the problem of arriving at a fair assessment of his influence on a country other than his own.

Further complicating the task is the fact that Dewey's teachings have as often been misunderstood and misapplied in China as in America. To determine which of the actions, utterances, and attitudes, even of those who regarded themselves as Dewey's disciples and followers, were in fact the result of his influence upon them, and which stemmed from the interplay of other forces which impinged upon them, would require far more data than are available, and greater discernment than we possess. Finally, we are handicapped by the fact that because of the situation which prevails on the Chinese mainland, many relevant documents are inaccessible to scholars. These circumstances combine to make it impossible to reach definite conclusions regarding Dewey's influence on China. In the face of such an array of difficulties, what we attempt here is to trace the broad outlines of Dewey's influence as it can be seen from the limited materials available—enough, we hope, to assist the reader in appreciating the importance of the lectures here presented for the first time in English. We anticipate that there will be later, more complete, and more definitive studies as the situation becomes clarified and as additional materials come to light.[26]

Dewey's influence on education was far more pronounced and lasting than it was on other aspects of the Chinese scene. That Dewey exercised a tremendous influence on China is universally admitted, and is especially attested by the virulence of the diatribes in which Chinese Communist writers attacked his philosophy. The question is, then, just how great that influence was, in what ways Chinese thought and education were affected, and what results can be discerned. Hu Shih wrote in 1921, "We can say that, since the meeting of China and the Occident, there has not been a single foreigner who has had such an influence on the world of

Chinese thought."[27] Ten years later, one of the translator-editors who shared in the preparation of the present volume ventured a first estimate of Dewey's influence on Chinese education:

> The influence of Dewey on Chinese education is general and even total. It was brought about by conferences with educators while Dewey was himself in China, and also by his publications, almost all of which have been translated into Chinese, and by the outstanding students, who are the leaders of Chinese education. Among these are Chiang Monlin, ex-minister of education and rector of the National University of Peking; Hu Shih, an ardent pragmatist, who inspired the movement for a New Culture and who was also a professor there at the time, and P. W. Kuo, the ex-rector of the National Southeastern University, Nanking. The renown and activity of these men have been very influential in bringing about popular acceptance of Dewey's teaching and putting it into practice.[28]

When we consider Dewey's impact on Chinese thought and education, we think first of the warmth of his reception in China. All who met him were impressed by his personality, his intellectual honesty, his enthusiasm, his simplicity of nature, his friendliness, and his sympathetic understanding of the Chinese people and their problems. All these characteristics contributed to his popularity both among the intellectuals and among the common people. On one occasion, Ts'ai Yüan-p'ei, chancellor of National Peking University, even likened him to Confucius.[29] Another factor which contributed to Dewey's popularity among the Chinese was that, as an American, he represented the one great nation friendly to China and opposed to its partition by the great powers.

The fact that pragmatism is congenial to the practical mentality and disposition of the Chinese people is also a factor of fundamental importance among those which contributed to Dewey's popularity. Unlike the Greek, the Chinese tradition has never exalted knowledge for its own sake, but rather for its usefulness to morality, society, politics, and culture. Finally, Dewey augmented his influence through that of his disciples and followers, among whom were numbered many who were already the intellectual leaders of the country.

Two important institutions were the main centers of Dewey's influence in China, both during his stay and after his departure. These were the National Peking University and the National Nanking Teachers College. Both had at their head men who had been Dewey's students, Chiang Monlin in Peking, and P. W. Kuo in Nanking. Hu Shih, Dewey's greatest Chinese disciple, involved Dewey in the New Culture movement while the latter was in Peking. In Nanking, Kuo and his colleagues in the Department of Education, especially T'ao Chih-hsing and Ch'en Ho-ch'in, spread the great educator's influence among their own students and followers. Many educational reforms followed as a result of their efforts.

Thus, it is reasonable to say that it was mainly Peking National University which radiated Dewey's more general influence throughout the country, and mainly from Nanking Teachers College that his influence permeated the entire educational community of China.

In addition to these two centers, two other important institutions of higher learning helped to extend Dewey's influence throughout China: Peking Teachers College, of which Li Chien-hsun was president, and Nank'ai University in Tientsin, of which Chang Pei-lin was president. Both Li and Chang had been Dewey's students at Columbia. With so many of his former students placed in high, key posts, there is little wonder that Dewey was so warmly received, or that his teachings were practiced by a rapidly widening circle of disciples and friends.

Even before Dewey went to China, the way had been prepared for his reception. *Hsin Chin Nien* [*New Youth* or *La Jeunesse*] (monthly), founded by Ch'en Tu-hsiu in 1915, and soon strongly supported by Hu Shih, opened an avenue for new ideas. The *New Education* magazine, established in January, 1919, and edited by Chiang Monlin, was inspired by Dewey's educational ideas.[30] *New Education*'s masthead read "Stands for Individual Development and Social Progress." The third issue of the magazine was a special issue devoted entirely to Dewey. Hu Shih, Chiang Monlin, and Liu Pei-ming, all of them to serve later as Dewey's interpreters, wrote on Dewey's philosophy, ethics, and logic, respectively, to introduce Dewey to the Chinese academic world. And shortly before Dewey's arrival, Hu Shih delivered four lectures on the pragmatic movement, emphasizing Dewey's major role in this movement.

Both during and after Dewey's visit certain national educational organizations also helped to expand his influence. The China Society for the Promotion of New Education was founded by Ts'ai Yüan-p'ei, Chiang Monlin, T'ao Chih-hsing, and others, in the same year that Dewey arrived in China, with the *New Education* magazine as its organ. The new education they promoted, as the magazine's masthead suggested, was inspired by Dewey.

The National Federation of Educational Associations was a council of provincial educational associations, with the Kiangsu Educational Association as its nucleus. It was extremely influential, and many educational reforms promulgated by the Chinese government were based on its recommendations. The Chinese National Association for the Advancement of Education, with T'ao Chih-hsing as its secretary-general, was also active in promoting Dewey's ideas in education.

It is interesting to note that Dewey did not gain followers among the professional philosophers on the faculties of Chinese universities, most of whom continued to follow the German and French schools of philosophy in which they had been trained in Europe. But Dewey's pragmatism as method, being congenial to the Chinese mind, was used with telling effect by other leading Chinese intellectuals as a weapon with which to criticize Chinese culture and the traditional Chinese value system. In the hands of these intellectuals, who were so implacably hostile to China's past and so determined that all vestiges of Confucianism must be extirpated if China were to become "modern," Dewey's pragmatism undoubtedly hastened the disintegration of traditional culture and values. Even though this pragmatism was not a tightly knit philosophical system in the sense in which contemporary philosophers used the term, its emphasis on methodology, logic, and practicality made it irresistibly attractive to the leaders of the intellectual revolution, or the New Culture movement, and highly useful in promoting many social, ethical, and economic reforms.

Dewey, who arrived in Shanghai on May 1, 1919, three days before the May Fourth rioting in Peking, had nothing to do with launching the New Culture movement; nor, for that matter, did Hu Shih, who was occupied at the time with preparations for Dewey's reception. But as the movement gathered force, the students, coming to the realization that China's political unrest, economic backwardness, and humiliating diplomatic posture were rooted in her culture and traditions, and that these were not adaptable to the changing world situation, rallied to the support of the intellectuals who had been proclaiming that the old Confucian-centered culture and tradition had to be critically examined and changed, and that Western thought and culture should be welcomed.

Dewey arrived on the scene when the time was exactly ripe. His pragmatism provided the movement with just what it needed: an effective method with which to criticize and reevaluate Chinese culture on the one hand, and a stimulus to the critical selection and adaptation of Western culture on the other. In the eyes of the students, Dewey virtually embodied the new thought, and represented a new hope for intellectual enlightenment and guidance. Hu Shih and his followers acted as spokesmen for Dewey, and by their speeches and writings transformed what otherwise might have been a simple student agitation into a more or less organized movement for cultural reform. The consequences of this fateful change were manifold and momentous: the literary revolution, the undermining of the authority of Confucianism, open-mindedness toward all philosophical, political, and social isms, the reform of the institutions of marriage and the family, reconsideration of the traditional value system, and the changed status of the individual in the family and in society.

All these consequences were advocated, supported, and encouraged by Dewey through his lectures and writings, as well as through those of his disciples. His greatest contribution to these changes, however, was a more reflective method of thinking, and a method of criticism and valuation, rather than a new program of action to replace the old.

Dewey's impact was thus primarily on political and social trends. In his lectures he advocated democracy—social, political, and economic. He opposed both laissez-faire individualism and Marxist Communism. While he proposed a general ideal, he refused to advocate any all-embracing ism or any concrete program for action. His principle of the primacy of method also dominated his social and political thinking. Hu Shih's article "More Study of Problems, Less Talk of Isms" was but an echo of Dewey's voice.[31] Through his advocacy of democracy as a socio-political goal and his urging a piecemeal attack on concrete problems as a method, Dewey did wield a practical influence on Chinese affairs which can be traced through certain events of the time.

Hu Shih was the first to accept and practice Dewey's social and political teachings. He and his friends published their writings in a number of periodicals such as the *Weekly Critic, Endeavor Weekly,* and the *Independent Critic*. These (and other) magazines were ostensibly founded to advocate democracy and study concrete social and political problems along the lines laid down by Dewey. But Chow notes that

> . . . when he classified in his lectures all social problems into three categories—economic, political, and intellectual—Dewey pointed out that economic problems were the most important, because, as he said, "economic life is the foundation of all social life."
>
> But the significant economic problem discussed by Dewey did not attract enough attention from his Chinese students and friends and other Chinese liberals. Chinese liberals at this time were preoccupied with educational reform, academic research, and the reevaluation of national classics. Few of them considered seriously the problem of the application of democracy in China in terms of economic organization and practice. This was undoubtedly

one of the major causes of their waning influence on the public following their dramatic rôle in attacking the traditional ideology and institutions.[32]

While Hu Shih was still an active supporter of *New Youth* magazine, he subscribed to an article of its manifesto which read "We believe that it is requisite for the progress of our present society to uphold natural science and pragmatic philosophy, and to abolish superstition and fantasy."[33] Ch'en Tu-hsiu and Li Ta-chao, who subsequently became co-founders of the Chinese Communist party, also subscribed to this manifesto. Later Hu Shih published a "Manifesto of the Struggle for Freedom" (1920) and "Political Proposals" (1922), both signed by a group of prominent intellectuals, including Ch'en and Li, and both obviously inspired by Dewey's advocacy of democracy as a goal, and of gradual reform as the method for reaching it. Although Hu Shih did not enter the political arena until after the outbreak of the Sino-Japanese War, a number of his associates did—men such as Chiang Monlin, Wang Shih-chieh, Chiang Ting-fu, and others. These men participated in the Nationalist government, and added a tincture of Deweyan liberalism to its nationalism.

The extent to which Dewey's influence on the liberal intellectuals led by Hu Shih contributed to the downfall of the warlord government in Peking and paved the way for the Nationalists' reunification of China in 1927 cannot be determined. The fact that men who acknowledged Dewey as their leader and inspiration were active in the process is warrant for the assumption that Dewey's influence was a factor; but the additional fact that a large majority of liberals of the Deweyan persuasion subsequently rejected the political aspects of the New Culture movement, and withdrew from participation in politics, casts doubt on the argument that this influence was anything approaching a *decisive* factor in the development of Chinese socialism, and the ultimate takeover by the Communists twenty-eight years after Dewey left China.[34]

Certainly Dewey's sympathy, support, and encouragement contributed significantly to the metamorphosis of the May Fourth incident into the New Culture movement. But with the passing of time, many Chinese youth, realizing that cultural reforms were not enough, and believing that practical action was required if the ideals of democracy were to be realized, flocked to Sun Yat-sen's standard and joined the newly organized Kuomintang. But "by this time Sun and his followers [had] allied themselves with the Soviet Union and the Chinese Communists in a joint effort to overthrow the Peking warlord government by force. The Dewey-ites actually opposed this, and refrained from joining in."[35] Whatever influence Dewey's pragmatism may have had upon the rise to power of the Nationalists, it is certain that neither he nor those of his followers closest to him were numbered among them, or that they supported or took part in the revolution which finally did overthrow the warlord government and establish the Kuomintang in power in 1927.

The extent and manner in which Dewey's participation in and influence upon the New Culture movement through his lectures was or was not a predisposing factor to the growth of Chinese Communism, and to its eventual assumption of control of the government of mainland China in 1949, is still a matter of controversy and debate. The May Fourth incident occurred within four days of Dewey's arrival in China. Forces destined to discredit traditional Chinese values had been at work for well over a half-century, and "Confucius . . . had just retired from the scene." Just what the differences in the direction and momentum of the New Culture movement might have been had Dewey not lectured in China for 26 months, in the midst of an intellectual revolution that was well under way when he arrived, is difficult to surmise. But the emphasis and consistency with which he rejected Marxian dialectical materialism, and the cogency and frequency of his warnings against wholesale adoption of any one ism as a cure for China's ills, support the conclusion that the drift toward the extreme left might have been swifter, and that the triumph of Communism might have come sooner but for his influence.

The Chinese Communist party was "created in secret in May 1920 . . . albeit it later officially set the date as July 1921."[36] This early version of Chinese Communism was vastly different from the doctrinaire Communism that was to take over the government three decades later. "Experimentalism both as a philosophy and as a scientific method, had in this period an upper hand over dialectic materialism. The idea of class struggle was also definitely rejected by Ch'en Tu-hsiu and most other Chinese leaders at the time."[37] Both the Ch'en to whom Chow here refers, and Li Ta-chao, although they were to become founding members of the Chinese Communist party the next year, joined with Hu Shih and others in December, 1919, in signing the "Manifesto of the *New Youth* Magazine," which was a strong statement of pragmatic philosophy. Drawing on Dewey's analysis of the development of American democracy and on his admiratiton for the traditional Chinese guild system, Ch'en even proposed "local government and professional unions as two units of the foundation for building democracy in China."[38]

Although Dewey's influence did not prevent Ch'en and Li from embracing Communism, his teaching and personal contacts did serve to dissuade many Chinese intellectuals and students who might otherwise have gone along with them from joining the Communist movement. In his lectures, Dewey took an unequivocally anti-Communist position, severely criticizing and pointedly repudiating Marxism. In a speech delivered in Fukien he blamed the Communists for neglecting critical thought and for their blind obedience. His anti-Communist strictures did, indeed, have their effect in "countering the budding interest of Chinese intellectuals in Marxism."[39]

Intellectuals who identified themselves with Dewey, commonly spoken of as "the liberals," increasingly dissociated themselves from the extremists both of the left and of the right. Hu Shih and his group withdrew from the *New Youth* magazine in 1921, in protest against the Marxist proclivities of other contributors. Hu Shih's advocacy of a "good men cabinet," and his founding of *Endeavor Weekly* proclaimed his stand for political reform or amelioration as opposed to class struggle and revolutionary violence. Subsequently he and a number of other liberal intellectuals did participate in the Nationalist government (he served as China's ambassador to the United States from 1942 to 1945), and their example attracted other intellectuals and students, diverting them from Marxism and possibly administering a temporary check to the Communist drive for power.

Since the Communists' accession to control of the Peking government in 1949, Dewey has been blamed by conservatives for "paving the way for the Communists," while at the same time he has been excoriated by the Communists for his opposition to their ideals and goals. Certain members of the Kuomintang on Taiwan, through articles in a periodical called *Hsüeh Ts'ui,* and through other channels, allege that Dewey's pragmatic method as utilized by the New Culture movement was responsible for the disintegration of traditional Chinese culture, and that while those in the movement engaged in negative criticism, they offered nothing in the way of a new system of thought or program of action to replace what they were destroying. The result, so these critics charge, was that the floodgates were opened for the importation of every kind of Western idea, and that the Communists were then able to exploit the cultural vacuum, and the intellectual zest of youth for everything new, to convert the populace to their way of thinking.

The fallaciousness of this criticism will be immediately obvious to the reader of *Social and Political Philosophy,* for he can see at a glance that Dewey did not advocate wholesale rejection of traditional Chinese culture, or the wholesale adoption of Western culture or systems of thought and value. Instead, Dewey repeatedly urged the critical evaluation of the old, and a careful examination of Western culture, and reiterated his hope that the outcome of such a process of reflective thinking would be the birth of a new culture which would have assimilated the best elements of both.[40] But these critics either have not read what Dewey himself said, or they choose to ignore it.

Very few of the liberals who were identified with Dewey defected to the Communist cause, but when the Communists began to push their own all-encompassing philosophical and political system, they did win over the younger intellectuals and students who had not heard or did not heed Dewey's oft-repeated warning against the indiscriminate acceptance of Western ideas and practices. Chinese conservatives were not the only ones to accuse Dewey and his followers of helping the Communists. Two Western critics level at Dewey essentially the same charge made by certain members of the Kuomintang:

> Dewey's message was that democracy could be achieved only through a slow process and that social objectives were relative. He was particularly interested in the scientific approach which he described as the search "for concrete methods to meet concrete problems according to the exigencies of time and place." In contrast to the apparent indefiniteness of his general social philosophy, the Communist theory provided the Chinese intellectuals with a system which also claimed to be scientific and to be based on a materialistic and antimetaphysical interpretation of human life. In addition, communist theory provided a program of action, definite goals, and an historically determined role for the elite. . . .
>
> The pragmatists helped to prepare the way for the spread of materialism in the next decades. By joining in the attack against Confucianism they discredited the traditional value system, but themselves offered no system of values. They proposed solutions to the problems of the day according to what Dewey called "exigencies of time and place." Because the pragmatists themselves tend toward a materialistic and utilitarian interpretation they offered little resistence to communist doctrine.[41]

At the same time that Dewey was being accused by critics of the right for "paving the way for the take-over of China by the Communists," he was being excoriated by Chinese Communists for having impeded their efforts. In December, 1954, Wang Jo-shui published an article in a Communist journal, *Jen Min Jih Pao*, "Hu Shih and John Dewey in the May Fourth movement." Wang's argument, according to the abstract made by T. S. Sun, was that

Dewey made the tour at the invitation of Hu Shih for the purpose of combating the rising tide of Marxism among Chinese intellectuals at the time. Dewey is accused of trying to lead Chinese intellectuals away from their interest in politics and to influence them to advocate revisionism instead of revolution.[42]

The following year Yin Fa-lu, another Communist, published "How Did Hu Shih, John Dewey, and Bertrand Russell Start to Sabotage the New Culture Movement in China?" Sun's abstract of this article reads: "He [Hu Shih] invited John Dewey to make a lecture tour of China at the time when the May Fourth movement swept the country, with the purpose of countering the budding interest of Chinese intellectuals in Marxism."[43]

Hu Shih, noting the difficulty of an accurate appraisal of Dewey's influence on China (for the same reasons that we have already enumerated), cites the volume of vilification directed at himself, and through him, at Dewey, in the Communist press in the middle 1950s:

> . . . in our present case, however, the Chinese Communist regime has given us unexpected assistance in the form of nation-wide critical condemnation and purging of the Pragmatic philosophy of Dewey and his Chinese followers. This great purge began as early as 1950. . . . But the purge became truly violent in 1954 and 1955, when the Chinese Communist regime ordered a concerted condemnation and purge of the evil and poisonous thought of Hu Shih in many aspects of Chinese intellectual activity—in philosophy, in history, in the history of philosophy, in political thought, in literature, and in histories of Chinese culture. In those two years of 1954 and 1955, more than three million words were published for the purging and exorcising of the "ghost of Hu Shih." And in almost every violent attack on me, Dewey was inevitably dragged in as a source and the fountainhead of the heinous poison.
>
> And in most of the articles of this vast purge literature, there was a frank recognition of the evil influence of Dewey's philosophy and method. . . . May we not accept such confessions from the communist-controlled world as fairly reliable, though probably slightly exaggerated, estimates of the "poisonous" influence left by Dewey and his friends in China?
>
> . . . I have brought upon my head and the head of my beloved teacher and friend, John Dewey, years of violent attack and millions of words of abuse and condemnation. But . . . these same millions of words of abuse and condemnation have given me a feeling of comfort and encouragement— a feeling that Dewey's two years and two months in China were not entirely in vain. . . . and that Dewey and his students have left in China plenty of "poison," plenty of antiseptic and antitoxin, to plague the Marxist-Leninist slaves for many, many years to come.[44]

Thus, while there is still disagreement—even controversy—over the exact nature of Dewey's influence on China, and over its extent and duration, the fact is indisputable that he did wield an influence that was both considerable and enduring.

Dewey's Influence on Chinese Education

Passing mention has been made in earlier portions of this introduction of Dewey's influence on Chinese education. There is no dispute about the fact that of all Western educators, Dewey most influenced the course of Chinese education, both in theory and in practice. While, as we have indicated, his influence on Chinese thought, politics, and society in general is a controversial matter not susceptible to precise determination, his influence on Chinese education can be documented and itemized.

We have already mentioned the fact that many of Dewey's former students at Columbia University held important positions in the Chinese educational world, chief among them being Chiang Monlin, P. W. Kuo, Tao Chi-hsing, and Ch'en Ho-ch'in. After he became minister of education in the Nationalist government, Chiang did a great deal to extend Dewey's influence. Kuo, Tao, and Ch'en were at National Nanking Teachers College during Dewey's sojourn in China, Kuo as president, Tao as head of the department of education, and Ch'en as professor of education. They applied Dewey's ideas in their preparation of secondary and normal school teachers, and these, in their turn, spread Dewey's influence in the schools in which they taught after their graduation, thus bringing it into play on all levels, from the college down through the middle schools to the elementary and primary levels. The graduates of Nanking Teachers College who became school inspectors and superintendents similarly carried Dewey's influence into school administration. From Nanking Teachers College as the center, Dewey's influence thus radiated through the entire country.

Of Dewey's disciples who were most responsible for spreading his influence in China, Tao and Ch'en deserve special mention because each developed his own system, taking Dewey's educational theory as his starting point. The teaching and practice of Tao Chi-hsing may be said to represent Dewey pushed to extremes.[45] Tao's contribution to the extension of Dewey's influence can be compared only to that of William Heard Kilpatrick. From his early Nanking days down to his death in 1946 Tao devoted his life to the cause of educational reform in China. He was the first of Dewey's Chinese followers to develop his own systematic educational theory and practice, and the first to seek to extend Dewey's influence from the college level down to the rural school.

Tao's oft-quoted statement bears witness to the fact that his concept of living education was a type of Dewey's own experience-centered education.

> "What is living education?" Tao asked, and answered his own question, "Living education is life-centered education. . . . Education which has no life-centered work is a dead education. Schools which have no life-centered activities are dead schools. Books without life-centered materials are dead books. People who deal with dead education, dead schools, and dead books are dead men."[46]

Tao also advanced the "Principle of Teaching-Learning-Doing Combination." According to Tao, teaching is essentially the art of helping pupils to learn by doing. Only when teaching, learning, and doing are combined as an educational method practiced in a life situation can living education be said to exist. On the practical side, Tao's experiments at Hsiao Chuang Normal School exemplified Dewey's educational ideas, and helped popularize Dewey's teaching throughout numerous normal and rural schools. Dewey and Kilpatrick were so impressed by Tao's work that on his death they jointly sent a telegram which read, "We honor Dr. Tao for his unsurpassed and heroic devotion on behalf of a better education for the common people of China. We who remain must keep alive his memory and his work."[47]

Ch'en Ho-ch'in, another influential Dewey disciple, was Tao's colleague, friend, and follower. Ch'en played an important role in modernizing Shanghai's municipal school system, and later followed up with his work with kindergarten teachers. Through his efforts, Dewey's influence reached to the most basic levels—the kindergarten and the elementary school. Ch'en's role in promoting Dewey's educational theory and practice was such a profound one that later the Communists forced him to make a public recantation as a means of combating Dewey's influence on Chinese education. In his public "confession," Ch'en declared: "As one who has been most deeply poisoned by his [Dewey's] reactionary educational ideas, as one who has worked hardest and longest to help spread his educational ideas, I now publicly accuse that great fraud and deceiver in modern history of education, John Dewey."[48] We will return to Ch'en's accusation later, but there can be no doubt about the important role he played in spreading Dewey's influence in the years prior to his "recantation."

We have said that Dewey's influence on Chinese education was general, and even total. As strong as this statement may sound, it can be substantiated. We may begin our development of this thesis by tracing Dewey's influence on Chinese educational theory.

Dewey's philosophy of education dominated the teaching of educational theory in all teachers colleges and in university departments of education for many years. His epoch-making textbook in the philosophy of education, *Democracy and Education,* was used everywhere, either as a text or as a work of reference. More than a dozen of his major works were translated into Chinese, and most of their translators were educators rather than professional philosophers. There were even several translations of some of these books.[49]

Numerous articles, books, and pamphlets were published to introduce and interpret Dewey's philosophy of education. Some of his most-used phrases—"education is life," "school is society," "learning by doing," "education for the needs of life"—were familiar to all levels of the Chinese educational world, and were so often quoted as to become educational clichés. No dissent was voiced to Dewey's views during the time of his visit, nor for many years afterward. Dewey became the highest educational authority in China, and there were many more converts to his views in Chinese educational circles than among professional philosophers.

The fact that Dewey's influence was exerted on practical reforms as well as on theory is attested to by a number of developments:

1. Chinese educational aims were reconsidered in the light of Dewey's thought. The first Conference for Educational Investigation, held in April 1919, was attended by sixty outstanding educational leaders, including Ts'ai Yüan-p'ei and Chiang Monlin, all of whom were appointed by the Ministry of Education. Dissatisfied with the old educational aims which had been promulgated in 1912, and which had emphasized military education, the conference suggested that the aim and spirit of American education should be adopted. The new aim was to be "the cultivation of perfect personality and the development of democratic spirit."[50] This sounds very much like the platform of Chiang Monlin's *New Education* magazine, which was inspired by Dewey.

The fifth annual meeting of the Federation of Educational Associations endorsed the new educational direction in the same year, and even went a step further in following literally Dewey's admonition that "education has no ends beyond itself; it is its own end," by advocating the abolition of all educational aims, and their replacement by a statement of the nature of education instead.[51]

In 1922 the New School System Reform Decree promulgated by the Chinese government made no provision for the establishment of educational aims; only general principles governing the school system were enunciated. This fact constitutes a clear example of the acceptance of Dewey's teachings.[52]

2. The national school system was reformed according to the American pattern. The Federation of Educational Associations proposed the reform while Dewey was still in China. The proposals were discussed by a Committee on School System Reform appointed by the Ministry of Education, and these discussions led to the promulgation in 1922 of a decree reforming the school system. This decree, which marked a new era for Chinese education, was the high-water mark of American, particularly Deweyan, influence on Chinese education. The school system was modeled entirely on the American 6–3–3 plan. The general principles of the reform governing the whole school system were as follows: (a) to adapt the education system to the needs of social evolution; (b) to promote the spirit of democracy; (c) to develop individuality; (d) to take the economic status of the people into special consideration; (e) to promote education for life; (f) to facilitate the spread of universal education; and (g) to make the school system flexible enough to allow for local variations.[53] A glance at this set of principles is enough to tell us that they reflect Dewey's educational philosophy as it is to be found in his writings, and in the lectures he delivered while in China.

3. Child-centered education predominated in the revision of the curriculum. The Federation of Education Associations met in Tainan in 1922 to discuss a thorough revision of the national school system and curriculum. According to Hu Shih, who participated in the meeting, Article 4 of the *New Educational System* proposed by the meeting read:

> The child is the center of education. Special attention should be paid to the individual characteristics and attitudes of the child in organizing the school system. Henceforth, the elective system should be adopted for secondary and higher education, and the principle of flexibility should be adopted in the arrangement and promotion of classes in all elementary schools.

Hu Shih rightly observed that "in the new school curriculum of 1923, and the revised curriculum of 1929, the emphasis was placed on the idea that the child was the center of the school. The influence of Dewey's philosophy is easily seen in these revisions."[54] Although the term "child-centered education" did not appear in the National School System Reform Decree, the spirit of such education permeated the document.

After its reorganization by Sun Yat-sen in 1924, the Kuomintang issued its *Political Programme,* Article 13 of which dealt with the "Promotion of Child-centered Education." When this program was put into effect after the Nationalists established their government in Canton, child-centered education was to be effectuated throughout the whole of China, regardless of the political differences between the North and the South.

4. New methods of teaching in accord with Dewey's pragmatic theory were initiated. The fifth meeting of the Federation of Educational Associations recommended reform in teaching methods, with Dewey's ideas as guiding principles. In its meeting in 1921, the federation urged the extension of the practice of the project method in elementary schools.[55] To help extend the practice of the project method, Dewey's great disciple and proponent of the method, William Heard Kilpatrick, was invited to lecture in China.

5. Experimental schools were multiplied. With Dewey's own Chicago Laboratory School serving as a model, a number of experimental schools were founded during and after Dewey's visit. The first to be mentioned was the Experimental School of Nanking Teachers College, under the direction of Yu Tze-yi, an educator who had been trained in Japan. Yu turned the school into an experimental school in which the project method was first practiced and the curriculum organized around it to give effect to the principles of the child-centered school. The school gradually became a model of the Dewey type, and attracted visitors from schools throughout the country who came to gain fresh inspiration and learn its method of teaching and its curriculum organization. These visitors adapted its practices in their own schools, a circumstance which further helped to extend Dewey's influence over Chinese education.[56]

6. Student government, about which Dewey made a number of speeches, was widely extended as a mode of school discipline.[57] Under Dewey's influence, the Federation of Educational Associations in 1920 suggested an outline of regulations covering the practice of student government. In its meeting of 1922, it reaffirmed its support of student government as the most effective means of school discipline. As a consequence, student government was widely practiced in colleges and schools at the time, and in

some cases was carried to such extremes as to produce unrest—a consequence which was later attributed by his critics to Dewey's teachings.[58]

7. Literary reform was encouraged, and elementary school textbooks written in the vernacular were adopted. Dewey spoke warmly on behalf of the literary reform promoted by Hu Shih and others. When the Federation of Educational Associations passed a resolution in 1919 on the use of the vernacular in textbooks for elementary schools, Dewey praised the resolution and considered the use of *Paihua* as a textbook medium a great step forward in Chinese education.[59] In the following year the Ministry of Education amended the Elementary School Ordinance, dropping the term *kuo-wen* in Articles 13 and 15, and replacing it with the term *kuo-yü*.[60] The ministry also ordered that *Paihua* textbooks be used beginning in the fall of 1920. In the same year, the Commercial Press began to publish twenty series of elementary school textbooks in *kuo-yü*.[61]

In 1925 the Ministry of Education ordered that all the lower elementary schools use textbooks printed in the vernacular. In the same year the Association of Elementary Schools attached to the Normal Schools of Kiangsu, Chekiang, and Anwei met to pass a resolution urging that all textbooks printed in literary Chinese be burned to show the country's determination to do away forever with all textbooks in classical Chinese.[62] Since that time, all textbooks for elementary schools have been printed in *Paihua*.

These examples are ample warrant for the conclusion that Dewey's influence on Chinese education was both profound and extensive.

The Decline of Dewey's Influence

From 1919 until 1927, Dewey's influence was dominant in Chinese thought and in Chinese education in particular. There is no question that Dewey's philosophy represented the mainstream of Chinese thought during this period. There were occasional critics of some of the more extreme tendencies advocated by some of Dewey's followers, but these were rarely heeded.[63]

Dewey's influence first began to diminish, however, after the May 30 incident in Shanghai in 1925. Disillusioned and humiliated, a number of educators were dissatisfied with the cosmopolitan and individualistic tendencies dominating educational thought and practice at the time. These critics advocated the preservation and dignification of national culture, and the cultivation of a national spirit. In response to this new development, subsequent meetings of the Federation of Education Associations gradually shifted the emphasis in education. Although opposition to Dewey's authority did not actually break out into the open, his prestige began to decline. After the Nationalists came to power in 1927, Dewey's influence was seriously undermined.

Despite the fact that Sun Yat-sen's revolutionary theory was compatible with and congenial to Dewey's pragmatic method, Sun was out of sympathy with the anti-Confucian trend of the New Culture movement. His *Three Principles of the People* called for the re-creation of a national spirit to assure national unity and independence. Upon their assumption of the reins of power, Sun's followers set themselves the task of rehabilitating Confucius, and of revising educational aims, curricula, and textbooks in accordance with Sun's goals. Adopting the resolutions of the First National Conference, the Nationalist government promulgated a statement of educational aims formulated in the spirit of the *Three Principles of the People*. A detailed program for realizing these aims was decreed, with emphasis on respect for the cultural heritage, cultivation of the old Chinese virtues, discipline and order in school life, physical culture, and the acquisition of modern scientific knowledge and technology. The traditional value system was also reaffirmed. In a word, the recently established authority of Deweyism was undermined in favor of the old Confucianism, and rather quickly a cultural restoration was under way. Chinese thought and education proceeded more or less along these lines from 1927 until the Communists' take-over in 1949.

After 1949, the Chinese Communists followed Soviet authorities and educators in their denunciation of Dewey and his followers. Formal notice of Dewey's influence on Chinese education was first taken in the October 1950 issue of *People's Education:*

> If we want to criticize the old theories of education, we must begin with Dewey. The educational ideas of Dewey have dominated and controlled Chinese education for thirty years, and his social philosophy and general philosophy have also influenced a part of the Chinese people.[64]

This is merely a statement of fact. But in 1951 the People's Education Press in Shanghai published an *Introduction to the Critique of John Dewey,* and followed this with more than three million words of derogation and condemnation of Hu Shih in 1954 and 1955, constantly referring, in this massive campaign of vilification, to Dewey as a major source of Hu Shih's thought.

The most violent attacks on Dewey were launched by his own disciple, Ch'en Ho-ch'in. Ch'en's first denunciation of Dewey occurred during the course of his public "confession of error" which he was forced to make at the second session of the First Conference of the People's Representatives of Kiangsu Province in February 1952:

> How was Dewey's poisonous pragmatic educational philosophy spread over China? It was primarily through his lectures in China preaching his pragmatic philosophy and his reactionary educational ideas, and through that center of Dewey's reactionary thinking, namely, Columbia University, from which thousands of Chinese students, for over thirty years, have brought back all the reactionary, subjective-idealistic, pragmatic educational ideas of Dewey.[65]

Ch'en charged that he had been wounded by three "gunshots" fired by Dewey. The first shot was Dewey's view of educational aims. According to Ch'en, Dewey's contention that "education has no end beyond itself; it is its own end," and his theory of growth in education were advanced "to overshadow the class struggle and with a base and shameless motive." In following Dewey's teaching in this respect, Ch'en confessed that he "failed to take into consideration in educational practice the right direction of social development, and cooperated with foreign imperialists in Shanghai and reactionary forces in Kiangsi in practicing education according to Dewey's pragmatic, reactionary philosophy."[66]

"Dewey's second shot," Ch'en went on, "was the theory of the child-centered curriculum." Following this theory, Ch'en had developed his own concept of "living education," taking nature and society as living subject matter, but never organizing them. These subjects were taught to children in a piecemeal way, with no systematic organization being provided. Ch'en formally accused himself, saying:

> The child-centered curriculum in living education has destroyed scientific knowledge's nature of system, design, and organization, debased the leading role of the teacher, obstructed the child's potentiality in world reconstruction through the mastery of scientific knowledge and consequently discouraged the will of the child and the youth to reconstruct the fatherland and defend world peace. This is the consequence of my being hit by Dewey's second gunshot, namely, his pragmatic, reactionary theory of the child-centered curriculum—school is society, education is life.[67]

Dewey's third gunshot, Ch'en said, was the child-centered method of teaching. In copying this method, Ch'en had eventually developed his own process of teaching, that is, "to learn through doing, to teach through doing, to make progress through doing." This method was a variation of Tao Hsin-chi's *Combined Method of Teaching, Learning, and Doing.* Ch'en explained that

> doing in learning and teaching was not the same as "practice" in Marxism-Leninism. "Practice" in Marxism-Leninism is social and purposeful, while "doing" in the Deweyan method of teaching is trivial, fragmentary, and splitting scientific knowledge in an attempt to subject the youth to slavery at the service of American monopolizing capitalists.[68]

Ch'en attributed the failure of his living education method to Dewey's pragmatic method of teaching, and considered himself to be a victim of Dewey's third gunshot, the method of learning by doing.

The Chinese Communists were not satisfied, however, with Ch'en's denunciation of Dewey's educational ideas, and required him to attack their philosophical base as well. Obediently Ch'en fired off three gunshots of his own at Dewey's pragmatism. According to Ch'en, Dewey's pragmatism consisted of three elements, namely, (1) idealistic empiricism, (2) a biological view of human nature, and (3) a vulgar evolutionist view of society. Ch'en's attack on Dewey's pragmatism is contained in his pamphlet, *Critique of the Philosophic Bases of John Dewey's Reactionary Pedagogy,* which is a highly technical performance from the philosophic point of view. Some critics, judging from Ch'en's academic training, have expressed doubt that Ch'en was actually the author of this work. The pamphlet attacks Dewey from the official Marxist-Leninist standpoint, and contains little not already set forth in similar works by Russian Communists. It is worth noting, however, that the virulence of the Communist attack on Dewey is one good indication of the force of his impact on Chinese thought and education, and of the degree to which the Chinese Communists deem it necessary to extirpate his influence, root and branch.

Thus it may seem that Dewey's thought is in eclipse in China, not only on the mainland where his followers have been liquidated by the Communist regime, but also on Taiwan, whose school system is still functioning under the decree of the Nationalist government which modified and revised the original Reform Decree of 1922.

But for all that, it must be admitted that Dewey's influence is still alive and felt on Taiwan. For instance, in a recent issue of *Education and Culture,* an official publication of the Ministry of Education, Ho Min-lin published an article entitled "The Influence of Dewey's Theory of Teaching Method and Subject Matter upon Chinese Education," which contains the statement that:

> Dewey was a reformer and a foreign philosopher; his educational theory has had a tremendous influence upon Chinese education. Dewey lectured in China between 1919 and 1921 during which time he made a great many constructive suggestions to the existing Chinese educational system and curriculum. Even the present educational system was established also directly or indirectly under his influence. In spite of the fact that his prestige has been rapidly reduced in America, his philosophy of education and his way of thinking are still worthy of study.[69]

Since these are the words of an ordinary teacher, they may reflect the general attitude of the average Chinese educator toward the great American philosopher and educator.

We may well conclude on a note of promise. The Elementary School Teachers In-Service Training Center in Taipei is headed by a follower of the Dewey school, and Dewey's educational philosophy permeates this institution. Hundreds of elementary school teachers have been trained under the influence of Dewey's pragmatism over the past several years. According to a recent issue of *Education and Culture,* twelve thousand in-service teachers will be trained by the Center on a rotation basis in the next five years. If its present spirit does not change, the outlook for a revival of Dewey's influence is by no means dim.[70]

The purpose of this translation back into English of the lectures which Dewey delivered in China is not to determine the exact nature or extent of Dewey's influence on Chinese thought, but rather to assemble the lectures for which texts exist outside Communist China, and to make available to those who read English but not Chinese, the text of these lectures as nearly as possible in the language in which they were initially delivered.

We hope that these lectures will be of interest and use to two groups of readers (not necessarily mutually exclusive). On the one hand, we hope that students of modern Chinese history will find it helpful to have at hand the text of Dewey's lectures, and that they will find reference to this text useful when considering conflicting estimates and interpretations of the influences wielded by Westerners on recent intellectual currents in China. We hope that this brief introduction has established the fact that Dewey did have a profound influence, even though it has begged the question of the exact nature and full extent of that influence.

On the other hand, we hope that students of Dewey's thought and writing will find it helpful to have readily accessible the text of the lectures which represent the bulk of his production during a twenty-six-month period of his development. The serious student of Dewey will find in these lectures not only echoes of ideas and positions characteristic of his earlier writing, but also intimations and foreshadowings of ideas that he was to develop in the next decade or more.

TRANSLATORS' NOTE

This project of returning to English the lectures John Dewey delivered in China in 1919–1921 had its genesis late in 1962, when Chung-ming Lu, of Taipei, a graduate student in the philosophy of education at the University of Hawaii, under a grant from the Center for Cultural and Technical Interchange between East and West (the "East-West Center"), came to the office of his adviser, Dr. Robert W. Clopton, with a copy of *Tu-wei Wu Ta Chiang-yen* [Five Major Lecture Series of Dewey in Peking], published in Peking in 1920 by *Ch'en Pao She* [the *Morning Post* (Peking)]. Mr. Lu was eager to find out where he could get an English translation of these lectures.

Reference to available bibliographies, including Milton Halsey Thomas' definitive *John Dewey: A Centennial Bibliography*, failed to yield any reference to an English translation. Consultation and correspondence led to the conclusion that no English translation existed. (It was also discovered that the copy which Mr. Lu had found in the Asian Collection of the University of Hawaii Sinclair Library was one of very few copies of the Chinese text in existence outside mainland China.)

As a result, Dr. Tsuin-chen Ou, of New Asia College in Hong Kong, an eminent Dewey scholar, was invited to come to Honolulu to work on the project of returning Dewey's lectures to English. Professor Clopton was also invited to spend his sabbatical year at the Institute as a senior specialist to work with Dr. Ou; and Mr. Lu, whose discovery of the Chinese text of the *Five Major Series of Lectures* had inaugurated the

31

project, was appointed as research assistant to make the literal translation from which the two specialists would work.

The project had been conceived merely as a translation of the lectures that Mr. Lu had brought to our attention. However, Dr. Ou brought to Honolulu with him reprograph copies of a number of single lectures by Dewey which had been printed (in Chinese) in the *Bulletin* of the Ministry of Education. Examination of this material convinced us that it should be translated along with the lectures in the book published by the Peking *Morning Post*. The undertaking thus grew rapidly to something more than twice the scope of the project that was originally envisioned.

In the Introduction we quote Hu Shih's description of the manner in which Dewey's lectures were interpreted into Chinese and recorded for publication in that language. We also note the fact that the brief English notes that Dewey prepared before his lectures have not been preserved—a fact which makes the translators totally dependent upon the Chinese texts.

Recording these interpretations in Chinese ideographs, however, posed problems. The possibilities of variation are illustrated by comparison of two versions of a single paragraph from the first lecture, "Social and Political Philosophy."

The first four lectures in this series were recorded by Wu Wang, and the first nine also by Kao I-han, a professor of political science at National Peking University, whose recording was used by *La Jeunesse*.[71] Returned to English Wu Wang's version reads:

> Mankind shares one universal characteristic: when a need occurs there is activity which seeks to satisfy the need. When we are hungry, we eat; when we are tired, we sleep. As events of similar character occur in experience, such actions become habitual. We do not ask ourselves "Why do we do it this way?" or "What would happen if we do it that way?"

Kao's version of the same passage, taken down at the same time from Hu Shih's oral interpretation, when translated into English, reads:

> Mankind shares one universal characteristic: when a need occurs there is activity which seeks to satisfy the need. When we are hungry, we eat; when we are tired, we sleep. When a need comes into being because of a particular event (or an event which we have not yet recognized as belonging to a category or class of events), we consciously try out and evaluate activities calculated to reduce the tension. As events of similar character occur in experience, however, and as the same or closely related activities prove effective in reducing a series of similar tensions, such actions become habitual. We no

longer think about what we do; we do not ask ourselves "Why do we do it this way rather than some other way?" If someone does raise the question, we reply that "everybody does it this way," or that "this is the way that it has always been done." As long as our way of dealing with a class of situations provides reasonable satisfaction, we do not need a theory to justify our actions.

It is immediately obvious to anyone at all conversant with Dewey's style of this period that the version of Kao I-han, the academician, is a much closer approximation to what Dewey probably said than is that of Wu Wang. Since the lectures in this volume (as well as most of those listed in Appendix B) were both interpreted and recorded by academicians who were familiar with Dewey's style and subject matter, there is warrant for assuming that the Chinese texts reflect what Dewey said more closely than the first example quoted above.

Our procedure was this: Chung-ming Lu made exact, literal translations from the Chinese, which Dr. Clopton rendered into idiomatic English. Dr. Ou then compared this version for fidelity to the Chinese text, after which Dr. Clopton incorporated Dr. Ou's suggestions for modifications.[72]

Dr. Milton Halsey Thomas, Archivist at Princeton University, and author of *John Dewey: A Centennial Bibliography,* kindly provided us with a copy of *An Open Letter to the Chinese People,* written by Dewey in 1942, translated into Chinese, and scattered by the U.S. Army Air Force over Chinese cities in the form of a seven-by-six-centimeter leaflet. We were unable at the time to locate a copy of the letter in English, so we proceeded to retranslate the leaflet into English. Several months later we secured from the National Archives a copy of the letter as Dewey had originally written it. Appendix A includes both the original English version, and our translation from the Chinese.

After we had received the original English text of the letter, we compared it carefully with the Chinese version, discovering in the process that most of the variations between the original and our retranslation were the results of alterations (and, in at least two cases, errors) made by the unidentified translator who prepared the Chinese version. When one takes account of the fact that this translator worked with a complete text before him, and compares this situation with the manner in which the 1919–1921 lectures were interpreted orally and instantaneously as Dewey delivered them, taken down by recorders who had to decide on the spur of the moment which ideographs to use, and who had no text (other than the sketchy notes mentioned earlier) against which to check their translation, he cannot but be aware of the possibility of significant alterations in meaning in such a process.

This single example—the only one in existence (of Dewey's writing) so far as we know, in which the original English, the Chinese translation, and the English retranslation are available for comparison—can provide the reader with a basis for estimating the degree to which this retranslation of Dewey's lectures in China approximates the form in which he originally delivered them.

The individual lectures which comprise the series in this volume were not titled in the Chinese texts. The translator-editors have supplied what they hope are appropriate titles.

For support in making these lectures available to the English-reading public, and for the privilege of working on the project, the translator-editors express their appreciation to the East-West Center, to its Institute of Advanced Projects, and to its administrative officers.

We should be remiss, indeed, if we did not also express our gratitude to Professor Chow Tse-tsung of the University of Wisconsin. Our dependence upon his monumental *May Fourth Movement* for much of the material in our introduction is obvious from the numerous notes. Our indebtedness to Professor Chow extends further, however, than our dependence upon his published scholarship. He generously took time for a detailed criticism of an earlier draft of the Introduction, and contributed a large number of helpful and constructive suggestions from which, with his permission, we have taken the liberty of quoting in the Introduction.

Robert W. Clopton
Honolulu, 1968

Tsuin-chen Ou
Hong Kong, 1968

NOTES TO THE INTRODUCTION

AND TRANSLATORS' NOTE

Material from Chinese sources, located and translated by Dr. Ou, is not, unless otherwise noted, available in English, except for references from Dewey's lectures. In this case, the reference is always to the Chinese source, even though these lectures are now translated either in this volume or in the typescript for which Appendix B is the table of contents.

1. "His influence on education was original, decisive, lasting. Not only in China but on a universal basis it is doubtful if anyone in this century has had as extensive an influence on the education programs of the world. If this influence has been delayed in making itself felt in Europe, in Asia it arrived much earlier. *Its greatest impact was in China."* (Emphasis added.) Thomas Berry, "Dewey's Influence in China," in *John Dewey: His Thought and Influence,* ed. John Blewett (New York: Fordham University Press, 1960), p. 214.

2. Hu Shih, "John Dewey in China," in *Philosophy and Culture East and West,* ed. Charles A. Moore (Honolulu: University of Hawaii Press, 1962), pp. 762–769.

3. *Tu-wei Wu Ta Chiang-yen* [Five major lecture series of Dewey in Peking], *Morning Post* [Peking, 1920], p. 3.

4. "Typing on his own typewriter, Dewey always wrote out his brief notes for every lecture, a copy of which would be given to his interpreter so that he could study them and think out the suitable Chinese words and phrases before the lecture and its translation. After each lecture in Peking, the Dewey notes were given to the selected recorders, so that they could check their reports before publication." Hu Shih, "Dewey in China," p. 765.

5. "Hsü-Kao-seng-chuan" [Supplement to biographies of eminent monks],

in *Taishō Shinshū Daizōkyō,* ed. Junjiro Takakusu, vol. 50 (Tokyo: Taisho Issai-Kyo Kanko Kwai, 1927).

6. Some of the material in this section of the Introduction, as well as some in other sections, also appears in Tsuin-chen Ou, "Dewey's Lectures and Influence in China," in *A Guide to the Works of John Dewey,* ed. Jo Ann Boydston (Carbondale: University of Southern Illinois Press, 1970).

7. John Dewey, *Reconstruction in Philosophy* (New York: Henry Holt & Co., 1920; London: University of London Press, 1921). The book has been translated into Arabic (1959), Bohemian (1929), Chinese (1933), Italian (1931), Japanese, Persian, Portuguese (1957), Spanish (1930, 1958), and Urdu. Translation data from Milton Halsey Thomas, *John Dewey: A Centennial Bibliography* (Chicago: University of Chicago Press, 1962), p. 90.

8. John Dewey and Alice Chipman Dewey, *Letters from China and Japan,* ed. Evelyn Dewey (New York: E. P. Dutton Co., 1920); John Dewey, *Characters and Events, Popular Essays in Social and Political Philosophy,* ed. Joseph Ratner, 2 vols. (New York: Henry Holt & Co., 1929).

9. Some of the material in this section of the Introduction was included in Robert W. Clopton, "John Dewey in China," *Educational Perspectives* (a quarterly journal published by the College of Education of the University of Hawaii), spring 1965. It is used here by permission of the editors of that journal.

10. Y. C. Wang, *Chinese Intellectuals and the West* (Chapel Hill: University of North Carolina Press, 1966).

11. Ibid., pp. 499–500.

12. Ibid., p. 200.

13. Ibid., p. 498.

14. Berry, "Dewey's Influence in China," p. 206.

15. Chow Tse-tsung, *The May Fourth Movement: Intellectual Revolution in Modern China* (Cambridge: Harvard University Press, 1960), p. 271.

16. Ibid., p. 279.

17. Berry, "Dewey's Influence in China," pp. 202–203.

18. Chow, *May Fourth Movement,* pp. 178–183.

19. Ibid., pp. 182–183.

20. These lectures, translated by Clopton and Ou, and briefed in Appendix B (which see), have been deposited in typescript form in the Gregg M. Sinclair Library, University of Hawaii. They may be consulted in the Sinclair Library or copies may be ordered from the Reprography Department of the Thomas Hale Hamilton Library, University of Hawaii, Honolulu, Hawaii 96822.

21. This list of Chinese publications, in both romanized transliteration and Chinese characters, also may be consulted in the Sinclair Library or copies may be ordered from the Hamilton Library Reprography Department.

22. *Tu-wei Wu Ta Chiang-yen* (see note 3).

23. John Dewey, *Democracy and Education: An Introduction to the Philosophy of Education* (New York: Macmillan Co., 1916). This book has been translated into Arabic and Chinese (1934), German (1930, 1949), Italian

(1949), Japanese (1952), Persian and Portuguese (1930), Spanish (1946, 1953), Swedish (1948) and Turkish (1928). (Translation data from Thomas, *Dewey Centennial Bibliography,* pp. 45–46.)

24. John Dewey, *Democracy and Education,* translated into Chinese by Ch'ang Tao-chi (Shanghai: Commercial Press, 1922).

25. Hu Shih, "Dewey in China," pp. 764–765.

26. A historical treatment of Dewey's reception in China, and of the turbulent years of his visit, was submitted as a Ph.D. dissertation by Barry Keenan at Claremont Graduate School in 1969.

27. Hu Shih, *Essays of Hu Shih,* 1st ser. vol. 2 (1921). We quote the English version of this passage from O. Brière, *Fifty Years of Chinese Philosophy,* translated from the French by Laurence G. Thompson (London: Allen and Unwin, 1956), pp. 25–26.

28. Tsuin-chen Ou, *La Doctrine Pédagogique de John Dewey,* 2nd ed. (Paris: Vrin, 1958), p. 252. We quote the English version of the passage from Berry, "Dewey's Influence in China," p. 216.

29. Kazuko Tsurumi, ed., *John Dewey: A Critical Study on the American Way of Thinking* [in Japanese] (Tokyo: Shun Zyu Sha, 1950), p. 186.

30. Chiang Monlin, *Tides from the West: A Chinese Autobiography* (New Haven: Yale University Press, 1947), p. 114.

31. *Weekly Critic,* 20 July 1919.

32. Chow, *May Fourth Movement,* p. 230.

33. Ibid., p. 175.

34. Ibid., chap. xiv.

35. Chow, correspondence, 16 February 1966.

36. Chow, *May Fourth Movement,* p. 248.

37. Ibid., p. 176.

38. John Dewey, "The Development of American Democracy," *Bulletin* of the Ministry of Education [Nanking], no. 7, 1919, pp. 1–5; *Tu-Wei Wu Ta Chiang-yen,* p. 64; *New Youth,* 7, no. 2 (December 1919).

39. *Tu-wei Wu Ta Chiang-yen,* pp. 57–65; John Dewey, "Habit and Thinking," *Bulletin* of the Ministry of Education, no. 10, 1922, pp. 34–41; *Historical Abstracts,* no. 3366, 1955.

40. John Dewey, "Habit and Thinking," *Bulletin* of the Ministry of Education, no. 10, 1922, pp. 39–41.

41. Franz H. Michael and George E. Taylor, *The Far East in the Modern World* (New York: Henry Holt & Co., 1956), pp. 232–235.

42. *Historical Abstracts,* no. 1560, 1955.

43. *Shih-hsueh* (Supplement of *Kuang Ming Jih Pao,* no. 51, 1955); *Historical Abstracts,* no. 3366, 1955.

44. Hu Shih, "Dewey in China," pp. 766–769.

45. Tao Chi-hsing later changed his name to Tao Hsing-chi to show his firmer conversion to the pragmatic philosophy of Dewey. The old name meant "doing after knowing," or "to know in order to do," while the new one means "knowing after doing," or "to do in order to know."

46. Tao Hsing-chi, "The Textbooks Prepared According to the Principle of

Teaching-Learning-Doing Combination," *Chung Hua Education Review,* 19, no. 9 (October 1930). Translated and quoted by Chu Don-chean in "Tao Hsing-chi and Chinese Education," Ed. D. dissertation, Teachers College, Columbia University, 1953, p. 92.

47. Chu Don-chean, "Tao Hsing-chi and Chinese Education," p. 23.

48. Translated and quoted by Hu Shih, "Dewey in China," p. 767.

49. The following works of Dewey have been published in Chinese translation: *Democracy and Education, School and Society, The Child and the Curriculum, My Pedagogic Creed* (two versions), *Schools of Tomorrow, Freedom and Culture* (two versions), *Sources of the Science of Education* (two versions), *Education Today, Reconstruction in Philosophy* (two versions), *Ethics, How We Think* (three versions), *Moral Principles in Education, Experience and Education* (two versions).

50. Hsin-cheng Shu, comp., *Chin Tai Chung Kuo Chiao Yu Shih Liao* [A collection of documents on the history of modern China], vol. II (Shanghai: Chung Hwa Book Company, 1933), pp. 113–120.

51. Ibid., p. 20.

52. *Bulletin* of the Ministry of Education, no. 10, 1922.

53. Ibid.

54. Hu Shih, "Dewey in China," pp. 765–766.

55. *Education Review* 11, no. 11 (1919), p. 108; ibid., 13, no. 11 (1921).

56. I I-tze, *An Elementary School's Ten-Year Endeavor* (Shanghai: Chung Hwa Book Company, "before 1937").

57. See Appendix B.

58. *Chung Kuo Ching Chi Shih Nien Lai Chiao Yü Chi Shih* [The record of Chinese educational events in the past seventy years], comp. Chih-pin Ting (Shanghai: Commercial Press, 1935); *China Year Book* (New Haven: Yale University Press, 1923, 1947), p. 1900; Chiang Monlin, *Tides from the West,* p. 124.

59. *Tu-wei Wu Ta Chiang-yen,* p. 251; ibid., p. 158.

60. *Bulletin* of the Ministry of Education, no. 2, 1920, p. 7. *Kuo-wen* is usually translated "national language" (Mandarin). *Kuo-yü* is "popular language" and is virtually synonymous with *Paihua,* except that the latter term customarily refers to printed material.

61. Cyrus H. Peake, *Nationalism and Education in Modern China* (New York: Columbia University Press, 1932), p. 143; Ting Chih-pin, *Chinese Educational Events,* p. 89.

62. *Bulletin* of the Ministry of Education, no. 2, 1925, p. 10; *Education Review,* 18, no. 1(1925).

63. Tsuin-chen Ou, *La Doctrine Pédagogique de John Dewey,* p. 253.

64. Hu Shih, "Dewey in China," p. 767.

65. Ibid.

66. Ch'en Ho-ch'in, *Critique of the Philosophic Bases of John Dewey's Reactionary Pedagogy* (Shanghai: New Knowledge Press, 1956), p. 44.

67. Ibid., p. 45.

68. Ibid., p. 47.

69. *Education and Culture* (Taipei: The Ministry of Education) no. 317 (April 15, 1964), p. 18.

70. Ibid., no. 319 (June 15, 1964), p. 44.

71. Wang Wu is a pen name used by a man whose identity we have not been able to establish, but who may have been a member of the editorial staff of the *Citizens' Gazette,* the newspaper which first printed these lectures in the version subsequently used by the *Morning Post* (Peking), both in its columns, and eventually in the paperbound volume, *Tu-wei Wu Ta Chiang-yen.*

72. For two years beyond the expiration of his appointment at the East-West Center, and while engaged in graduate study in Canada, Mr. Lu continued to translate additional lectures as they came to light. In 1968 Mr. Lu was awarded the Ph.D. degree by the University of Alberta, Edmonton, at which time he changed his name to Henry C. Lu. Dr. Ou was recalled to Hong Kong early in 1965; after that time collaboration continued by mail in the pattern described.

PART I SOCIAL AND
POLITICAL
PHILOSOPHY

INTRODUCTORY NOTE by Hu Shih

Dr. John Dewey has recently completed two series of lectures in Peking, one on "Social and Political Philosophy," the other on "A Philosophy of Education." Dr. Dewey's philosophy of education is so well known that no introduction to it is required; but I do wish to make a few remarks about his lectures on "Social and Political Philosophy."

The philosophy of pragmatism, with which Dr. Dewey's name is identified, has been the subject of a number of systematic statements, among them the work of William James in psychology, the work of Dewey himself and of Ferdinand Canning Scott Schiller in logic, the work of Dewey and James Hayden Tufts in ethics, and, of course, Dewey's own monumental work in education.

Only in the field of political philosophy has there not yet appeared any single systematic work which treats the subject from the viewpoint of pragmatism. It is true that the political theory of Graham Wallas and Harold Laski in England, and of Walter Lippmann in the United States of America, strongly reflects the influence of pragmatism; but, until now, a formal, coherent statement of a pragmatic philosophy of politics has been lacking.

It was for this reason that I suggested to Dr. Dewey, earlier this year when he and I were discussing his forthcoming lecture series in China, that this might be an appropriate opportunity for him to formulate a coherent statement of a social and political philosophy based in pragmatism, elements of which have been suggested in his writings increasingly during the last decade.

Dr. Dewey thought that my suggestion was a good one, and the result is this series of sixteen lectures. I hope that those who were in the audiences when these lectures were delivered, as well as the readers of the printed version of the lectures herewith presented, are cognizant of their rare good fortune in sharing in Dr. Dewey's initial formal statement of his social and political philosophy.

As Dr. Dewey delivered his lectures in English I interpreted them sentence by sentence into Chinese for the benefit of members of his audiences who did not understand English. My Chinese interpretation was recorded by my friend, I-han Kao.* Dr. Dewey intends to revise and expand his original lecture notes for publication in book form. When his manuscript is complete, I hope to translate it into Chinese, so that both English and Chinese versions can be published at the same time.

It is inevitable that in material so complex as these lectures on-the-spot oral interpretation and simultaneous recording should result in certain inaccuracies and inadequacies. For such errors and omissions Professor I-han Kao and I offer our apologies, both to Dr. Dewey and to the reading public.

November 1919

---

* As a matter of fact, Professor Kao recorded only the first nine lectures. The remaining seven were recorded by Sun Fu-yuan, then an editor of the *Morning Post* (Peking).

THE FUNCTION OF THEORY

The topic for this series of sixteen lectures is "Social and Political Philosophy." This means that I shall be talking about theories dealing with the collective life of mankind. Theory, as an explanation of the way things are constituted and of the ways in which they work, always comes onto the scene quite late. We do not ordinarily ask why or how we do certain things until we have been doing them a long time. People had been eating and digesting food for millions of years, for example, before they formulated theories about physiology and hygiene; they had been talking—and even writing—for hundreds of generations before they devised theories of grammar, rhetoric, and logic to explain the behavior of language as they and their ancestors had used it.

The case is the same with social and political philosophy. We do not philosophize—that is to say, we do not construct theories—about our customs and habits and institutions until some sort of difficulty or obstruction raises questions in our minds about the ways in which we have been carrying on our group activities. It is always the social institution which precedes the theory; not the theory which precedes the institution.

Mankind shares one universal characteristic: when a need occurs there is activity which seeks to satisfy the need. When we are hungry, we eat; when we are tired, we sleep. When a need comes into being because of a particular event (or an event which we have not yet recognized as belonging to a category or class of events), we consciously try out and evaluate activities calculated to reduce the tension. As events of similar character occur in experience, however, and as the same or closely related activities prove effective in reducing a series of similar tensions, such actions become habitual. We no longer think about what we do; we do not ask ourselves "Why do we do it this way rather than some other way?" If someone does raise the question, we reply that "everybody does it this way," or that "this is the way that it has always been done." As long as our way of dealing with a class of situations provides reasonable satisfaction, we do not need a theory to justify our actions.

Even when conditions change and our individual and group habits prove less effective and less satisfying than they formerly were, there is a general tendency to shy away from examination and speculation—that is, from theorizing—and to become annoyed at or resentful toward people who insist upon raising the questions of what? and how? and why? Men who have raised such questions have often been unpopular, and some who have persisted in pressing their questions about existing institutions have even been put to death for their pains. The classic example, of course, is Socrates, whose "Why this?" and "Why that?" so exasperated his fellow Athenians that they finally condemned him to drink the hemlock, alleging that he had misled the public and corrupted the youth with his questionings. From that day to this, most societies have disliked theorizing and have penalized theorizers.

In spite of the fact, however, that people in general seem to prefer not to think about their problems, times come when they cannot avoid doing so. Were this not so, we should be following the habits, customs, and institutions of our ancestors, and there would be no social and political philosophy.

So long as accustomed actions serve reasonably adequately to meet situations which we encounter and to reduce tensions, people can and do get along well enough without giving conscious thought to their behavior. One need not think much about eating, for example, so long as he has enough food before him and does not suffer from loss of appetite or indigestion; nor does he need to think about walking as he goes about his day-by-day affairs. But when afflicted with nausea or loss of appetite, a man does think about eating; when a sprained ankle hinders his walking, he does have to make a decision about whether to call a taxicab or take a bus.

Generally speaking, thinking occurs only when we encounter difficulty, only at those times when habitual or institutional ways of acting prove insufficient to the situation at hand. This is as true of the attitude of human beings toward social institutions and politics as it is in the simpler matters of eating and walking. It is only when existing customs and institutions cease to function adequately that we tolerate—and even then, quite unwillingly in many cases—questioning as to their form and function. When our laws, customs, and institutions no longer serve the purpose for which they were originally evolved, we are forced to ask "What's the trouble?" or "Why aren't they working?"

Analogy with the human body is instructive. Not only do we think when the body fails to function as it should, but the thinking done by qualified observers is ultimately combined to form theory, and we have first the art, then the science of medicine. Treatment of disease creates the need for antecedent theory to provide answers to questions raised by medicine, and so we have theories about, and sciences of, anatomy and physiology, and eventually theories such as those which identify the origins of diseases in germs and viruses, the theory of immunology, and the many branches of biochemistry.

The parallels with society and politics are obvious. When social life becomes disordered, we cannot but make the attempt to find out what causes the trouble. And, thinking of the art of medicine as restoration of the body to its former condition of well-being, we seek methods by which we hope that we may similarly restore society to the wholeness or health which our memories attribute to its earlier stages. The body of theory which we evolve and formulate as we conduct this search constitutes our social and political philosophy.

Generally speaking, in the Eastern World as much as in the Western, political theories have been expounded only when a society is in disorder and appears to be threatened with distintegration. By the end of the fifth century before Christ, for example, the legal institutions and social customs which had provided centuries of stability for the Greek city states were proving increasingly inadequate and ineffective for the regulation of civic and social life in the period of economic and moral confusion which followed two generations of warfare with the Persians. One effort to meet the need—and no one could deny that there was a need—was the philosophy of Plato; another was the philosophy propounded by Plato's pupil, Aristotle.

Unless I am misinformed, the social theories which have patterned Chinese thought and society for so many centuries must have arisen the same way. Lao-tze was born at a time when chaos marked social, political, and moral life; and later Confucius came along when there was still such distressing disorder that the people of China recognized the need for, and eagerly accepted, a philosophy which afforded the basis for a stable society for more than two thousand years.

So much for the origins of social and political philosophy. What can we say about the effects of theories after they have been formulated and propounded? Even when we grant that social and political theory comes into being only when a society is out of kilter, the question remains whether the theory can merely describe the symptoms, or whether it can be a means toward the cure of the disease. Analogously, is medical science limited to diagnosis, or does it include prescriptions for cures? Or does the science of dynamics, as applied to steam, for example, have to do only with the potential power of the vapor produced when water is heated, or does it include the harnessing of this power to drive locomotives?

These are examples of the same sort of question as "What effects can a theory have in practice?" or, in our present inquiry, "What is the practical use of social and political philosophy in social and political practice?" As obvious as the answers to these questions may appear at first glance, there exist two schools of thought on the matter—answers which are antithetical and contradictory. While there are shadings of opinion within each camp, we may for convenience and at the risk of oversimplification designate the points of view as extreme idealism and extreme materialism.

The extreme idealist emphasizes the ideal, holding that everything results from theory. Because of his preoccupation with ideals, he tends to ignore the effects of nonintellectual factors, and to conclude that all institutions and habits result in one way or another from application, explicit or implicit, of theories. He sees, for example, the recently concluded World War* as the result of conflict between irreconcilable theoretical positions.

The extreme materialist, on the other hand, holds that a theory is an effect, not a cause. It results *from* something, but cannot result *in* anything. For him, the war in Europe was the result of material conflict. In his view, all major events of the world are the results of struggles of various interests in life. He does not limit this conclusion to politics and economics, but extends it even to the fine arts.

From the viewpoint of the historical materialist, the World War can be explained in terms of economic competition. He repudiates the idea

* In all thirty-two lectures, whenever Dewey refers to the "recent World War" or the "World War" he is, of course, referring to World War I.

that the war might have resulted from conflict between theories, and insists upon interpreting it as material conflict. In prewar Germany industry had produced such huge surpluses that it had to seek overseas markets for its excess output. At the same time the economic development of England depended chiefly on maritime commerce. Thus, according to the materialist, the conflicting interests of these two great nations inevitably resulted in war, and talk of conflicting ideals is nothing more than the use of high-sounding phrases to entice the populace into participation in the war. He points to the successful efforts of German militarists to incite the people with references to *"Kultur,"* and with slogans such as *"Sturm und Drang"* and *"Deutschland über Alles";* and to appeal by leaders of the Allied Nations to "freedom and justice," to "making the world safe for democracy," and like catchwords. The materialist denies that these terms represent ideals at all; he regards them as nothing more than devices employed by capitalists and militarists to further their ends. And with this denial he rules out the possibility of conflict between ideals.

I have mentioned these antithetical points of view not to criticize either of them, but rather to set the stage for your consideration of the effects which social and political philosophy might have upon the practical affairs of life. Rather than dispute either of the two points of view I have described, I advance a third one.

According to this third theory, hypotheses and theories are, in their initial stages, the results rather than the causes of practice. But—and this is the essential difference from the two points of view discussed earlier—as soon as an hypothesis is formed, or a theory begins to take shape, no matter how crude, it becomes part of the practice which produced it. This is to say that when people begin to think about what they've been doing, the very act of thinking changes the doing. Further practice clarifies or modifies the theory; the clarified or modified theory alters practice, then theory is still further clarified, and so on until a coherent and adequately descriptive theory is achieved.

In the social and political realm, as in other aspects of living, thinking occurs when we encounter difficulties and dissatisfactions; and as is the case with individual action, once thinking occurs it results in some change in customs and institutions. These changes are not always immediately discernible, but people are influenced and changed, often more than they recognize; and the changes are reflected in their behavior, their habits, and their characters—more, in many cases, than in their utterances.

Thus it is not very significant to talk about the different philosophies of England, France, and Germany from the purely theoretical point of view; for, from the practical point of view, the differing philosophies of these countries are exemplified in their people's behavior, attitudes, and habits.

Since commonsense observation convinces us that ideas can and do influence human actions, it becomes important for us to observe what sorts of effects are wrought by what sorts of ideas. We must concern ourselves with the question of which ideas are good and which are bad.

The first function of theory is to give permanence to that which is initially temporary or accidental, to provide stability for ways of thinking and doing which are wavering and shaky. A presumed good, without theoretical support, may disappear within a relatively short time; but this same good may be embodied in principle or established as doctrine with the aid of theory, and so become permanent and stable.

This fact may conduce either to good or to evil. A prime example in history is the adoption by the Roman Catholic Church of Aristotelianism (as interpreted by St. Thomas Aquinas) as its official philosophy. Now why should the Catholic Church adopt the theoretical constructs of a non-Catholic as its official philosophy? It was simply because in the thirteenth century, theological controversy, and the challenge of competing philosophies, threatened the very existence of traditional Christian theology, and Aristotle's systematic philosophical framework afforded the means of crystallizing Christian doctrine and perpetuating it in a stable and transmissible form. China offers other examples. Many Chinese institutions, under the aegis of Confucianism, have remained unaltered and unchallenged for more than two thousand years. When theory results in rigidity rather than in stability, it interferes with progress, and can thus prove dangerous.

A second function of theory, particularly in those cases in which theory constitutes an ideal, is that in time of crisis it can generate faith, and cause people to sacrifice their property, and even their lives, for something in which they believe deeply. We have mentioned the use of slogans by both sides in the recent World War. Even if the extreme materialists are correct in their allegation that militarists capitalized upon the use of such slogans to manipulate the populace to their ends, they must recognize the fact that such terms were, somehow or other, attached to ideals (dimly comprehended in many cases, but ideals nevertheless) in the minds of people who were influenced by them. Human behavior is, in fact, influenced by theory on one or another level, quite as much as by the material conditions of existence. In a time of crisis a few abstract terms can set the world on fire, a notable indication of the power of theory.

The two functions of theory which we have mentioned are obvious to all of us. Theories can be both good and bad, and both good ones and bad ones have their effects in human behavior. Even superstitions and hallucinations are effective in controlling human actions.

Now let us discuss the ways in which a theory produces its effects, and inquire whether our present age demands a reconstructed social and political philosophy.

Generally speaking, social and political philosophies, like human character, can be subsumed under two broad categories, the radical and the conservative.

The typical radical is dissatisfied with and sharply critical of existing social institutions. He deplores what he sees about him, and proposes idealistic utopian schemes. He is not interested in improving what exists, but advocates replacing it with something entirely new and different. His theories tend to be destructive rather than constructive. The conservative always appears later than the radical. For example, in classic Greece the conservative Aristotle followed Plato, the radical. In *The Republic,* Plato, with utter disregard for the institutions of his society, proposed a Utopia in which property, wives, and children would be common possessions of all citizens. This extreme radical statement was followed by the conservative theories of Aristotle, who in his *Politics,* his *Ethics,* and his other books, set forth theoretical bases for the perpetuation of the social and political schemes of his time. The same thing was true in China: the radical theories of Lao-tze were followed by the conservative theories of Confucius.

The radical puts his emphasis upon individuality and individual conscience, demanding that existing institutions, which he alleges to be stifling to individuality, be replaced by idealistic constructs. The most extreme radicals believe that if each person is permitted to follow his own conscience and develop his individual character, he will be able to govern his actions; that the need for government will disappear and that a utopian society will come into being.

The conservative is also dissatisfied with existing institutions, but he recognizes the fact that each institution evolved to serve a human need, that it has what might be called an original meaning. A given institution may have deteriorated because people lost sight of the purpose it was originally intended to serve. Governments, for example, are essential institutions, but when a ruler fails to exercise his power in such a way as to serve the purposes for which the government was instituted, we call this bad government.

With this thought in mind, the typical conservative, when he judges an institution, undertakes to identify the need which brought the institution into play in the beginning, or as he might express it, "to look for the original meaning of the institution." He assumes that the task at hand is to restore this original meaning rather than to replace the institution.

Aristotle was a conservative because he held that the ideal for an improved society was to be found within existing social institutions, and not, as Plato had advocated, in some Utopia outside the existing society. In the early phases of the French Revolution the Jacobins were extremely radical, advocating the destruction of existing institutions—governmental, ecclesiastical, class-structural, even calendric. But after the fall of Napoleon I there was a reversal of the trend, and efforts were extended to preserve much of the institutional framework of government and society as this had existed prior to the revolution. We see a similar picture in Confucius, who held that all institutions had their ideal standards, and that if men would rediscover and act upon these ideals there would be no need to destroy or replace the institutions.

Of these two theoretical ways of looking at the world, the first—radicalism—emphasizes the ideal of individuality, and finds in the human person the measure of right and wrong. The second position—conservatism—places less trust in individuals, noting that individual judgment is fallible, and holding that the wisdom of the past affords the only reliable basis for action. The former theory deprecates existing institutions and seeks their replacement with new arrangements, while the latter postulates a fundamental validity for existing institutions and concentrates on clarification of their purpose, or discovery of their original meaning. The former relies on individual initiative and intelligence, the latter looks to the ancients; the former puts its faith in reflective intelligence, the latter calls for analytical study of the past.

There have been, of course, many different theories in the field of social and political philosophy, but all of them may be subsumed under one or the other of the two categories I have described. If I have oversimplified and exaggerated, it is not because I wished to ridicule either position, but rather to focus attention on a basic weakness in classical and contemporary social and political philosophy, and so to prepare the ground for a third theoretical position which is different from both those I have described.

From time immemorial mankind has been subject to two errors, deficiency and excess. In times of crisis men have tended to be either too radical or too conservative. They have fallen into the trap of either-or, tending to regard everything they see around them as either good or bad.

Yet our common sense and our everyday observation tell us that the problems of human life cannot be solved either by completely discarding our habits, customs, and institutions, or by doggedly hanging on to them and resisting all efforts to modify and reconstruct them.

What mankind needs most is the ability to recognize and pass judgment on *facts*. We need to develop the ability (and the disposition) to look for particular kinds of solutions by particular methods for particular problems which arise on particular occasions. In other words, we must deal with concrete problems by concrete methods when and as these problems present themselves in our experience. This is the gist of what we call the third philosophy.

The common weakness of extreme radicalism and extreme conservatism as I have described them is their dependence on sweeping generalizations. The former holds that all institutions are evil, and calls on men to discard them and build a paradise forthwith. The latter holds that all institutions are basically sound if we can discover and stick to their original meaning. Both fail to focus on the concrete problems which arise in experience, allowing such problems to be buried under their sweeping generalizations.

To conclude, the present problem of social and political philosophy is that of discovering ways in which human behavior can be controlled and guided by human knowledge and intelligence, and directed toward ends which are justified by human reason. What instruments can be devised with which to deal with our present environment? These are the problems of the third social and political philosophy, and will be the subject matter of the next lecture in this series.

SCIENCE AND SOCIAL PHILOSOPHY

B roadly speaking the social sciences—the sciences which deal with associated human life—came into being in Europe in the nineteenth century. The laws and principles which were originally developed in natural science were only gradually applied to individual human life, and still later to the problems of human society. What we call the social sciences are the result of applying to social problems the spirit and methods which had evolved as man sought a sounder understanding of nature.

My topic for today is the influence of this scientific spirit on the third social and political philosophy which I mentioned at the conclusion of my first lecture as an alternative to extreme radicalism or extreme conservatism.

It is interesting to note that in its beginnings modern science dealt with subject matter which was about as far from the immediate problems of human life as it was possible to get—astronomy. Then man brought the methods of science to bear on his immediate world, and modern physics and chemistry were born. It was only after this that we had a scientific approach to living things, and developed the life sciences of botany and zoology. It was only comparatively recently that it dawned on us that the problems of associated living were susceptible to investigation and ordering by the same methods which had proved so useful in dealing with the objective world.

Once man recognized that scientific methods could be fruitfully applied to the study of social events, we had the birth of the social sciences. For example, the science which deals with the origins of human races, with evolution, with customs, and with adaptation to environment is called anthropology; the science which deals with the production, distribution, and utilization of material goods is called economics; the science which deals with the institutions by which men seek to regulate the behavior of themselves and their fellows in their relationships in village, city, state, or nation is called politics; the science which investigates man's efforts to relate himself to his universe, to study his beliefs and values, is called religion; the science which explores man's past efforts to cope with situations which have confronted him is called history; the science which deals with the means of communication of ideas among human beings is called linguistics. These and others are the social sciences which apply the laws and methods of the natural sciences to the problems of associated human living.

The social sciences have developed at various rates and have achieved varying degrees of success in their efforts to order knowledge of human behavior. At times some of them have advanced conclusions which subsequent investigation showed to be invalid. Regardless of these circumstances however, one statement can be made about the social sciences as a group—they have made a tremendous change in people's attitudes and in their habits of thinking. No longer does any educated man suppose that scientific laws and theories can be constructed only for the natural sciences such as mathematics, physics, and chemistry, or that the irregularities of human life exclude it from the domain of the sciences. We have accepted the fact that the physical, psychological and social behaviors of man are susceptible to investigation and explanation in the same ways (if not always with the same degree of exactitude) as natural phenomena are explained.

Yet, strangely, many of the very men who are creating the social sciences take a dim view of social philosophy. They appear to believe that sciences follow fixed natural laws and deal with hard facts, but that philosophy, as mere speculation, is beneath their notice.

I had not intended to criticize social scientists, but there is one matter to which we must give consideration at this point: when the subject matter of scientific investigation is a category of human behavior, the principles and theories are ordinarily derived from the study of a particular situation during a particular period of time. These principles and theories may provide an accurate and adequate description and explanation of the behavior observed in that situation and at that time. Too often, however, social scientists undertake to make the application of such principles and theories general and universal, and to assume that they are equally applicable everywhere and at all times.

Let us look at economics as an example of this tendency. Economics was not developed as a social science until the eighteenth and nineteenth centuries. Its general principles were formulated as a result of study of economic conditions and behavior in a limited portion of Western Europe. The questions for which early economists sought answers were: "How can more goods be produced at lower costs? How can these goods be most effectively distributed? How can demand be stimulated so that consumption is increased?"

These were questions which were of major concern in a certain region in Western Europe, but after economists formulated general principles which were applicable to the time and place in which they were derived, they tended to regard them as universal laws which could be used equally well all over the world and for all time. As a matter of fact, three major aspects of the nineteenth century economics situation in Western Europe differentiated it from situations which existed in other places at that time, as well as from the situation which is increasingly replacing it on its own ground: (1) nineteenth century European production was by means of a capitalistic system, composed chiefly of huge units; (2) economic development was competitive, not cooperative; and (3) the purpose of economic organization was frankly profit and without reference to the welfare of the public.

Economists studying a situation of which these factors were characteristic came up with a statement of principles which seemed to them to have the status of universal law, and which they assumed to describe all economic activities of human life. One example of such a "law" was that of supply and demand, which was presumed to describe the inexorable operation of the processes of production and consumption. This law might result in hardship or unhappiness; grinding poverty for some, affluence for others; it might be deplored, but according to the economist, it had to be accepted. It was as immutable as the orbits of the planets.

Then Carlyle, Ruskin, and other social thinkers of their time, horrified at the poverty and degradation which they saw, and unwilling to grant the status of natural law to the pronouncements of the classical economists, demanded the abolition of such a tragic sort of science. Out of the controversy arose a new school, the "historical economists," who recognized historical facts and systems and who concluded that principles and laws derived from the study of particular facts in history are relative to those facts, and are not absolute and universally applicable laws.

History affords us another example of the fact that general principles are formulated on the basis of particular events. Facts change, and the shift to a different set of facts creates the need for a new statement of principle, a new theory. A case in point is the fact that the nature of European society was, at one stage, chiefly that of city-state. Subsequently it was a feudal society; then later it became an industrial society. It is obvious that principles that may have been entirely appropriate to and adequate for a city-state could not have been applied in a feudal society, and that principles that may have worked well in a feudal society become useless, obsolete, or harmful in an industrial society.

What I have illustrated by reference to economics and history is equally true in the other realms of human behavior which constitute the subject matter of the social sciences. The situations in which people live differ from generation to generation, and it follows that generalizations and principles derived from the study of these situations must also differ in one or another degree. There is no such thing as a social theory which is absolutely and always true, or which is immune to change.

I have mentioned views of nineteenth century social scientists for two reasons. The first of these reasons has both a negative and a positive aspect. On the negative side I meant to explain that society is still developing, and that history, which is a human creation, is still in process. We must bring philosophy to bear on our present situation. Science operates from a purely objective viewpoint. It can describe and record natural phenomena, but it cannot guide them or change them according to human ideals. But social philosophy cannot stop with mere recording and description; it must direct with thoughtful understanding the conclusions and recommendations which grow out of the records and descriptions of science. A certain amount of speculation is, therefore, necessarily present in social philosophy.

On the positive side is the tremendous change in the psychological attitude of people in general following the development of the social sciences. We have come to regard human activities as something from which law and principle can also be formulated, rather than something erratic and unpredictable. The social sciences have introduced the scientific spirit into social philosophy. Philosophy, formerly purely speculative, has been brought down from the clouds to dwell among men.

Among the significant results of this shift, we see men judging on the basis of fact rather than armchair speculation, deciding on the basis of evidence rather than presumed "natural law," becoming experimental in attitude rather than having closed minds, and regarding scientific laws as hypotheses rather than as universal truths. Increasingly, with the development of the social sciences, social philosophy has become imbued with the scientific spirit.

The second reason I mentioned the development of the social sciences is that I wanted to show how it was only after the scientific spirit had been introduced into social philosophy that the third school of the latter could come into being. This third school of social philosophy is characterized by three important features:

1. Emphasis on experimentation. Classical philosophies have tended to depend on ideas, to be generally conservative, and to be isolated from the cold, hard facts of human experience. This third philosophy holds that ideas and theories must be tested by practical application. The truth or falsity of an idea has to be determined by experimentation. If experimentation demonstrates that an idea is valid, it can then be applied as a guide to human conduct.

2. Emphasis on the study of individual events. Classical philosophers have either advocated the replacement of existing institutions on the one hand, or sought to conserve them in their entirety on the other. The third philosophy does not resort to such sweeping generalizations. It is concerned with individual cases in particular situations. It does not advance panaceas or universal laws.

3. Emphasis on application of knowledge and intelligence to social change. The third philosophy advocates neither the total reconstruction nor the absolute conservation of existing institutions. Its purpose is to cultivate knowledge and intelligence by use of which men may remedy particular disorders and solve particular problems.

There are two branches of science—pure science and applied science. Pure science deals with facts; it describes and formulates theories about events as these can be observed and recorded. Human will and desire, ideally speaking, should not be involved in scientific descriptions of natural processes nor in theories that explain scientific observations. Applied science, on the other hand, since it is application of the findings of pure science to the field of human will and desire, must of necessity not only involve man's preferences, but must generate theories to satisfy those preferences, to save them from suppression or perversion.

In pure science man can study an event only with the attitude of a spectator. In astronomy, for example, he can say whether the moon is full or on the wane, whether it is rising or setting. He can construct theories which account for the behavior of the moon, but he cannot have it remain full, or cause it to wax rather than to wane, to return to the eastern horizon instead of setting in the west. But the case is quite different with applied science. Man is not only closely related to applied science; he is, in fact, one of its components. Consequently, in applied science, man conducts research with a perfectly legitimate subjective interest, not with the attitude of a spectator. In medical science, for example, the doctor is part of his own research. His theories deal with the cure of diseases, but his choice to work for the recovery of his patients rather than to let them die is an act of his will. Theory is not established, and the end of applied science is not reached, until human desire and will are satisfied.

This is also the way social philosophy must operate. It must provide man with a sense of direction so that he moves toward a goal rather than wandering hither and yon. All social sciences are applied sciences, the sources of theories which should direct human conduct and enable man to achieve those ends in life which his reflection makes him desire. This is the attitude of instrumentalism, or the experimental method.

Social philosophy is an applied science, not a pure one. Thus it is not sufficient for social philosophy merely to describe the phenomena of experience—it must also contribute to the realization of the ends which men desire. It is not enough, for example, for economists merely to describe the production and exchange of goods, and stop there; they must indicate the directions, based upon their study of economic situations and events, in which men are to move so that the greatest number of people may achieve the maximum satisfaction. Or take political science as another example: it is not sufficient for it to record and analyze present and past political events and trends. It must also provide the material by means of which man can improve his lot and move toward the goal of peace and happiness. The social sciences such as economics, political science, and the others, are in actuality technologies, the application and assessment of which are functions of social philosophy. The relationship between the social sciences and social philosophy is thus one of interpenetration.

Of course there are many sorts of technologies, some of them good, some of them not; and man is constantly confronted with the necessity for choosing. In medicine, for example, there is treatment of disease by sorcery; and there is medical science which utilizes physiology and bio- chemistry in its technology. The same is true of the other social sciences. When, for example, there was no coherent and consistent body of theory in political science, good government was pretty much a matter of chance. Under a strong ruler or a group of talented and dedicated public officials a country might flourish, but history is replete with examples of deterio- ration and chaos when less capable persons acceded to positions of power. Now, with principles and theories of political science derived from experi- ence, political behavior is more likely to be guided by scientific intelli- gence, and governments are less subject to fate, good luck, or mere chance.

There are two reasons for insisting that social philosophy must incorpo- rate scientific method. The first of these is that we have finally arrived at a stage at which we can observe and investigate political and other social situations all over the world. Modern developments in transporta- tion and communication have brought all regions and all peoples into some degree of contact, and have made it possible for social scientists to survey and record their behavior. We are now in a time when failure to utilize the findings of scientific research could result in a single incident which might totally destroy the human culture that has been so labori- ously built up over countless centuries. The very preservation of mankind demands that we seize every possible opportunity to carry on research, and to derive from it theories which can serve as instruments for guiding human conduct.

My second reason for insisting upon the incorporation of scientific method into social philosophy is to direct attention to the characteristics which differentiate this third type of philosophy that we are discussing from its predecessors. Earlier social philosophies were general, abstract, and idealistic. They built their arguments around general concepts such as individualism, socialism, or communism. They resorted to sweeping generalizations—"government is useful," "government is useless," or "the institution of private property is bad." Modern social philosophy eschews doctrinaire positions such as these. It deals with individual cases, with particular events, and with the relationships between the individual cases and generalizations. Its task is to formulate tentative general principles from investigation of similar individual cases, and then to check the generalizations by applying them to still further actual cases.

Philosophers who still resort to vague, sweeping generalizations are behind their times. The modern philosopher does painstaking research on individual cases. This is the reason that social philosophy must incorporate scientific methods.

Let us look at some examples which illustrate the basic fallacy involved in exclusive dependence on methods of abstraction, generalization, and idealization. Our first example is hypothetical, and patently absurd, but fundamentally no more so than the others, which are observable historical developments.

What would we think of a railroad builder who adopted the abstract idea of an ideal railroad as his construction plan? Would investors provide funds if he were to build his bridges where they appeared on his ideal plan instead of where actual rivers occurred in the landscape? Or if he bored tunnels where the ideal plan called for tunnels, instead of where actual mountains made tunnels a practical necessity? Or if he failed to take account of the real commodities produced in the area to be served by his railroad, and of the location of the markets for these commodities? Yet such a procedure would be quite consistent with the exclusive use of generalizations and idealizations by the social philosophers of an earlier day.

Now for an actual example from history: Chaotic conditions in seventeenth-century Europe—religious wars, rivalries among principalities, struggles for ascendancy among emerging nations—created the need for law and order, and above everything else, for absolute national sovereignty. Political theorists, finding justification for their theories in the fact that they were effective in meeting the problems of the time and place in which they were devised, concluded that the same theories should hold good in all countries and for all time. This "law" of absolute national sovereignty is unquestioningly accepted by all too many people, even in the twentieth century—and with results that have proved supremely tragic. To insist upon applying to a later time or another region, to require universal acceptance of "laws" which succeeded in meeting the needs of a particular period, is, as this example illustrates, to invite disaster.

A third example: means of production and distribution of goods underwent a tremendous change in the late eighteenth and early nineteenth centuries when steam power was substituted for muscle power in manu-facturing. This change brought into obsolescence a number of laws and practices of government regulation which had been needed in earlier phases of economic development, and gave rise to the demand for laissez faire—the doctrine that unrestricted competition, completely free from governmental interference, would result in a balanced economy.

Now it happens that laissez faire was a workable and effective theory at a time when modern capitalism was coming into being. But it was by no means a universal truth; and when people did take it to be universal and immutable, it metamorphosed into a tough individualism that was ruthlessly invoked to suppress the powerless, to keep wages down, and to serve the aggrandizement of men of power and wealth.

We could multiply examples which illustrate the danger of taking a method or a theory which may have been successful in meeting a par-ticular need at a given time and trying to make it permanent and insist on its universal applicability. But I believe that these few examples illus-trate the point sufficiently.

Unlike older philosophies which either attacked or defended existing institutions *in toto,* the third philosophy which we are discussing ac-knowledges that it is better to work for progress in particular situations rather than to try to defend or attack existing institutions. But such prog-ress is not automatic, nor is it progress *en bloc;* it is cumulative, a step forward here, a bit of improvement there. It takes place day by day, and results from the ways in which individual persons deal with particular situations; it is a step-by-step progress which comes by human effort to repair here, to modify there, to make a minor replacement yonder. Prog-ress is retail business, not wholesale. It is made piecemeal, not all at once.

Nowadays there are men who propose grandiose schemes by means of which they would reconstruct the world once and for all. But I, for one, simply do not believe that the world can be reconstructed totally and on a once-for-all basis; it can be reconstructed only gradually and by indi-vidual effort.

Here in China a number of people have asked me, "Where should we start in reforming our society?" My answer is that we must start by re-forming the component institutions of the society. Families, schools, local governments, the central government—all these must be reformed, but they must be reformed by the people who constitute them, working as individuals—in collaboration with other individuals, of course, but still as individuals, each accepting his own responsibility. Any claim of the total reconstruction of a society is almost certain to be misleading. The institutions which make up the society are not "right" or "wrong," but each is susceptible to some degree of improvement. Social progress is neither an accident nor a miracle; it is the sum of efforts made by individuals whose actions are guided by intelligence.

We do not always know how to start in dealing with human problems; and when we do get started, we make mistakes, whether or no. This is true because our problems are so numerous and so complicated. If we approach our problems one by one, and seek to solve them individually rather than by rule, we will still make mistakes; but we will not make nearly so many, nor such serious ones.

I imagine that most of you in the audience today are students; and as students, you must be peculiarly aware of the truth of what I have been saying. You know from your experience that the accomplishment of a series of small tasks results eventually in significant achievement. Sometimes, perhaps, the simple task at hand does not seem very relevant to our larger goals. But if each of us does his duty and faithfully performs the various small tasks which confront him, the final result can be the reformation which all of us desire. But if we focus our attention on this reformation alone, losing sight of the myriads of minor undertakings of which we are capable, I fear that little—more probably, nothing—will be accomplished.

I n my first two lectures I described three schools of social and political philosophy: the radical, which advocates the overthrow of existing institutions; the conservative, which defends existing institutions; and a third approach which emphasizes concrete problems instead of attacking or defending existing institutions by resort to sweeping generalizations. Today I shall talk further about this third type of theory, making comments on the first two as the occasion demands.

The fundamental concept of this third approach is that theory originates in man's attempts to deal with unresolved situations. The function of theory, in this view, is to correct errors and satisfy deficiencies which are perceived as man deals with social situations, as well as to resolve conflicts which occur among the component elements of the society. In such cases, emphasis on concrete problems, while essential, is not sufficient; we must also have a framework of general conceptions to guide us in our consideration of the total situation.

A sailor, for example, must have at least a map and a compass, the former to help him set his destination, the latter to provide a sense of direction. By analogy the social philosopher must also have general guiding principles to serve him as map and compass as he observes and seeks the causes of conflicts and instabilities in the social scene, and then contrives approaches which promise to resolve or alleviate the difficulties which the concrete problems present.

However, a "general guiding concept" as I use the term here is not by any means the same sort of thing as sweeping generalizations, serving as virtual absolutes, about which I made comments in earlier lectures. The general guiding concept is, in fact, a *general* concept, and in each case it derives from concrete events of the sort to which it is to be applied.

Classical philosophers have resorted to generalized antinomies when they have dealt with social conflicts—the individual versus society, the people versus the government, authority versus freedom. The actual bases of social conflicts were obscured rather than clarified by this manner of dealing with them. We should seek the origins of conflict in interpenetrating relationships among groups rather than in these abstracted antinomies.

From our point of view, social conflict cannot be defined merely as disagreement between one entity and another. For practical purposes it is useless, or worse, to postulate such oppositions as the individual versus society, the people versus the government, or authority versus freedom. Society is made up of many groups, and the lines of demarcation are ill-defined and overlapping. Conflicts among these groups are therefore complex and difficult to define.

By "group" I mean a collection of people who are united by common interests. People who have common interests naturally form themselves into groups, as, for example, people interested in baseball form baseball teams—or, in a more extended sense, become fans of one team or another. And since a society is made up of a multiplicity of groups each of which is constituted on the basis of at least one interest held in common by its members, social conflict is not, in any real sense, conflict between the individual and his society, but rather conflict between classes, occupational groups, or groups constituted along ideational, or perhaps even ethnic lines.

Let us be more specific about what we mean when we say that people with common interests naturally form themselves into groups, and see how each such group serves to meet some of the basic needs of human beings. One of the most fundamental urges in man (as in all animals) is sex. The satisfaction and regulation of this drive, and the need to provide for the children who are born, throws people naturally into groups which we call families, and gives rise to the institution which we call the home. Commonness of interest among the generations and among people of varying degrees of blood relationship calls into being the institution of the clan.

Again, because people need to eat, to keep warm, and to be protected from the weather, we have occupational groupings—farmers who produce food, merchants who sell it; men and women who spin, weave, and make our garments; those who transport goods from the regions where they are produced to the places where they are consumed; and so on. In a broader sense, because human nature is such that conflicts inevitably do arise, the need for regulation of human activities when association becomes complex is met by the formation of governments on the local, the provincial, and the national levels.

Human nature seems also to need religion, since most people are not content with a day-by-day existence, but want some sort of definition of their relationship as individuals with the universe. People who share common definitions of this need, or who postulate similar answers to the questions it poses, constitute religious groups—and so we have churches, temples, and mosques. We could engage in endless multiplication of examples of the plain fact that when people share interests in common they will form themselves into groups through which they give expression to their common interests.

We have been speaking of the origins of human groups; now let us look at the bases for conflicts among these groups. Social grouping is a complicated and overlapping phenomenon. No group is independent and isolated, and no person is ever a member of only one group. A single individual, for example, is a member of his total society; at the same time he is a citizen of his nation, his province, and his city or village. He may also be a member of a church, an employee in a given trade, a devotee of a particular sport. Another person may share membership in certain of these groups with him, but at the same time belong to different (and possibly antagonistic) groupings in relation to his other interests.

Society is in a state of imbalance because these many groups do not and cannot develop equably. Sometimes one group oppresses another. As decades and centuries pass, things may appear to run smoothly, and the subordinated group may, on the surface, appear complaisant and aquiescent. But history is replete with instances of revolts of apparently complacent groups—revolts which often revealed submerged antipathies and suppressed hatreds.

Now let us look at examples of cases in which certain groups have achieved privileged status, and, in suppressing other groups, have contributed to disorder and generated social conflict. Religious leaders constitute one obvious case. The Roman Catholic Church dominated a thousand years of European history, between A.D. 500 and 1500. During this period the Church exercised control over the family, the arts, education—and, as long as it was able to do so, even over the state.

While the family did persist as a basic institution during this time, it functioned, in general, on a lower level than had been the case in pre-Christian Rome. Christian theology postulated a conflict between man's spiritual nature and his physical needs; and the Church, applying this view, required that its clergy be celibate. Marriage and family were tolerated for the laity; but since the married state was scarcely more than a concession to those who did not have the spiritual strength to assume the burden of celibacy required of priests, monks, and nuns, little if any attention was devoted to the improvement of the quality of the family as an institutional unit.

The creative arts which had reached a high level of development in the classical "pagan" world suffered decline almost to the point of extinction during this period—or, at least, until other forces began successfully to challenge the domination of the Church toward the end of the age. Many of the early Church Fathers inveighed against the arts—particularly against those which portrayed the human figure—alleging that the sensuous appeal of sculpture and painting might inflame bodily desires—which were by definition (*their* definition) evil and to be avoided. It is true that the Church did encourage certain of the arts, notably architecture, and subsequently music—but primarily for the service that these arts were supposed to render to religion, not for what they could be presumed to contribute to the enhancement of human life.

With a very few notable exceptions ecclesiastics were antagonistic to the development of science, since they feared that science would challenge the "truths" of religion. Educational opportunity was restricted, and such education as there was served the needs and interests of the Church rather than of the populace. Ecclesiastics were jealous of the power of dukes, princes, and kings—and since neither the state nor the Church would alter its position, there was virtual warfare between the two for a thousand years. As a matter of harsh fact, there are remnants of this particular conflict even in the present day.

I know you will understand that in saying these things I am merely calling your attention to the frequency with which history shows us the domination of ecclesiastical organizations over other groups, largely because of the special respect and status that has been accorded to them. The sort of situation I have described occurs all over the world. The only three exceptions which come to mind are ancient Greece, China, and the

United States of America. In classic Greece there was virtually no institutionalization of religion, and consequently no priestly domination over
other groups. In China there has never been a state religion. At the time
the United States was established as a nation, its founders, well acquainted
with the history of conflict between church and state in Europe, wrote
into their constitution safeguards which guarantee complete and permanent separation of church and state. The American people have reaped
what their ancestors sowed; with this exception and the other two noted,
social progress has been impeded by the domination of organized religion.

Another group which has held a privileged position and has often sub-
dued others to its control is the political establishment. The story is told
of a Westerner who, arguing with a Hindu about the reasons that Oriental
countries are underdeveloped, averred that "Oriental countries are underdeveloped because the natives are too conservative, and stick to traditional
habits too persistently. For example, people in India used to carry things
on their heads because they didn't have wheelbarrows. Then when they
were introduced to wheelbarrows, they loaded them with coal and carried
the wheelbarrows on their heads. This is an example of the fact that
Orientals are the victims of habit and tradition to such an extent that
they cannot hope to reform their countries." To this the Hindu replied,
"It is true that Oriental peoples are bound by habits and traditions; but
it is also true that Western people depend too much on government.
Their mistake is that they use the government as a wheelbarrow—they
do not know how to put on their heads the things that belong there.
They dump everything into the wheelbarrow of government; and this
puts them at a disadvantage compared to us, because we still know how
to use our heads for carrying on our business."

The Hindu had a point. Westerners do, typically, place too great dependence on government. During the recent World War, for example,
the powers of Western national governments were extended to include
control of railroads, mining, many industrial enterprises—even of human
life itself. All institutions—commerce, industry, education—were subjected
to government control. The process went so far that a reaction against
big government set in, and thoughtful people began to question the wisdom of concentrating so much power in government, of subjecting other
institutions so completely to its control. Such doubts are increasing, and
will continue to do so.

Economic factors also often exercise undue dominance. Westerners in
particular seem to put a disproportionate value on the material things of

life. They like to make money; and the man who has made a fortune is almost automatically accorded respect and admiration. The Chinese are critical of this tendency, and are especially critical of the American people because Americans tend to put so much emphasis on economic factors.

The vast natural resources of the United States have contributed quite naturally to the rapid development of large-scale industry and commerce, and from this development has emerged a group of powerful capitalists—men so powerful that they exercise disproportionate control on governments, even at the national level. American capitalists have so often controlled government and exploited its power to their own advantage that people sometimes wonder where the real government is to be found, whether in legislative halls or in the board rooms where directors of giant corporations hold their meetings. This overemphasis on the economic aspects of life has had unfortunate consequences. In literature, in philosophy, and in the fine arts, America lags far behind Europe. Thus again we see the results of one group in a society gaining more power than is its just due, and so retarding the development of other groups and other activities necessary to a healthy society.

Even the family as an institution cannot escape some measure of censure when we seek to account for social imbalance. Especially in less complex societies, the family, because of the intimate association of its members, can embrace within itself economic interests, governmental institutions, organized education and organized religion. Originally economics, as the etymology of the word indicates, had to do with the management of affairs in the home and on the farm. Whether we think of the East or the West, it has been only a relatively few years since the production of food and the spinning and weaving of cloth were centered largely in the family unit. Slaves, cattle, horses—even women—were family possessions and under the control of the head of the household. For generations—until comparatively recently, in fact—the family provided the most significant aspects of the education of its children.

When the family became extended to form the clan, and the heads of individual households became subject to the authority of the head of the clan, it began to have a semipolitical character. In ancient times—and even among some modern peoples—the head of the family or of the clan led the family in prayer and worship, and thus the family assumed a religious function. It is not surprising that the family, as the fundamental social institution, has throughout history been able to resist, at least in a measure, the attempted domination of other groups. There is, indeed, ground for considering the family as the most important of all social groupings and institutions. The basic moral concepts of compassion, love, friendliness, nurture of the young and protection of the weak, respect for the human person as a person—could never have developed except within the intimacy of family living.

The positive contributions of the family as an institution are, however, to a measure offset by liabilities, of which I shall mention only two, namely conservatism and inequality. The family system is inherently conservative. The head of the family seeks to retain certain rights and privileges for himself, or for a favored son, and so imbues other members of the family with the importance of observing customs and traditions. As time passes and conditions change, these customs may lose their utility, but family pressure dictates their continued observance. All too often, outmoded traditions become the dead hand of the past, retarding progress in the present. Similarly, in most families the various members do not enjoy equality of privilege and opportunity. Some members exercise the authority, while others simply obey. Slaves are never accorded equal treatment; women, seldom.

The fifth and last group we will consider today as we look at the problem of social imbalance and conflict is one which we might designate the geographical group. People are neighbors when they live near one another. Extending this concept, we come to the concept of fellow countrymen, by which we may mean people who live in the same city, the same district, the same province, or the same nation. Even when people hold to differing religious or political convictions, they form groups based on geographical relationships. Positively, this fact helps to mitigate the conflict which might be generated from religious or political differences, by embracing such differences under an overarching sense of community. Negatively, geographical loyalties can and do degenerate into provincialism, so that people living in neighboring towns or provinces regard each other with suspicion or animosity. An extreme example is the fact that wars have often started over the question of national boundaries.

We have cited these instances to demonstrate that social reformation and the achievement of social stability require knowledge of the sources of conflict in the social order. In earlier times the various tensions tended to counterbalance one another, and society and its institutions developed without much conscious planning. It is only when society ceases to operate in a reasonably satisfactory manner, when we discern maladjustment or corruption, that we become concerned with finding methods for correcting the ills we observe.

The time has come, however, when we can no longer afford to wait for our society to become disjointed and then seek means of putting it back together again; we must rather devise methods and instruments to forestall disaster, to prevent infection rather than waiting to try to cure it when it occurs. We need to observe, first of all, the causes of social conflict, to find out what groups have become too dominating and have come to exercise disproportionate power, as well as to identify the groups that have been oppressed, denied privilege and opportunity. Only by making such an accurate diagnosis can we hope to prevent social infection and build a healthier society. We must devise means for bringing the interests of all the groups of a society into adjustment, providing all of them with opportunity to develop, so that each can help the others instead of being in conflict with them. We must teach ourselves one inescapable fact: any real advantage of one group is shared by all groups; and when one group suffers disadvantage, all are hurt. Social groups are so intimately interrelated that what happens to one of them ultimately affects the well-being of all of them.

I hope that you will give careful thought to this matter of social conflict as we have discussed it today, and that you will recognize the need to work out concrete methods for dealing with it in ways that will be effective in producing a happier and healthier social order. I submit that the theory that I have discussed with you holds immeasurably more promise for bringing about improvement than either of the two approaches we discussed earlier—the radical approach, which attacks existing institutions, or the conservative, which undertakes to defend and perpetuate them.

I n the earlier lectures in this series I have developed two important points: (1) theory originates at times when society is disordered and when the normal processes of social interaction are disrupted; and (2) social conflict occurs when the interests of certain groups are achieved to the disadvantage of other groups and to the suppression of their interests. A disproportionately privileged position of certain groups at the disadvantage of others constitutes injustice which generates conflict.

This point of view is a departure from that which has generally prevailed in social and political philosophy hitherto. Those who are familiar with the history of social and political philosophy will immediately recognize the difference. Earlier theories fall into three broad categories: (*a*) individualism, which stresses the freedoms, the rights, and the dignity of the individual person; (*b*) socialism which emphasizes law and order as the means to the well-being of the body social conceived in its entirety; and (*c*) a position which undertakes to strike a middle ground between these extremes, expressing a concern for the freedom and rights of the individual on the one hand, while at the same time asserting the necessity for law and order and the smooth functioning of the society on the other. This third point of view postulates an opposition between the rights and freedoms of the individual on the one hand and the demand for social stability on the other, and sees the origins of social conflict in this opposition.

All three of these viewpoints are quite different from the one I am advancing for your consideration. We are saying that it is more useful—that is, that it conforms more nearly to what we can see to be the case when our observation is thoughtful and careful—to think of society as being constituted of people in many sorts of groupings, rather than being made up of collections of individual persons considered as entities. And we are saying that social conflict occurs not because the interests of the individual person are incompatible with those of his society, but because the interests of some groups are gained at the disadvantage of, or even by the suppression of, the interests of other groups.

If our approach to the problem is a valid one, then philosophers of the past three or four hundred years have been mistaken; and the standard definition of social conflict as disparity between the interests of the individual on the one hand, and of his society on the other, involves a basic misinterpretation of the facts of the case, as the recently developed social sciences enable us to observe and interpret them. Let us see, then, whether there actually is a practical and fundamental difference between hitherto accepted theories and the one we now propound, or whether the difference is merely terminological and theoretical.

Let us look once more at our basic problem, social conflict. As we have said, the instrumentality of the social sciences now enables us to see that society is composed of many groups of people, not merely of individuals in the aggregate. From this definition follows the definition of social conflict as disparity among the interests sought by groups of people.

When one group achieves a position of recognized privilege and power, when it becomes the dominant group in a society, its members tend to define all those interests which do not pertain to their group as the interests of individuals, and their own as the interests of society. In other words, in its own view, the dominant group *is* the society, its interests *are* the interests of the society, and the welfare of the dominant group is identified with the welfare of society. Members of the dominant group do not recognize interests disparate to or competitive with their own as being the interests of other groups, but almost invariably attribute them to individual persons, and thus postulate conflict between such individuals on the one hand, and society (which, in their own view, is synonymous with their group) on the other. It was obviously the fact that this sort of definition was uncritically adopted by earlier social philosophers that led them to perpetuate a fallacious definition of social conflict.

To repeat then, in our present view social conflict occurs when one or more groups enjoy a degree of freedom and rights which deprives other groups of their just due. It is not, as we have seen, a conflict between individuals on the one hand and their society on the other. It is not a conflict between freedom and rights on the one hand and law and order on the other. In our view the person who initiates a move for social reform is not necessarily a radical, but one who seeks modification or revision of existing institutions; in the classical view, he is invariably looked upon as a deviant who has taken up his cudgels to engage in warfare with his society; he is the culprit in social conflict.

But in our theory, social conflict is a matter of groups in conflict—and groups are, by definition social. The group on one side of the battle believes just as strongly that it is fighting for the welfare of the total society as does the group which opposes it on the other side. If it were legitimate to attribute the actions of the unpopular or subordinate side to dissident individuals, it would be just as reasonable to point out that the superordinate group is also composed of individual members and to attribute to them as individuals the defense they make of the status quo. The practical difference is, as we have indicated, that the interests of the dominant group tend to be implicitly identified with the interests of society, while the interests being sought by a subordinate group are customarily not so recognized. This fact explains why leaders of reform movements are so often designated trouble-makers.

We may again refer at this point to the conflict between the state and the church which was such an obvious aspect of the history of the Middle Ages in Europe. After the relative chaos of the Dark Ages, when the Church emerged as the stabilizing agency in most of the areas of Western Europe, it was natural enough to identify the interests of this institution, and soon, the interests of the ecclesiastical establishment which governed the Church, with the interests of society. Political leaders—dukes, princes, even kings—were generally subservient to the Church, ostensibly, at least, accepting the identification of its interest with those of society at large.

As emerging political institutions began, however, to develop interests and to serve functions which were incompatible with ecclesiastical polity, the result was conflict which was defined in terms of rebellion by upstarts against the established order. This definition was asserted not only by the ecclesiastical establishment, which identified its own interests with those of society, but continued to characterize the prevailing outlook even after considerable numbers of people began to conclude that the interests that were close to their hearts could be better served by secular political institutions than by the Church as such. The interests of the Church were publicly recognized; those represented by its slowly emerging competitors did not yet enjoy such public recognition, and hence were largely regarded as being individual rather than social in nature.

A further and similar example is the conflict between religion and science in the period following the one of which we have been speaking. Even after political institutions achieved a measure of independence of Church control, the Church retained tremendous power. Its creeds, embodied in laws, were enforced by the state; it retained, in a large measure, control over education, and the curriculum continued to be dominated by the scriptures and theological commentaries and speculations; it influenced legislation, and was able to reserve as its own prerogative a wide range of matters in the determination of which judgments of ecclesiastical courts were final. The Church was the major conservative force in society, throwing the weight of its influence toward preservation and perpetuation of existing customs and traditions. In its eyes, the maintenance of social stability was a responsibility to be assumed and discharged by a relatively small aristocracy, whose interests were assumed to be identical with the interests of the total society. Independent thinkers, and especially innovators in science, were rebels and enemies of society whose nonconformity posed a threat to stability. The fact that even those demands for social reform, the justification of which nowadays seems so completely obvious, were routinely rejected on the allegation that they were against the social interest is illustrative of the degree to which selfishness can blind members of a group whose long-continued dominance has resulted in their thinking of themselves as being society, and of their narrow interests as being those things which would best serve the needs of the entire body social.

Let us leave Europe, and for our final, and possibly most telling illustration of the point we are making, look at the Oriental family. The family is the basic unit of Oriental society, and consequently it is natural enough that family interests are widely regarded as being synonymous with social interests. In the family organization the elders occupy positions of status, and exercise considerable power. Often the elders inhibit the interests of the women and the younger men in the family to the point at which the latter belong to the family only in a sense which virtually relegates them to the status of possessions—or, at best, as agents for obeying the orders and carrying out the purposes of the elders.

When, in response to changing conditions, sons and younger brothers begin to express their own opinions and to insist upon choosing their own occupations, determining their own faith, and selecting their own spouses, their elders see these demands as something contrary to family interest, and, therefore, as threats to social stability. In their view, safeguarding the interests of society requires that the interests of the family must first be safeguarded; and the interests of the family require that sons and younger brothers be held in check. The elders cannot understand that the demands of the sons and younger brothers also represent a kind of social interest. The demand to choose one's job, to elect one's faith, to select one's spouse, is in essence a demand for social equality, for equal opportunity for free development; such demand seems to threaten disaster for the simple reason that it has not yet been accorded sufficiently wide public recognition by society at large. This is another illustration of the fact that the interests of groups which are still subordinate to the dominant groups, who identify their own interests with those of their total society, are generally opposed or disregarded—at least until the subordinate group grows large enough to enforce its demand that it, too, be recognized as an operating component of the larger society. I believe that every instance of social conflict in history can be shown to have had this sort of origin.

To repeat: social conflict is never a contest between the individual and his society, but conflict between two groups, one of which has been publicly recognized by the larger society, the other of which has not yet achieved such recognition. The dominant group, which in its own eyes is the society, cannot see that the demands of still-unrecognized groups do, in fact, constitute a sort of social interest. This fact becomes clearer when we note the circumstance that every major reform movement in the world has gone through three phases.

As an illustration and means of defining these phases, let us look at the movement to achieve women's rights which took place in Europe and America in the late nineteenth and early twentieth centuries. Having from time immemorial occupied an inferior position in Western society, women began to demand their rights to participate in industrial, economic, and professional life on their own terms and in jobs of their own choosing, rather than in the sharply delimited spheres to which they had, from time to time, been admitted by their masculine-dominated society. They demanded the opportunity to share in social obligations, and this meant that they would have to have political power; this, in turn, meant that they must gain the right to vote. This movement for the emancipation of women from the restrictions that had always been imposed upon them went through the three phases which we have postulated as being characteristic of every major movement for social reform.

First, of course, there is the period of tacit acceptance of the status quo. Since women always had been subservient to men, they tended to accept the inferiority of women as an established fact. (Even today, in Great Britain, a married couple is, in the eyes of the law, one person—and that one person is, of course, the husband.) Inequality between men and women was regarded as a fact of nature—unalterable, and therefore to be accepted.

The second phase is one of challenge. Society undergoes changes, and these changes create new demands. New knowledge comes to light, and people begin to think in ways different from those to which they have been accustomed. "Facts of nature" turn out not be immutable after all, and presumed "universal truths" begin to totter.

Until fairly recently, necessity dictated that most women remain in their homes, doing household tasks, and producing many of the material goods of life such as handicrafts (textiles are a good example). But the invention of machines precipitated the industrial revolution, and machine production in factories replaced handicrafts. Women left their homes to work in factories; and as wage-earning participants in an expanding industrial milieu, they began to see themselves in a different light.

The industrial revolution also created the need for more generally available schooling than had been necessary in earlier days—and this schooling, at first in the rudiments alone, but eventually on higher levels, was gradually made available to girls as well as to boys. It was not as easy for educated women to acquiesce in the assumption of female inferiority as it had been for their grandmothers to do so. More and more women became aware of, and then resentful of, the injustice of their being deprived of the right to vote and hold office, and so to participate directly in the improvement of society through political channels.

But old institutions are rigid; old moral concepts are persistent; old customs are tough. The number of women actively participating in the movement for women's rights was at first small, and the larger society either disregarded the movement or, at best, looked upon it with tolerant amusement. The few leaders were ridiculed as unwomanly females—aberrant individuals engaged in quixotic combat with the established order of society. But, undeterred, these leaders stuck to their guns, propounding the doctrine of natural rights, and arguing that these rights extend to all people, even women. In the later stages of this second phase, a movement gains converts, and while in the general public eye the advocates of change may still appear to be a conglomerate of individuals in opposition to their society, participants in the movement itself begin more and more to conceive of themselves as a social group, fighting for freedom and right, against the larger society which still does not accord it public recognition.

The third phase through which a reform movement goes might be termed the period of fruition. The movement involves greater numbers of people, it gains power, and the possibility of achieving its goals is enhanced. The character of the movement undergoes a change from the second phase when one side claims to fight on the side of morality and order, the other on the side of sacred and inviolable freedom. Now there is general recognition that the demands made by the movement are actually matters of social interest, not the vagaries of quixotic individuals. The leaders of the movement, demanding opportunities for its members to meet and fulfil their obligations, begin to be able to demonstrate that society's failure to grant these opportunities is to its own disadvantage. Society, in its turn, recognizes the social validity of the demand. The interest which was initially characterized as antisocial comes to be regarded as social, and—usually not all at once, but nevertheless inexorably—the demands of the movement are met and reform is achieved.

Every reform movement in history has gone through these three phases. In every case, during the second phase, one side claims to protect and preserve the social order; the other demands rights; and at this point the conflict appears to be between individuals on the one hand and their society on the other. It is not until later that people recognize that the conflict is in fact one between differing social interests, and not between individuals and their society.

The labor movement is another apt illustration of the fact that every reform movement goes through this same succession of three phases. In the first phase, which coincided with the beginnings of the industrial revolution, laborers in general took the capitalists' treatment of them as a matter of course. In the second phase they developed an awareness of their own humanity and consequently a conviction that they were entitled to certain human rights. Here the concepts of the dignity of labor, of equality of treatment, and of opportunity were formulated and propounded. In the third phase people became aware of the fact that the labor problem is not just one of individuals, but a social problem; that meeting the demands of the movement not only enhances the welfare of the individuals involved, but promotes the welfare of the total society.

We could multiply examples, but there is really no need to do so. We have said enough to indicate that the traditional definition of social conflict as a contest between individuals and their society is a fallacious one. (A single person may, at times, be out of accord with and unable to adjust to the norms of his society, but when such a situation does occur we classify it as an instance of psychopathology, and not social conflict.) Social conflict is, as we have seen, a tug of war between the interests of one group of people and those of another group. The group which professes to defend the interests of society is always the one that has achieved public recognition, and freqeuently one which identifies its interests with those of the total society. In the view of this dominant group, the challenging group takes a position antithetical to the interests of society, and it is only as the subordinate group gains numbers, strength, and public recognition that it becomes apparent that the things they demand can be defined as genuine social needs. Because the demands of the subordinate group are at first voiced by relatively few individuals, there is ground for the superficial description of the conflict as being between these individuals and the society against which they direct their protests. A more realistic appraisal of the situation (an appraisal that is the easier to make as a reform movement moves into its third phase) leads to the valid definition which we have just expounded, namely, that the conflict is in actuality between groups, each of which conceives its goals to be consistent with, if not indeed identical with, the welfare of society.

Let us turn now to our second question, that of the difference, if any, between traditional theories of social conflict and the one we have developed here. Is the difference merely terminological and theoretical, or is it a practical and fundamental one? I believe that it should be clear by this time that the difference is not a superficial one, but a very practical one. The traditional definition of social conflict as a contest between individuals and their society deprives not only the public, but the reformers themselves, of an adequate context within which to consider the facts of the case. If social theorists insist on regarding the leaders of reform movements as aberrant individuals, as trouble-makers, and as enemies of society, it is not only possible, but likely, that the leaders may take the same view of the situation. If they are enemies of society, what more natural than for them to conclude that society is their enemy? In such case the development of deep animosities is inevitable, and the exercise of dialogue between the competing parties all but impossible. Each side sticks to its guns the more determinedly, the one vowing to defend to the death the status quo, the other advocating violence and revolution. Victory for the former results in further ossification of custom and tradition; victory for the latter, in "reformation" of that which does not need to be reformed, in discarding that which should be retained, and in rejection of much that is essential. Either of these results, as history demonstrates to us over and over, is wasteful to the point of tragedy.

The alternative theory which we have propounded, however, provides a framework within which leaders of reform movements may adopt an attitude of inquiry by which they can dispassionately determine which needs of their society are not being reasonably met; which elements in the society are not being afforded opportunity to develop themselves so as to contribute to the enrichment of the total society; and what sorts of abilities are being wasted or inadequately utilized. When leaders of reform movements can thus thoughtfully diagnose the ills and deficiencies of their society, reform becomes a matter of advocating methods for correcting ills and satisfying deficiencies, and not of revolution which undertakes to scrap the whole structure of existing institutional arrangements. Instead of regarding society as their enemy because it has insisted that they are its enemies, leaders of reform movements operating in this contest of theories can see themselves as helpful participants in an ongoing process of social reconstruction.

Our theory also provides for the whole public, as well as for the dominant groups within it, a framework for an approach that can be immeasurably more profitable than anything that was possible under the traditional definition of social conflict. If the people on one side of an issue adopt an attitude of calm inquiry, it becomes less difficult for those who hold opposing views also to adopt a rational approach to the problem. Evaluation of proposed alternatives becomes possible, and openness to conviction replaces intransigeance. To be sure, conflict will not be eliminated, but it can be ameliorated; and its outcomes can be tremendously less costly and wasteful than has so often been the case in the past. When critical intelligence is called into play, and when scientific methods of investigating actual situations are substituted for sweeping generalizations, social reformers no longer need to look on themselves as messiahs or martyrs, and society no longer need see them as trouble-makers. The function of reformers then becomes that of advancing diagnoses of social ills and of formulating and propounding suggestions for changes which will improve the situation; and, given the theory we have advanced, they can then join forces with other elements of society in assessing the accuracy of their diagnoses, and the probable efficacy of their proposed remedies.

In light of what we have been saying, it seems abundantly clear that the difference between traditional definitions and theories and those set forth here is much more than terminological. It is, judged by the results of application to actual situations, a very practical difference.

CRITERIA FOR JUDGING

SYSTEMS OF THOUGHT

I n my preceding lecture I contrasted the traditional view that disorder in a society results from conflict between individuals on the one hand and organized society on the other, with my own theory that social conflict originates in sharp imbalance among the interests and advantages of the groups of people which collectively constitute a society. To the question of whether there is significant difference between traditional views and the one I developed, I answered an emphatic, "Yes, there is a tremendous difference, and one of great practical import."

As long as we persist in defining social disorder in terms of conflict between individuals and their society, we evoke animosity on the one side and intransigeance on the other; we encourage the one to dogged conservation of existing institutions, at whatever cost, and encourage the other, in desperation, to agitate and work for the indiscriminate abolition of existing arrangements and their replacement with something entirely different; and finally we set up a situation such that no matter which side wins, the concrete problems which need to be dealt with are lost to view, buried under a welter of sweeping generalizations and emotional reaction.

Our alternative theory is really quite different, holding that the ends of both parties in social conflict can be defined as social interests, the difference being that the position of one party is publicly recognized as a social interest, while that of the other has not yet been accorded this recognition. This view makes possible rational and dispassionate discussion of contending ends, and their evaluation in terms of probable advantage to the whole social fabric. It encourages inquiry to determine which aspects of the society stand in need of reformation, and which ought to be conserved—that is to say, it puts a premium upon the application of scientific methods to social problems. Surely these considerations give to our theory an incalculable advantage over traditional definitions and outlooks.

In contrast to our theory, the traditional view perpetuates the tendency to view individuals and society as antithetical entities. When such a view prevails, the conservatives in society react with a blanket protectiveness when any of their values are challenged. Instead of examining and appraising, instead of differentiating between those arrangements which perhaps ought to be changed and those which certainly ought to be preserved, they resort to sweeping generalizations and rally to the defense of what *is,* identifying traditional with good, and anathematizing those who disagree with them as enemies of society. Advocates of social reform, on the other hand, goaded by this reaction in dominant groups, tend toward extreme radicalism and become revolutionaries, demanding that customs and institutions which restrict human freedom be discarded as wholly evil. They, too, as long as this old view prevails, are incapable of dispassionate examination of actual situations, of scientific determination of the locus of needed change, and of intelligent decision about what ought to be conserved.

Naturally we do not attribute this traditional theory, in the oversimplified form in which we have presented it, to all social theorists who have gone before us; but we do contend that their approach, pressed to its logical ultimate, tends toward the results we have indicated. And we must repeat at this point our insistence that we are not attempting a reconciliation between the radical outlook and the conservative, between the theoretical position which emphasizes individual rights and freedom, and the alternative position which exalts law and order. The theory which we are developing here calls for a new method of judgment, one which will apply the methods of science to our efforts to distinguish the better from the worse, and to decide what should be reformed and what should be retained. It encourages us to identify and diagnose concrete problems and to devise scientific solutions to these problems.

Let us look for a moment at the example of anarchism. The anarchist would dispense with all governing rules and institutions. He would abolish all government, all law, all private property, even the family—because each of these puts some restriction on individual freedom. He has lost sight of the fact that ought to be obvious, namely, that some forms of government do unduly restrict individual freedom, while other forms of government enhance the opportunity of the individual to grow and develop his potentialities, and that some laws are restrictive, others liberative. He does not understand that the absolute freedom for which he fights is a chimera, and that any freedom that means anything is the result of, not the antithesis to, appropriate regulation of human conduct. Traffic rules, to take an everyday example, do impose certain restrictions and tell us on which side of the street we may drive and on which side we may not; but their total effect is to facilitate movement, not to restrict it. They provide us with freedom to get to our destination more rapidly and more safely than we could possibly do if we were free to drive wherever our fancy of the moment happened to dictate. The same principle applies to government in general. The scientific attitude calls for the assessment of governments and laws by the criterion of their contribution to human welfare and freedom; it makes possible the amendment or repeal of specific laws which impose undue or unnecessary restrictions, but it is altogether antithetical to the attitude that would dispense with all law because some laws were inappropriately framed or have become outmoded.

Having said this much by way of introduction, let us return to the central problem of method and attitude, the act of judging. We cannot judge what is good or what is bad, what is better or what is worse, unless we have criteria on which to base our judgments. I shall mention several criteria which are available to us as instrumentalities when we engage in the act of judging.

First, however, a word about criteria in general. The theorists whom we have been criticising had their criteria. All theorists do. In fact, theory without criteria is a contradiction in terms. Too often, though, theorists have selected as their criteria ideals, archetypes of what ought to be, utopian conceptions. Because these ideals so frequently have no perceptible relationship to conditions which actually do confront us, and because they are so remote from our experience that we cannot discern any significant relationship between them and the specific improvement which we want to make now in the confronting situation, they are scarcely more useful in directing the act of judging than they would be if they were wholly imaginary. In our view, on the contrary, criteria derive from experience and are subject to our control. How utterly ridiculous it would be, for example, for a navigator simply to announce his destination and hoist his sails, without informing himself about ocean currents, prevailing winds, or the location of shoals, and without compass and map! But how often do we in politics formulate our goal in terms of an ideal—comparable to the navigator's destination—and set forth to achieve it, without adequately informing ourselves about the currents of conflicting group aspirations, the prevailing winds of ideologies, the location of the shoals of tradition and custom; without consulting the map of history on which are plotted both successful and disastrous political voyages of the past; and without the compass of critical intelligence to help us plot our passage so that the dangers of the route are minimized.

No, we must deal with facts—and our facts must be derived from our experience with human nature. (When we speak of human nature we do not refer to the idle logomachies about man's inherent goodness or his innately evil nature, but rather to objective study of observable human behavior and scientifically derived hypotheses about its changing trends.) Through the study of facts we determine human needs, make plans for meeting these needs, and identify the rules which will apply to and regulate our efforts. On the basis of these findings we devise our approaches to and methods for solving human problems.

There are three broad categories of human activity in which we seek criteria for our acts of judging: (*a*) habits and customs; (*b*) social institutions; and (*c*) associated living (by which phrase we do no more than point to the simple fact that every human being lives in—and can live only in—some sort of association with other human beings).

A habit is a regulated pattern of individual behavior derived from prior experience. A custom is a habit which is common to the members of a society. When custom becomes regularized, systematized, and consciously insisted upon, we call it tradition. When social arrangements reach the degree of systematization which is characterized by delegation of responsibility, division of labor, and the necessity for cooperative endeavor, we have an institution. These two categories, however, are of secondary importance; the chief source of our criteria for judging lies in associated living, inasmuch as cooperation and interaction are possible only when people live in associated groups with shared interests.

HABITS AND CUSTOMS. Psychologically speaking, habits and customs are the most economical means of getting cumulative value from the common experiences of life. If we had to take care about everything we did, if we had to think about each of the innumerable actions we perform every day, our entire energy would be expended upon merely keeping alive (if, indeed, we could keep alive!), and we would have no time,

thought to the way you manipulate them, can concentrate on enjoy-
seen a little child just learning to walk. He has to pay attention to every
step he takes, to devote his energy to maintaining his balance; in effect,
to make a decision about each separate step. And we have all noted that
when this child really wants to get somewhere—let us say, to reach a
favorite toy on the other side of the room—he flops down and crawls.
Crawling is already a habit, he doesn't have to think about it; walking,
for him, has not yet become a habit. You who are in the audience have
made a habit of eating with chopsticks, and without giving any particular
thought to the way you manipulate them, you can concentrate on enjoying your food. I, on the other hand, have to pay so much attention to the
way I hold my chopsticks that sometimes I hardly know what I am eating.

Every person has thousands of habits; every society thousands of customs. If it weren't for the economy of effort that these make possible, we
simply could not get along.

When customs become consciously recognized and regarded as good,
they become systematized, and we have such things as the family system,
the property system, the marriage system, and so on. Such consciously
recognized customs can have great utility. Not all customs are stable or
uniform, even though they are means for channeling common human
needs; but when they become systematized and raised to the level of traditions, they do tend to become fixed and more or less uniform. People
generally accept traditions as standards to which their behavior should
conform. Conventions embodied in custom and tradition afford a common power which regulates conduct among individuals and reduces the
incidence of conflict which would prevail if each person followed his own
whims. The way Thomas Hobbes put it was, "Hereby it is manifest,
that during the time men live without a common power to keep them
all in awe, they are in that condition which is called war; . . . all other
time is PEACE."* While we cannot accept Hobbes' assertion without
qualification, it is generally correct to say that there can be no peace in a
society without conventions and that where the social formalities operate
successfully, there tends to be peace.

Customs have both advantages and disadvantages. A custom might be
compared to the shell of a crustacean, which protects the animal from
attack, but which at the same time inhibits growth because it is hard and
inflexible. Analogously, customs arise to preserve that which has been

---

* W. Molesworth, ed., *The English Works of Thomas Hobbes*, 11 vols. (London:
J. Bohn, 1839–1845), 3:112–3. [The word *peace* is in capitals in this text.]

learned from experience, but how often we lose sight of this purpose and make the maintenance of the custom an end in itself. Then, like the shell, the custom grows thicker and harder, obstructing social growth and development, until finally it occasions social conflict which can eventuate in revolution so violent that it destroys not only the custom itself, but even the value which the custom was originally intended to serve. Revolutions of this sort are not initiated by malcontents, but are mass reactions against the determination of a society's conservative elements who blindly insist upon trying to preserve a dying society surrounded by an already dead shell.

The alternative to revolution as a means (and almost always an expensive and wasteful means) to social progress is a system of habits, customs, conventions, traditions, and institutions flexible enough to permit adjustment to changing environments and conditions. And such flexibility requires thinking—the exercise of individual intelligence in discussing and appraising, in choosing, in judging, and in testing. Habits, customs, and systems can remain viable only when they are the objects of intelligent thinking. This first criterion is useful in the adjustment of habits, customs, and institutions to the realities of human nature. Here we emphasize individual freedom in choosing, criticising, and judging, to the end that such habits, customs, and institutions do not become dead weights, impede progress, and excite revolution.

SOCIAL INSTITUTIONS. Habits and customs come into being without conscious planning, but social institutions are deliberately devised. An institution may be compared to the body, in which each part carries out its own function in interaction and cooperation with all the other parts. An adequate system of social institutions naturally increases a society's capacity for survival, when, as often happens, it finds itself in competition with another society. Social institutions afford to the society the same economy and efficiency that habits and customs provide for the individual person.

Everybody acknowledges the organizing ability of the German people —although we have our doubts about them in other regards. The Germans make use of scientific methods to control their institutions and to design plans to be accomplished within specified periods of time. This much is to their credit. Difficulties arise when the role of institutions is overemphasized. Such overemphasis tends to restrict opportunity for free development, and to inhibit creativity. Organization is, of course, indispensable in the operation of a factory, an industry, or an army. Sometimes, however, the organization is of such a sort that a small number of persons assume responsibility for total administration, relegating the rest of those involved to the status of automata. In some religious organizations dependence upon elaborate ritual has stultified the spiritual development of adherents. In some armies extreme regimentation and the rigidity of regulations have stifled initiative in the men in the ranks, making them little more than robots. Germany is a good example both of efficiency in organization and of carrying the process to the point at which the results are to be deplored.

Organization, by definition, requires structure. Accountability and responsibility have to be centralized—in boards of directors and managers in industry, in central staffs and field commanders in armies. In such situations where power is centralized, there is a tendency for people to think of the men at the top as human beings, and to consider (possibly without being conscious that they do so) all the rest as cogs in the machine. This attitude, which results in inhibiting free development of individual creative ability, is not limited to Germany, but is rather generally characteristic of Western peoples. Some people say that there is too much freedom in the United States, but as a matter of cold fact even America is rapidly becoming victim to overorganization and extreme institutionalization.

As with most other questions which we must face, the answer to the problems of organization and institutionalization cannot be in terms of either-or. We might as well face up to the fact that just as there are no universal truths in the world, no panaceas, there are also no institutions which operate automatically and perfectly. Institutionalization can, on the one hand, exercise too rigid control over our actions; on the other hand it may fail to provide sufficient direction to our efforts. Germany has gone too far in one direction; China has lagged near the other end of the scale. Germany plans too minutely and too rigidly; China tends to wait till the problem is upon her before making any plan at all. While it is undeniably true that there is such a thing as too much organization, it is equally true that maximum efficiency requires an optimum degree of organization.

The second source from which we derive our criteria, then, is an examination of the situations in which we are involved as broadly as we are able to conceive them, an intelligent appraisal of the need for organization and institution, and a judging of the extent to which component elements of the situation call for organization, and the degree to which our actions are to be subject to such organization.

ASSOCIATED LIVING. As my time today has run out, I will say only that associated living is characterized by cooperation, and that it is to the mutual advantage of everyone concerned in it. It is like friendship. Friends help each other, exchange knowledge and insights, with the result that their lives are richer and more meaningful. Associated living is the highest ideal of social development, and all societies should strive toward this ideal. Our search is for criteria by means of which we may intelligently judge whether and to what extent a given proposal seems capable of promoting associated living. Our task is to devise means which will promote free exchange of knowledge and insights, and which will enable and dispose us to promote the fullest possible development of associated living. Of this, more in our next lecture.

COMMUNICATION

AND ASSOCIATED LIVING

I n my preceding lecture, after raising the question of the ultimate criterion by which we are to judge habits, customs, and social institutions, I indicated that this was the degree to which the matter being judged could contribute to the development and qualitative enhancement of associated living. I said that a habit, a custom, or an institution is to be judged good when it contributes positively to free intercourse, to unhampered exchange of ideas, to mutual respect and friendship and love—in short, to those modes of behaving which make life richer and more worth living for everybody concerned; and conversely, any custom or institution which impedes progress toward these goals is to be judged bad.

There are societies in which one segment is kept rigidly separated from the others. Ancient Egypt and contemporary India are examples of societies characterized by caste systems, in which the members of one caste have virtually no communication with members of other castes. Not only is intermarriage between members of different castes forbidden, but communication of knowledge, feeling, thought, and emotion among the different castes is all but impossible. This sort of society not only fails to develop associated human living, but imposes actual blockages to its development.

While there are certain technical differences between the caste systems of ancient Egypt and modern India, and the class system which has been characteristic of European societies, the practical effects in the realm of which we are speaking are markedly similar. The land-owning aristocracy has little effective communication with the entrepreneurial middle class, and all but none whatever with the working classes; communication between the middle classes and their betters on the one hand, and the working classes on the other, is minimal and concerned solely with practicalities; while the working classes have virtually no communication whatever with either of the classes superior to them in the social structure. Wherever the class system is rigid and a dominant characteristic of a society, associated living cannot be a relevant consideration for the whole society, although approaches to it may be discerned in the intragroup relationships of the more or less isolated groups that make up the total society.

The same sort of thing is essentially true of a strong paternalistic family system, in which communication of thought and sharing of feeling are all but impossible between the head of the family on the one hand, and the other members who owe him respect and obedience on the other. The authoritarian state is another example—it is the authoritarian family writ large. Associated living in such situations is not a relevant ideal; in the authoritarian state the government decides what is best for the inhabitants, who are to accept the decisions; in the authoritarian family or clan, the elders decide, the others accept.

Even in religion, especially when the clergy constitute a special class as they do in many countries, they may become so preoccupied with the offices and rituals of their profession that they lose effective contact with the laity, concern themselves too exclusively with spiritual matters while laymen follow secular interests. In such cases, communication of thought, feeling, and sympathy dwindles.

The all-too-common phenomenon of alienation of the untutored masses from the educated members of their own society is another pertinent illustration of the same principle. When people who have had the advantages of schooling deprecate workers and farmers, deride them as yokels because they are illiterate, or ridicule them because their accents or dialects are different, the latter may tacitly concur in the inferiority so attributed to them, and shy away from any effort to communicate or associate with their betters.

All these are illustrations of the ways in which alienation (which is an antonym of associated living) contradicts the very purposes for which institutions were originally founded. The function of religion is to establish meaningful relationships between man and the world in which he has his being; when antinomy between the spiritual and the secular is postulated, this purpose is defeated. The function of education is the perpetuation and the revivification of society; but when the educated and the uneducated draw apart the one from the other, and live their lives in different spheres, this purpose is also defeated. In commerce and industry, profit-making ideally is subordinate to the social purposes of the exchange of commodities and transaction of ideas; when arrangements result in managers and workers living in different worlds, out of communication with each other, basic purposes are again defeated. In these, as in all other aspects, the society which we desire is one in which there is maximum opportunity for free exchange and communication. This is the ultimate criterion by which we judge the worth of any sort of institutional arrangement.

What we are really saying is that free and open communication, unself-seeking and reciprocal relationships, and the sort of interaction that contributes to mutual advantage, are the essential factors in associated living. To aid in understanding what we mean by these things, let us look for a moment at a mode of living in which the operation of these factors is at a minimum, namely the relationship between masters and slaves. This master-slave relationship is not limited to situations in which one person "owns" another, as was true in parts of America at the time of my birth. It refers to any system of relationship which effectively places one person in subjugation to another—children subject to their parents, wives to their husbands, subjects to their rulers, laborers to their employers.

When people exist under arrangements which call for some to rule and others to be ruled, some to command and others to obey, integration of the society cannot proceed, nor can the society hope to remain stable, because this disparity of status and function breeds conflict and induces disorder. At the same time, this pattern of dominance-subservience makes the development of personality extremely difficult, if not impossible—and strangely enough, this is as true of members of the dominant group as it is of those in the subservient group.

Some people are surprised when I say that a society organized along the lines I have indicated contains within itself the potentials of its own disintegration. They argue that although social stratification does inevitably infringe to an extent upon individual freedom, the advantages of such an arrangement outweigh this disadvantage. They contend that stratification contributes to, rather than threatens, social stability; that one cost of stability is the sacrifice of a measure of individual freedom; that some individuals must suffer so that the whole society can benefit.

What these people overlook is the fact that a stratified society depends upon force for its existence. In this age no society that depends for its existence on sheer force can remain stable or become integrated. The ingredients of social crisis are present in it, and will sooner or later manifest themselves in overt conflict, to the hurt both of the society as a structure and of the individuals who compose it.

Authoritarian political theory and democratic political theory are diametrically opposed. The essence of democratic political theory is that it promotes social communication, cooperation, and interaction among individuals. A democratic society depends for its stability and development not on force, but on consensus. In such a society each member is entitled to develop his abilities, pursue his own interests, and seek to achieve his own purposes. An authoritarian society, on the other hand, because it inhibits initiative and discourages cooperation, and because it resorts to force to suppress dissent, can never be stable in any true and lasting sense.

Why must it be that a society that does not value nor foster associated living must resort to force in its efforts to maintain stability? It is simply because the members of such a society are not aware of their stake in it. Even the appearance of unity and integration is dependent upon force—and any weakening of this force is immediately followed by disorganization in the society. It's like a schoolroom in which order is maintained by the rod; let the teacher leave the room, and pandemonium reigns. Or take the history of China: transition from one dynasty to another was always attended by political and social disruption—disorder which continued until the appearance on the scene of some person forceful and powerful enough to subject contending factions to his control. Right up to the end of any given dynasty there may have been the appearance of complete stability, but the fact that the establishment of a new dynasty was invariably attended by violent disorder is in itself evidence of the inefficacy of force as a means of achieving any lasting sort of stability. Constitutional democracy, on the other hand, incorporates within its very structure guarantees that its members will have opportunity to pursue their own interests. And since members of such a society recognize that they do have a stake in it, social order persists relatively unimpaired when there is a change in government.

As a result of the recent World War—the most devastating war in history—a number of nations have gone to pieces, while others, equally subject to the calamities of war, have managed to retain their integrity. What's the difference? Broadly speaking, the nations that are suffering the most acute internal disorder are those that have had authoritarian governments, such as Russia and Germany. Russia, with a longer history of autocracy, is undergoing the more severe dislocation. In the democratic nations, on the other hand, reasonable order prevails. But this is order which is not and has not been maintained by force. It is order which was built up by the free participation of the members of these societies in social and political activities, and which is maintained by their realization that their governments represent rather than control them. It is order based in the general will, the common feelings, and the mutual interests of the people. The reciprocal helpfulness generated in societies that have treasured and fostered associated living enabled these nations to survive the same calamitous experiences which caused authoritarian nations to disintegrate.

Authoritarian governments do not see associated living as a relevant goal, nor do they seek to foster communication of feelings, sharing of interests, or free interaction among the members of their societies. On the contrary, a fundamental tenet of democratic political theory is government by the consent of the governed. People naturally feel themselves to be a part of the country when its government is based upon their consent and is the instrument for the realization of their desires and aspirations. Recognizing that rights entail obligations, they are willing to do what they are called upon to do. This is the most stable foundation on which a nation can be built. True, there have been authoritarian governments that have existed for a century or two; but their lives have still been very short in comparison with the long history of mankind. It is the part of wisdom to work toward a permanently stable society characterized by associated living, and not to be enticed by the lure of the apparent benefits of an authoritarian government which, at best, can operate efficiently for only a relatively brief period of time.

Viewed superficially, an authoritarian government may appear to be solidly grounded and strong, but in point of actual fact, it is always weaker than a government based on the values of associated living. Again to the superficial view, a democratic government, based as it is on the will of the people, may seem inefficient and unstable—but, subjected to the acid test of war—even the ignominy of defeat—it can maintain its integrity and restore its equilibrium far more effectively than can its authoritarian neighbor.

The same principle is illustrated in industry. Recent studies by efficiency experts have determined that the average worker in American factories works at less than fifty per cent of capacity—that is, he produces less than half as much as he could produce if he put forth his best efforts. This is fairly conclusive evidence that workers in general lack interest in what they're doing, and that this lack of interest stems from the fact that they have no share in determining the purposes of the factory where they work. This is an illustration of the degree to which the power of authoritarian management is vitiated by an inherent weakness. Workers aren't likely to put forth their best efforts when they are working only to make a living; when they not only do not share in, but frequently know nothing about, factory operations other than those in which they happen to be engaged; and when they have no opportunity to appreciate the significance of the total enterprise, ranging from procurement of raw materials, manufacturing, marketing, and distribution, to disposition of surplus value created in these processes. This lack of interest on the part of workers may be evidenced in apathy or in deliberate slowdown, in carelessness and wastage of material, or in outright sabotage.

Workers are much better off in America than in China. Their wages are better, and are still increasing; their working hours are shorter. But, far from being satisfied with their lot, American workers are now demanding a voice in determination of policy, not only in the particular industries in which they work, but for the economy as a whole. To the degree that this demand is met, it is an application of democracy to industry. Wages are only part of the picture. Workers in a democracy must feel interested and involved in their work. They want work that will afford opportunities for development of initiative and ability, and that will enable them to feel that they, themselves, are integral parts of the processes in which they are involved—they want to belong. The problem goes far deeper than mere wages and hours; it has to do with the human spirit. Man is not a machine, but a being who thinks and feels. The demands which modern industry makes on physical energy are far less than its demands on feeling and thinking. When social organization (and industry is one type of social organization) creates conditions that encourage men to devote themselves to the welfare of society, then we have a society that is far more stable than one based on compulsion can ever be.

Let us look now at the effects upon human personality which may be observed in a society that fails to prize and seek the values of associated living. We must consider separately the effects first on the subordinated or "inferior" members of such a society, and second on the privileged or "superior" members.

The first and most noticeable effect upon the inferior members of a society in which the values of associated living are subverted are psychological in nature—feelings of dissatisfaction, dislike, hatred, and deprivation—frequently approaching the level of neurosis, often of psychosis. Modern psychology tells us that neuroses result from the suppression of normal desires, the inability to meet normal needs. When a person is relegated to a permanently inferior position in a social hierarchy and suffers chronic frustration in his efforts to satisfy his normal needs and desires, his mental health is almost bound to suffer.

The second evil effect of the failure to cultivate the values of associated living is the inhibition of individual potentialities. Even a genius, to say nothing of an ordinary man, can live up to his potentialities only when he has the opportunity to do so. Without opportunity for exercise and development, the potentialities of even a genius—in politics, in management, in science, or in the arts—are likely to atrophy; or, with their positive, normal, and desirable development inhibited by socially-established blockages, potentialities may develop negatively and with antisocial results. In this kind of situation, people who might have become contributors to social progress become, instead, drags upon progress; men who might have become capable and admirable become, instead, mean and despicable. A caste society of master and slave produces two kinds of meanness in the latter: first, acquiescence, servility, obsequiousness, and sycophancy; second, craftiness, cunning, deceitfulness, and evasion of authority by whatever means.

It is deplorable—and absurd—that so many people defend a caste-oriented society on the basis of the very evil effects which stem from the institution itself. They argue that because the inferiors are dependent, crafty, servile, ignorant, and obsequious, they are thereby incapable of participation in associated living, and that thus a caste society of one or another sort is the only social organization that is feasible. They cannot—or will not—see that servility, ignorance, craftiness and obsequiousness are not innate qualities, but are the fruits of a system which forces men into subservience. Evil institutions bear bitter fruit, and this bitter fruit is then used to justify the institutions which produced it. This particular confusion is one of the most terrible tragedies in the world.

As regrettable as we may regard the effects on the inferiors in a society which deprecates the values of associated living, the results in the lives of the superiors may, in the long run prove to be even worse. The more obvious evil is that which is exerted upon moral dispositions. "Absolute power corrupts absolutely"; and the more power a man has, the more cruel, despotic, arrogant, and extravagant he is likely to become. Now, cruelty, arrogance, and extravagance are no more innate than servility, ignorance, or obsequiousness—all are fruits of the same evil institutions. The damage to the superiors, however, is the more insidious. Their privileges make them comfortable, and they tend to become insensitive to the needs and feelings of people who live in circumstances different from their own.

The evil effects on the moral dispositions of the superiors are matched by the hampering effects of a caste-oriented society on their intellectual dispositions. Even though they have access to education, their knowledge is likely to be one-sided and limited in scope, because the sources of their learning are limited, lying as they do so largely in the domains of their equals. This can be equally true of a father, a teacher, a plant superintendent, or the president of a corporation, if they all live in a society that does not put a premium on the values of associated living, or if they work in situations in which there is not free communication between them and their subordinates.

What I have just said is illustrated by the difference between the kind of self-seeking politician to whom we refer as a demagogue on the one hand, and the politician who approaches the stature of a statesman on the other. The former, to gain power, or to maintain himself in power, learns to entice or intimidate men to serve his ends. He may become quite adept at this sort of thing, but we still recognize it as shrewdness rather than as wisdom—or, in the terms in which we were speaking, a narrowly based and limited sort of knowledge. The potential statesman, however—and especially so in a democratic society—takes into consideration the hopes and aspirations of all members of his society, aiming to secure for all of them common opportunities for the development of their potentialities. He seeks counsel and creates channels for free communication between himself and all segments of his society, and thus his expertise is broadly based, his knowledge derived from many sources.

Another serious evil in a caste-oriented society is that members of the ruling class so frequently become decadent, dissipate their talents as well as their material resources, and sometimes even exhibit a notable lack of ordinary common sense. In the history of China, for example, we note that the first emperor of each dynasty was always a strong leader, gifted with imagination and initiative, capable of accomplishing needed reforms, and interested in the people over whom he ruled. But we also note that as an emperor's successors insulated themselves against all contacts other than those with the inner circle of palace courtiers, they became a class unto themselves, following their own desires and whims, without reference to what was good for their country. And the story goes on, time after time, in dreary repetition—*their* successors finally became so completely estranged from the populace, so uninterested in meeting the needs of the people, that they were eventually overthrown, and a new dynasty was instituted, again headed by a strong leader who knew what the country needed, and who could meet those needs. My point, of course, is that if the ruling families had encouraged associated living and profited from free communication with all sectors of their society, they would not have become so decadent and so unable to perform their functions as rulers.

I have been illustrating my philosophy of democracy. Now what kind of society would result if this philosophy were to become generally operative? It would be a society in which there would be opportunities for individual development, opportunities for free communication of feeling, knowing, and thinking. The foundation of such a society would be free participation by each member of the society in setting its goals and purposes, full and willing contribution by each person toward the fulfillment of those goals.

Such a society may not always appear to run as smoothly or to be as stable as an authoritarian society; but we have enough experience of history to convince us that it is, in fact, more stable and better able to forestall the evils of which we have spoken, than is a society in which free communication among its members is lacking.

ECONOMICS AND SOCIAL PHILOSOPHY

I n this series of lectures I have talked about the nature, the scope, and the function of social and political philosophy. I proposed a criterion for criticizing such things as habits, customs, and social institutions. But these discussions have been in general, and, I am afraid somewhat vague, terms. Beginning today, I shall deal with some of the more concrete problems with which social and political philosophy must concern itself.

We can group these problems under three headings, for the sake of convenience. Under the first heading, political problems, we consider the nature of politics and the scope of law and government. We seek answers to such questions as: What is government? What are the proper functions of a particular government? What sort of government is best? Is authoritarian or aristocratic government better than democracy, or the other way around? What is the extent of and limit upon the authority of a government? What should government undertake to do, and what should it leave to other agencies? What are the things that a government can do for its people, and what are the things that it cannot be expected to do?

There are even more questions. Authoritarian governments claim to be—and often appear to be—effective, but how far does this effectiveness go, and what is its cost, measured in human values? Why are laws necessary? Just what is law? Why do we have, and how do we use criminal law? Which of the contentions of anarchists can we reasonably accept?

All these questions, and scores of others like them, are subsumed under the heading of political problems.

Under the second heading we embrace the problems of the cultural and intellectual life of man—second in order of listing, but primary in importance. Man's basic problems are those of his culture, under which we include such things as religion, literature and the fine arts, and learning and scholarship. Here we ask such questions as: What roles do authority, tradition, and individual freedom play in the area of belief? In different kinds of society, what roles are assigned to freedom of thought, opinion, publication, and association? (One view of history is that it is the story of man's struggles to achieve freedom.)

Under the third heading fall the problems of economics. Here we ask about the roles and status of capital, and of labor. We examine the issue of private ownership of property versus some form of collectivism. We look into the question of whether economic life should be thought of as being primarily competitive or primarily cooperative.

I am going to discuss problems under all three of these headings: political problems, cultural and intellectual problems, and economic problems, one by one. But today I am going to talk about the last one. If you wonder why I take this last heading first, it is simply because the level of civilization which a people reaches, and the kinds of social institutions which man creates, are to a great degree functions of the nature and scope of his economic arrangements. Just as a man cannot live without food, a society cannot flourish when its basic needs are not satisfied. I take it as axiomatic that the ways in which a people meet their economic problems determine in a large degree what they do about their other social problems.

When we talk of economic problems, we have to think on three levels: (*a*) efforts to satisfy the basic desires that are common to all men—the need for food and drink and protection from the elements; (*b*) the instrumentalities which men devise, the more effectively to meet their basic needs—machines, if you will, provided that you remember that the term "machine" embraces such disparate things as a stick used as a lever and a great ocean liner; and (*c*) the production and distribution of commodities which serve to meet human needs.

The most dangerous luxury in which social and political philosophers can indulge—and one in which a number of such philosophers have indulged—is to deprecate economics, to suppose that because its subject matter is no more than the mundane business of production and distribution of goods it does not call for philosophic examination. Such philosophers apparently ignore the correlation of civilization and economics. In fact, one of the primary distinctions between savagery and civilization is the economic one. A savage has few desires and needs; consequently he devises relatively few and simple instruments and arrangments for the satisfaction of these needs. On the other hand, a man who lives in a complex civilization, having many desires and a variety of needs, devises a multitude of instrumentalities by means of which he meets his needs. The development of religion, literature, and the fine arts can be seen in historical perspective always to have been associated with refinements of the economic arrangements by which men have ordered the bread-and-butter aspects of their lives.

Philosophers have defined man in a number of ways: as the talking animal, or as the rational animal. Attention has even been called to the fact that man is the only animal capable of laughing. Recently the French philosopher Henri Bergson has proffered the definition of man as the tool-making animal—a particularly apt definition, in my opinion. Bergson's definition directs attention to man's ability to devise from the materials of nature instrumentalities for the satisfaction of his desires—a characteristic which lower orders of animals do not possess, and which is therefore unique to man.

Up to this point we have done no more than to assert the importance of economic arrangements, and to hint at the futility of trying to understand political problems and cultural and intellectual problems without first exploring the economic substructure upon which other social institutions are erected. As a civilization becomes more complex, both in its economic arrangements and in other respects, we note the increasing importance of two phenomena, both of which are primarily economic in nature: division of labor, and cooperation.

If each separate member of a society were suddenly required to devise for himself all the instrumentalities with which to cope with his environment, civilization would soon revert to savagery. Even if it were possible for each person to take care of himself—and there would be only a few cases in which it would be possible—men would soon be savages again, simply because under such conditions there would be no cooperative social life, no need for cooperation except on the simple level of the cooperation practiced in the family through the natural association of blood relatives.

The prime advantage in division of labor is that each person may cultivate a specialty of his own, concentrating his energies in a particular direction. Even in farming: nowadays the farmer customarily cultivates one or a few crops, looks to other people for care of his other needs, and is thus enabled to apply to his own specialty the results of a highly developed technology and, of course, to produce yields beyond anything his forefathers conceived to be possible.

In industry the advantages of division of labor are even more obvious. Blacksmiths, silversmiths, painters, engineers—all engage in the areas of their own specializations. If they couldn't do this—if each had to dissipate his energies in a multitude of tasks—they would never really develop their potentialities.

Division of labor not only facilitates the development of specialized technologies, but it promotes cooperation in social life. The complexity of social life in an advanced civilization renders cooperation indispensable, simply because the greater the complexity, the more demanding the necessity for ever finer distinctions and the greater numbers of divisions in the total responsibility for producing the goods and services of life. The farmer produces foodstuffs and fibres; the industrial worker transforms these into consumers' goods; the merchant manages the exchange and distribution of the produce of the farm and the manufactured goods of industry. Each is dependent upon the other; the segments of society are interconnected, and the society is by nature a cooperative one. A society without rather detailed division of labor remains a primitive one, and exists in relative isolation; but the more complex society in which division of labor is the rule takes on an organic quality, with the activity of any one part necessarily affecting all the other parts in a way that is quite comparable to what happens in the individual organism.

These justifications for division of labor are commonplaces; something everybody knows; things that really go without saying. I labor the point in order to call attention to the fallacy involved in the common practice of assigning economic questions to a somehow inferior order of inquiry, and of assuming that they are far removed from the spiritual life of man. Even in Europe today there are still those who lament that the development of the material aspects of civilization is accompanied by—if indeed it does not cause—decadence in the spiritual aspects. My own position is exactly contrary to this: that dichotomizing the spiritual and the material aspects of life is bound to be misleading. The cooperation in social life of which we have been speaking certainly has to do with the material conditions of life, but in a very real sense it is also an important foundation of the spiritual life of man.

We have voiced our disagreement with philosophers who deprecate the importance of economic questions deeming them to be inappropriate subjects of philosophical inquiry. We must, however, now glance briefly at a group of theorists who went to the other extreme. When in the late eighteenth and early nineteenth centuries certain British scholars became enamored of the concepts of division of labor and of economic cooperation, they fashioned one basket of these ideas and put all their eggs into it. They advanced the proposition that all political problems are fundamentally and in essence economic problems.

In the latter half of the nineteenth century Herbert Spencer was a powerful advocate of social Darwinism, expounding the view that the evolution of social institutions, and particularly of economic arrangements, was analogous to organic evolution as Darwin had described it. He was optimistic in his insistence that division of labor opened up opportunities for individuals to develop their potentialities, and that the increased producton and exchange of commodities made possible by this division of labor would naturally result in cooperation, and ultimately in the elimination of hostilities.

This was the doctrine of free trade. Free trade, its advocates contended, would eliminate war because enhanced economic development would cause people to recognize the costliness of war; free trade would obviate international tensions, both diplomatic and political, and would usher in an era of peace. Free trade (nowadays more commonly referred to as free enterprise) would not only reduce international hostilities to the vanishing point, but would also, its advocates held, promote internal cooperation within a given country. Their theory was that it would be equally to the advantage of seller and buyer to encourage free competition by relaxation of all governmental interference with natural economic processes.

These theorists postulated selfishness as a universal human characteristic, and they admitted that selfishness was the root of many of the evils that afflict society. But they made a distinction between naïve or unthinking self-seeking on the one hand, and what they called rational or enlightened selfishness on the other. They were confident that people in general would soon recognize that the former always had harmful effects, and that, as a result of this recognition, they would turn to rational or enlightened selfishness, which in the nature of things, would require the practice of cooperation.

We cannot judge this theory on the basis of its practical effects, because it has never been put to the test. There is not, and never has been, a country which could afford completely free trade independent of government regulation or support. But even though there are no practical effects on the basis of which to render a judgment, there are obvious weaknesses within the theory itself. The fundamental weakness of the theory lies in its assumption of a condition which is impossible, namely the assumption of equality of ability among individuals or nations involved in competition. Neither people nor nations have, or ever have had, equal ability when it comes to economic competition. If such equality could exist, the doctrine of free enterprise might be tenable, but the brute fact is that it does not. Differences in native endowment, in natural resources, in development of the means of exploiting these resources, in available capital, and in other factors are too obvious to ignore. Nor is it reasonable to expect that rational or enlightened selfishness will automatically replace thoughtless self-seeking apart from the guidance which comes from commitment to valid and consistent moral principles. As things stand, were the theory of free enterprise to be put to the test, the outcome would certainly be that both among individuals and among nations, the ones more richly endowed with resources and expertise would overpower their less fortunate neighbors; selfishness would breed selfishness, and the end result would be inequality, injustice, and tyranny.

This theory gained its greatest currency about the middle of the nineteenth century. Its weaknesses became more and more obvious between 1880 and 1914, the period of imperialism, when the industrial nations of the West dominated and exploited the weaker countries which had fewer and underdeveloped economic resources. In addition to the exploitation of smaller and weaker nations by the larger and stronger ones, there were conflicts among the great nations themselves. With each nation pursuing its own advantage under the guise of free enterprise, the industrial nations of northern Europe produced more than their people could consume, and their competition for markets—notably markets in the less developed nations—brought them into sharp conflict with one another. Instead of the united and peaceful world envisioned by the prophets of free enterprise, we saw in 1914 the outbreak of a war which ultimately involved the entire world.

Just as attempts to put the theory of free enterprise into practice on the international level led to the debacle of war, efforts to make it work on the national level resulted in a variety of ills. Nowadays, of course, there is a degree of cooperation among individuals in commercial and industrial enterprises, but this cooperation is overshadowed by competition, and in this competition, discrepancies in ability and resources give advantage to the stronger, and result in inequality and injustice.

With the transition from handcraft production to machine production, control over the lives of workers is concentrated more assuredly than ever before in the hands of capitalists. Accumulation of capital in the hands of the capitalists gives them control over not only the means of production, but of distribution as well. The disposition of manufactured goods is an intricate affair, and it takes time. The man with a great deal of capital at his disposal can afford to hold on to commodities until the market is in his favor; the man with less capital must let his stocks go for whatever the market can bring, because he cannot afford to hold on to them until prices go up. Under such conditions the wealthier competitor crowds the weaker to the wall and is soon in position to buy him out at depreciated prices—and then to make greater profits than ever.

To put the matter bluntly, in theory, capitalists and workers can cooperate with each other, but in fact, under a system of free enterprise and in the absence of governmental controls, the capitalist nearly always takes advantage of the workers. One reaction to this state of affairs was the organization of labor unions, the major concern of which is to ameliorate, if not eliminate, the worst of the inequalities and injustices engendered by free enterprise. Labor now sees these results as a denial of human rights, and defines the problem as one which calls for radical solution. Capital, on the other hand, citing as its justification the economic theories advanced in the eighteenth and nineteenth centuries, views free enterprise as a wholly natural and completely irreversible phenomenon. Without adopting either position in its entirety, I do offer two suggestions:

First, cooperation in modern economic life has had both positive and negative effects. In earlier ages when life was more isolated, and when there was a minimum of communication, there was also relatively little conflict. But cooperation has promoted communication among people, and has thus accelerated the development of culture. This is its positive effect. The negative is that along with promotion of communication and development of culture has come conflict among people—and in the present case, we refer to conflict between the capitalists on the one hand and the workers on the other. The present problem is one of devising modes of cooperation which will produce the effects we desire, and which will at the same time inhibit or eliminate the negative effects which we deplore.

Second, we must recognize that liberty and equality do not go hand in hand. The slogan of the French Revolution at the end of the eighteenth century was "Liberty, Equality, Fraternity." The theory was that if liberty were granted to everyone, equality would automatically follow. The century and a quarter since that revolution has been a period of liberty to a degree not known before in the world, but it has also been a period in which gross inequality has been so commonplace that many now argue its inevitability. And inequality *is* inevitable when those who can enjoy unrestricted liberty do so. The present problem is one of devising appropriate limitations on individual liberty, to the end that every person may enjoy both liberty and equality in the kind of balance which will afford him maximum opportunity to develop himself to his full potential.

CLASSICAL INDIVIDUALISM

AND FREE ENTERPRISE

I n the preceding lecture I noted that economic life of any degree of complexity involves both division of labor and cooperation. I also discussed the emergence of a new kind of political philosophy stimulated by the industrial revolution in Europe—a philosophy which was not only the first to recognize the basic importance of economic factors to the other aspects of life, but which went so far as to to predicate the possibility that all national and international problems could be solved by proper economic organization. Advocates of this point of view held that economic free enterprise would necessitate cooperation; that it would produce an enlightened self-interest which would lead people to abandon irrational self-seeking; and that it would bring people to a realization that warfare, because it was so expensive to both parties to conflict, was a nonsensical way of dealing with disputes. These economic philosophers painted a utopian world that would come into being as soon as their theories were adopted.

Their ideal, of course, has never been realized—and it cannot be, simply because it is based on assumptions that are contrary to the facts of the case. Unregulated competition, the basis of the theory of free enterprise, would be possible only if parties to the competition were equal in ability. But people aren't equal in ability, and the inequalities which do exist all too frequently result in "competition" in which one side has the advantage from the beginning. Attempts to put the theory of free enterprise into practice resulted in exploitation of labor by capitalists within nations, and in wars between nations.

The question with which we are faced today is that of the degree to which competition can be free, and at the same time just to the parties concerned in it. This is one of the more difficult problems which the industrial revolution is bringing into focus.

Let us review some of the consequences of the industrial revolution. As we noted in our last lecture, the industrial revolution substituted mechanical power for muscle power, and machine production and mass manufacture for production by handcraft. One of the consequences of the replacement of human muscle by steam, coal, and electricity was a new type of political philosophy—individualism. Individualism emphasizes not only freedom in the choice of occupation, but in a much broader sense, one's right to determine his own destiny. A central concept in the philosophy of individualism is the idea of contract, as distinguished from the idea of status which had permeated earlier philosophies. A contract is entered into by the consent of, and on the basis of the willingness of, the individuals or groups involved. The famous British historian, Sir Henry Maine, puts it this way: "If then we employ Status, agreeably with the usage of the best writers, to signify these personal conditions only, and avoid applying the term to such conditions as are the immediate or remote result of agreement, we may say that the movement of the progressive societies has hitherto been a movement from Status to Contract."*

Now, status refers to the position one occupies in his society by virtue of heredity, or by the title which is conferred upon him. The most obvious examples, as we have earlier noted in another connection, are the caste systems in ancient Egypt and in contemporary India—systems which afford virtually no opportunity for communication among members of the different castes. The same thing was true, perhaps on a somewhat less rigidly formalized basis, of the feudal system in medieval Europe, in which people for the most part spent their entire lives in the classes into which they happened to be born. Although Western societies no longer officially subscribe to status systems, it is easy enough to observe vestiges of such social arrangements in the unequal treatment of persons, no mat-

* Sir Henry Sumner Maine, *Ancient Law* (London: George Routledge & Sons, n.d.), p. 141.

ter where one looks. Only comparatively recently (in terms of historical perspective) have we abandoned the doctrine of the divine right of kings, according to which a ruler, without any reference whatever to his capacities or abilities, exercised absolute power solely by virtue of his status. Members of the royal family—and indeed, of several orders of the nobility—were above the power of the law, for no other reason than the status which their birth conferred upon them. The concept of status permeated the whole structure of society, so that even the relationship of the tiller of the land to his landlord was rigidly prescribed. With minor variations, status was the hallmark of social relationships throughout most of the countries of the world.

The fundamental characteristic of a society based upon status is the fact that each person is born into, and remains a member of, a particular social class. Typically a man followed his father's occupation; a woman married a man whose work and station in life were similar to her father's. We have noted that, particularly in industrial nations, the status orientation of society is undergoing rapid erosion, but this development is not the result of political revolution nearly so much as it is the natural outcome of radical changes in economic organization. As an example, the movement for women's rights did not become a political issue until the industrial revolution had taken women out of the home to produce in factories the same goods (largely fabrics, in the initial stages) which they had formerly produced by hand in their own homes. Economic factors were primarily responsible for the change in women's status; political action served chiefly to ratify what economics had already accomplished.

It is important to note the difference between the Glorious Revolution in Great Britain in 1688, and the French Revolution exactly a century later. The former was a political revolution; the latter, a social as well as a political revolution, which not only overthrew the Bourbon dynasty, but also dealt the deathblow to an anachronistic class system which was a vestige of feudal times. When Maine wrote of the movement from the age of status to the age of contract, he meant that in the natural order of development a society will slough off the status system when that system no longer functions effectively, and will adopt a contract system, under which individuals and groups freely negotiate and come to agreement.

As we have already noted, these social changes brought forth the new political philosophy of individualism. The central concept of early (or classic) individualism was that any person was completely free to enter into any sort of contract with any other person or group, and that the primary function of law was to see to it that contracts, once entered into, were enforced. These classic individualists took as their motto, "That government is best that governs least." They looked to the government to require fulfillment of the terms of a contract, but rejected the idea of any other sort of interference by government. This movement tended to equate political philosophy with economic organization, and to regard political reform as being either of negligible significance or as a natural and inevitable consequence of economic developments.

Now this view that the solutions to political problems inhere in economic processes is diametrically opposed to the philosophy of Plato, which had dominated Western thought for more than two thousand years. Plato's perfect society was firmly based in the conviction that the stability of the state was best served, and could be maintained, by a clearly defined status system. In such a society each person would make his contribution within the prescriptions of his own class, and best fulfill his own destiny by serving in the status to which he had been assigned.

But Plato was by no means a diehard reactionary. He was not at all satisfied with the status system which prevailed in Greece in his day. He argued that the existing system not only could not be expected to maintain the stability of the society, but that, unless radical reforms were effected, the end would be social chaos. He proposed that the basis upon which a person would be assigned a particular status be a rational one, rather than one depending upon accidents of birth or fortune. First, the needs of the society would be determined; then the classes that are indispensable in meeting these needs would be constituted; then each man would be assigned to a class or accorded a status in which he could make his most effective contribution; and finally, each child would be educated according to his ability and assigned to that class for which his nature suited him.

Plato's society would consist of three classes of men. At the apex would be his men of gold—the philosopher-kings who would make the laws. The great task of governing a state by law could not be left to the common people; rather, there must be those who are qualified to exercise the faculty of reason, those who can grasp the universals, for laws are the universals which embrace the particulars of experience. In this utopian state, kings would be philosophers—and philosophers would be kings; their status would be the highest.

The second group—Plato's men of silver—would be the auxiliaries, or the guardians, who would have the responsibility of enforcing the laws enacted by the philosopher-kings. These guardians would also defend the state. By nature they would be generous, outgoing, assertively courageous. They would occupy a status second only to that of the legislators, or philosopher-kings.

The third group would be the merchants, traders, and laborers, Plato's men of bronze. In some persons, according to Plato, appetites naturally dominate; these, he said, were to be assigned to the laboring and trading class which supplies the goods for human consumption. Theirs is the lowest status in the social hierarchy. Plato held that the state would exist in peace when each of these three classes fulfilled its own function.

Plato's scheme was a radical one, probably more so in the educational system he proposed than in his plan for social stratification. He argued that the class to which a person is assigned could not be determined by the accident of his birth, but rather by his innate capacities and by an education devised to discover and develop these capacities to their full potential. In *The Republic* Plato deals with education in considerable detail. He holds that education, if properly planned and conducted, should be able to select and train the wisest persons for the status of legislators and rulers, and to identify persons endowed with courage and capacity to understand the law and train them for the second class of guardians and warriors. Those incapable of learning, or who are ruled chiefly by desires and appetites, would be the hewers of wood and drawers of water —the great faceless mass of the common people. But Plato constantly reiterated that status was not to be hereditary—the son of a man of gold might merit no more status than that of a man of bronze, and on the other hand, it was quite conceivable that prospective men of gold would be identified among the offspring of men of bronze or of silver. It was to be the task of education to identify the potentials of each child, and groom him for the station in life for which his capacities suited him.

Plato's ideal is completely utopian, but we can use it as the starting-point of our discussion, because in the history of philosophy, Plato is one of the few philosophers who set forth a complete plan for the state. *The Republic* can stand as the type statement about a society based firmly on the concept of status. It is, of course, an instance of state socialism, with the needs of the total society and each of its parts being determined by an oligarchy. He subordinates economic concerns to those of the spirit, and deprecates any theorizing about the economic aspects of life.

The economic theory that developed in England and France during the late eighteenth and early nineteenth centuries is, of course, a direct antithesis to Plato's philosophy. The new theory saw economic operations as the basis of, and most essential element in, social development. It based its hope for eventual peace on free enterprise, which involved complete freedom of persons to compete with one another. People do not need, according to this view, the advice and counsel of sage and wise and virtuous people, because enlightened self-interest will naturally make them know what they want and enable them to decide which things are best. Free enterprise, it was claimed, could encourage full and free individual development far better than could the advice of Plato's philosopher-kings. If each person, knowing what he wants and needs, can pursue his own advantage, the net result of the total advantages pursued by all persons will add up to the advantage of society taken as a whole. Advocates of this outlook pointed to the fact that the person pursuing his own economic advantage is not acting in a purely individualistic and isolated manner; on the contrary, his interests are in actuality intertwined with those of others. When a contract is made, they argued, it has to be arrived at by common discussion and be mutually advantageous, else one or the other party would refuse to subscribe to it. Hence, they claimed, the result would not be merely personal and individual welfare, but also social welfare in the larger sense, and the promotion of peace and harmony.

When it was pointed out that an ostensibly free contract between persons might in fact involve grossly unequal competition, the reply was that this circumstance had to be tolerated because of the workings of the law of the survival of the fittest. The argument was even advanced that social development would be accelerated by application of the law of natural selection. In short, the advocates of free enterprise were fully convinced that the practice of free contract resulted in individual freedom, that the good society could be constructed without interference by the government, and most particularly, without the government's interfering in any way with industry and trade. The only warrant for government action, according to this view, would be otherwise irreconcilable social conflict, or correction of flagrant corruption in making contracts, or punishment for violation of a contract. This theory is commonly referred to as laissez faire, or sometimes as the police theory of politics, since the major function of the government would be that of policing contracts.

This theory holds that a hands-off policy in government is good not only for economic development, but also equally good for the cultivation of moral character. Free enterprise, it is held, encourages individual initiative and adventure; competition builds toughness of character, moral stamina, and creates zest for struggle. All in all, what was good for economic development would at the same time and to the same degree be good for the spiritual elements in the social process.

This outlook must obviously have considerable appeal here in China, where there has traditionally been so much interference both by the state and by the family elders. There seems to be a rapidly growing trend nowadays to reject the authority of the head of the clan, to have members of the family work more independently and responsibly, and to object to arbitrary interference in personal affairs by officers of the state.

There is, of course, certain merit in the view we are describing. It does, to a degree, encourage the development of character in individuals, and it does lead them to trust each other more than they have done under older outlooks. The theory does have a certain usefulness, both in associated business enterprises, and in the more general sphere of associated living. When we look at the matter historically, we can see that the development of free contract in trade has resulted in people's being able and willing to trust each other. It is probably true that the fact that Europeans in general trust others as much as they do is a result of the development of free contract.

Having looked at some of the merits of this theory, let us turn to its demerits.

The first weakness of the theory is that it ignores the fact that the parties to a contract must be of equal ability, if the contract is in reality to be an agreement reached willingly and freely. When there is this equality, the contract can be made freely, but to talk about a contract made by the free will of both parties when there is marked disparity in ability is to make a bitter joke. Let us take an illustration. A capitalist, let us suppose, owns everything—buildings, machinery, raw materials—everything except workers. But there are more workers available than the capitalist could possibly use. They all want work, so the capitalist can hire as many workers as he wants, and pay them as little as he pleases. If the workers don't like it, they can quit, and the capitalist can hire others for the same wages he has been paying. Under such circumstances, one can say that the contract between the capitalist and the worker is the result of the exercise of free will; but in actual fact, the worker accepts the contract only because he and his children have to eat, and his choice is to work for whatever the capitalist will pay, or else see his children go hungry. There is not even a pretense of equality of ability in the two parties to such a contract, nor does a contract such as this promote either the individual development of the worker or the improvement of the society.

Contracts such as this, where the disparity of ability between the two contracting parties is so pronounced, have two inevitable and deleterious results. The first of these has to do with hours of work. Nobody really wants to work sixteen or seventeen hours a day, as is sometimes demanded by the capitalist. And when the capitalist argues that workers are willing to do so because they have signed the contract, he is being less than honest. As a matter of fact, the workers sign the contract under the force of circumstances, and not by the exercise of free will.

The second evil effect has to do with the conditions of work and the treatment of workers. Workers handling dangerous materials may be crippled, disabled by exposure to poison, or even killed. When they ask for compensation, their employer argues that, by signing the contract (that is, by taking the job) they agreed to work under existing conditions. Again, you can call this the exercise of free will, but again, to do so is to repeat the gruesome joke we referred to a moment ago.

In the early nineteenth century most of the industrial nations rescinded laws which interfered with individual freedom, putting their faith in the asserted virtues of free enterprise. But by the end of the century, these same nations began to enact laws which set limits on hours of work, regulated the treatment of workers and imposed certain standards of safety, and even prescribed minimum wages. Other laws restricted the work that women were permitted to undertake, and proscribed certain sorts of work for children, as well as forbade employment of children under a certain age. The end of the nineteenth century also marked the beginning of the end of laissez faire economic theory and political philosophy, and the emergence on the scene of a theory that government had a proper role to play in the regulation of industry, even at the cost of seeming to interfere.

The second weakness of the doctrine of free enterprise lies in the assumption that a contract is a purely personal affair between the parties who agree to it. It seems to us today incredible that reasonable men could have operated on such an erroneous assumption. No contract is ever just a matter of personal relationship; on the contrary, all contracts have social connotations. Let us suppose for example that a group of a hundred men were willing to engage in work which would clearly be injurious to their health. Their agreement to undertake such work would not be a mere personal concern of these hundred men, but could harm their whole society. Parents whose health is impaired may give birth to defective children who become a burden on society, or who in their turn may further beget defective children. No man lives to himself; his welfare is part of the welfare of his society; his suffering is always at society's cost.

A specific example will clarify what I mean. One of the states of the United States of America enacted a law which set a maximum on the number of hours per day and per week during which women could be employed. Certain people objected that such a law was interference with the rights of women who might want to work longer hours and make more money, and that it was a restriction on their freedom. The courts, however, upheld the law, on the grounds that it was in the public interest that women should not be so weakened by working too long hours as to jeopardize their health, or to increase the likelihood of their bearing weakly children. In other words, the rights of society in this case were given precedence over the freedom of women workers to spend too much time at their jobs, as well as over the freedom of employers to take advantage of their need for additional earnings. The question is now recognized as a public one, not a private one. In Western Europe there has come to be fairly general recognition of the need for unemployment insurance, workmen's compensation laws, and laws protecting the interests of the aged and the incapacitated. The circumstance that Germany had the most comprehensive and forward-looking system of labor legislation was not unrelated to the strength and tenacity she showed during the recent World War.

We have been speaking of the situation in Europe and America, but the issue between laissez faire and government regulation of industry should be of real concern to China, too, particularly at a time when the country is beginning to industrialize so rapidly. Problems of limiting hours of work, of regulating the conditions under which labor operates, of controlling the employment of women and children—these and other related problems must be planned for before the situation becomes serious. To wait until these foreseeable ills have grown to huge proportions before taking measures to forestall them would be shortsighted, foolish, and, in the long run, very costly to the society.

Today we have discussed some of the basic issues between the classic individualism which grew out of laissez faire economic theory on the one hand, and principles of government control and regulation on the other. When government regulation reaches a certain stage of development, we sometimes refer to it as socialism. We have devoted most of our attention up to this point to the merits and demerits of individualism; in our next lecture I shall similarly examine socialism.

I n the preceding lecture I discussed the merits and demerits of the classical individualism to which laissez faire economic theory gave rise, and pointed to some of the problems which inhere in this theory. While there is considerable and growing opposition to laissez faire individualism, this opposition has not, as yet, been formulated into any one coherent statement of a point of view. In general, those who demand alternative theories agree that some form of governmental control and direction must be exercised to the end that economic development can be planned and directed toward specifiable ends. They agree that the rationale for economic development is to be found in the welfare of society rather than in the satisfaction of individual desires—an exact reversal of the position of the classical individualists. Beyond these broad principles, however, there is great divergence.

In today's lecture we will deal with some of the social and political philosophical points of view which are emerging in reaction against the defects and excesses of classical individualism. Advocates of one or another of these positions attack virtually every aspect of existing social organization. The present organization of economic life is probably the target for the greatest number of, and the most virulent, attacks; more specific attacks are directed toward the industrial system; other attacks challenge the institution of capitalism—some call for drastic reorganization of politics and government, while others go so far as to demand the abolition of private ownership of property. All are agreed in being opposed to some parts—or all—of existing systems, but when we come to their proffered cures for the ills they oppose, we find such a wide range of advocacies that it is all but impossible for us to say what "socialism" really is—although each of these solutions is characterized as being social- istic.

Despite all the differences, however, we can categorize the various types of socialism under two pairs of general groupings (each of which cuts across the other, so that either of the first pair may contain representatives of either of the second pair, and vice versa). The line of demarcation be- tween the two schools of thought represented in the first grouping lies in assumptions made about morality. English and French socialists, by and large, find their axioms in morality, criticizing the evils of industrial cap- italism and unequal distribution of property because of the immoral ef- fects of these institutions and conditions. Marxian socialism, on the other hand, eschews morality as an irrelevant criterion for criticizing social and economic institutions, calls its point of view scientific, and postulates a determinism in which the natural law of cause and effect will automati- cally bring about revolutionary changes.

The other line of demarcation which divides socialists into two schools —the vertical line as it were, if the differentiation indicated in the fore- going paragraph be visualized as a horizontal division—is the attitude toward the state as an institution. One group (which, we repeat, may contain representatives of both the moral socialists and the scientific so- cialists) would retain and strengthen the state as the agency for organiz- ing and directing economic activity—with such organization frequently being in the direction of some form of collectivism. The more extreme advocates of Marxian determinism, on the other hand, along with a mi- nority of the moralists, disillusioned by the excesses of classic individual- ism, and tending to identify government with the existing capitalistic sys- tem, advocate a social organization voluntarily and spontaneously formed by the individuals who make up society. Pressed to the logical conclusion this becomes anarchic communism. The former group puts its faith in the reform of the state; the latter, in its abolition.

Even though there are these fundamental differences among the groups, we have warrant for referring to all of them as variants of socialism. Despite their differences, they all hold the conviction that economic ac- tivities should be conducted to the end of the common welfare, not pri- marily for individual profit. All join in attacking classical economic theory because it depends too largely on abstractions and fails to take account of the general welfare of society. This neglect of social welfare, and its overemphasis on the profit motive resulted in such a variety of ills that the socialists agree that the classical theory must be discarded and superseded by other forms of political, governmental, and economic organization. They point to the fact that classical economic theorists emphasized abstract concepts and closed their eyes to concrete problems; they saw labor and capital as abstract terms, rather than as concerns of two different groups, each composed of living, feeling human beings. In reaction, socialists of all stripes tend to concentrate exclusively on what they conceive to be the welfare of the total society.

I cannot, at this time, deal in detail with what we might call moral and ethical socialism, but I must say a word or two about it. Moral socialism had its greatest influence in the early nineteenth century, and the revolutions in various European nations in 1848 were obviously the results of its influence. Marxian socialism became more influential in the latter half of the century, and continued to be popular until the end of the recent World War. There are now, however, indications that people are tiring of Marxism, and turning again to the moral and ethical socialism of the early nineteenth century.

Marx attacked moral socialism, deriding its advocates as sentimentalists. He repudiated the idea that the defects of the industrial system were in any sense at all related to moral issues. He was convinced that the existing system would fall under its own weight, and that a new system would evolve automatically—that individualistic capitalism would disappear, and in the nature of things would be replaced by socialism.

Marx conceded that private ownership of property had been justified in the preindustrial period. When most of the population was engaged in agriculture, producing their own food, and handcrafting commodities which they, themselves, could sell, Marx thought it was proper that each man should own his own property, and receive the income from the goods he sold. But with the advent of the factory system, people no longer carried on their business on an individual basis; with the resulting division of labor, commodities were machine produced through the cooperation of many people. No one person could possibly be involved throughout the process from the production of the raw materials to the processing of these materials into manufactured commodities and their distribution. These facts, Marx contended, meant that wherever there was factory production, manufacture and distribution of goods were in actual fact socialized, but that while production and distribution were already socialized, the operation of the economic system remained as it had been in the pre-industrial period. This, he contended, rendered current economic organization anachronistic, and justified the demand that the structure and organization of economic activity should undergo radical change, with social welfare being the central criterion for the reorganization.

After the invention of the machine and the organization of factories, business enterprises became larger and larger. In a system of free competition, smaller companies with lesser resources tended to be absorbed by larger corporations with their greater capital resources. The large corporations became steadily larger, with the ultimate result being the formation of huge trusts, such as we see today in the United States. In this prediction at least, Marx seems to have been correct, namely that the end result of unregulated competition would be the elimination of competition, with larger companies absorbing the smaller ones, until all major enterprises would be in the hands of monopolies.

We may summarize the salient points of Marx's theory under four headings:

1. Marx regarded private ownership of property as an anachronism. With the advent of the machine and the development of the factory, private ownership lost its raison d'être.

2. The system of economic competition was suicidal, with control naturally gravitating into an always smaller number of hands.

3. Capital in private hands begets more capital; the rich become richer, the poor become poorer, and exploitation of labor is an inevitable concomitant of this process. A natural result would be the disappearance of the middle class, with only the very rich and the very poor remaining; such a state of affairs would eventually and inevitably result in class struggle. Parenthetically, we might point out that people are mistaken when they accuse Marx of fomenting class struggle. It wasn't that he advocated such a struggle; he merely predicted that it would happen naturally, as an inescapable consequence of forces already in operation.

4. Marx, as other theorists before him had done, identified labor as the sole source of economic value. If all economic value derives from labor, then the profit taken by the capitalist must be viewed simply as a reduction in the workers' wages. For example, when a worker produces goods worth a dollar, the capitalist may withhold ten cents as his share, paying the worker the other ninety cents for the support of his family. In this process the capitalist becomes richer and richer, and in his greed for still

more profit, might well increase production to such a level of surplus as to induce economic crisis. It is at this point that Marx predicted that social disorganization would invite class struggle, and that this struggle would make it necessary for the government to take over all economic enterprises, since it would no longer be possible for private enterprise to function effectively or to produce the profits which are its dynamic.

This is a very brief, but I believe fair, summary of Marx's position. When he advanced it—and even for many decades thereafter—it seemed plausible, and gained many adherents. Since the recent World War, however, its popularity is waning, and it is being subjected to increasing doubt and adverse criticism. Two major factors have contributed to this circumstance. The first of these is the fact that most of Marx's predictions have not proved to be accurate. It is true, as we said a moment ago, that his prediction that capital would become concentrated has become fact; but events have run counter to his prediction that the rich would become richer, the poor poorer. Since the end of the war, the standard of living of the workers of Europe and America has become higher than ever before. Wages are higher than they have ever been; workers live better than ever before.

A second factor is that many of Marx's calculations were based on false assumptions. He predicted that socialism would come first to the most highly industrialized nations, since the very social disorganization and class struggle which would precipitate the revolution would be the results of industrialization itself. Historical developments have proved him completely wrong in this regard. He predicted that Germany and the United States, the two most advanced industrial countries of the world, would be the first to become socialist. But the fact is that Russia, the least highly industrialized nation of Europe, was the first to adopt a socialist form of government. If Marx had been correct, socialism would have been impossible for Russia; the fact that history so quickly and so thoroughly contradicted this one of Marx's most unequivocal pronouncements has shaken people's faith in him. If he could be so completely wrong about this, people wonder if he may not have been equally mistaken in other regards. It is small wonder that socialistically minded people are reconsidering the moral and ethical socialism which preceded Marx's.

Again I cannot take time now to deal in detail with some of the arguments used by capitalism to discredit Marxian theory, but I must mention one of them. A highly successful American business man, Herbert Clark

Hoover, was chosen by the Allied Nations to administer food control measures during the World War—and we must admit that Mr. Hoover discharged the obligations of his office with both zeal and efficiency. After some time in Europe, Mr. Hoover returned to America where in public lectures he told his audiences that European socialism was bankrupt. He said that the nations that had adopted socialism had suffered declines in production and could not produce enough food to feed their peoples. Hoover's explanation was that socialism removed the incentive to competition; that this was then reflected in lowered production and in increased difficulty in all-round economic development. He called attention to the fact that this situation was most obvious in Eastern Europe, and advanced it as convincing evidence of the failure of socialism.

This was faulty reasoning on Mr. Hoover's part. In the first place, a few months' observation could not afford an adequate basis for such a sweeping conclusion. In the second place, he failed to take account of other factors which could have contributed—and undoubtedly did contribute—to the suffering and desolation which preoccupied him. Even so, his argument has a point—and one which we should not neglect. Even some socialists have attacked Marx's concept of national socialism, opposing his insistence that economic activities should be under government control. As a matter of fact, even some who accepted Marx's basic doctrine entertained doubts about certain aspects of his theory. Among the reasons for this we may note in the first place that in some instances in which Marx's advocacy of government control of all economic activities was given effect, there did actually seem to be a diminution of individual initiative, a reduction of spontaneity, a lessening of incentive, and a resulting apparent regression to feudal arrangements. In the second place, even when the total economic life is nationalized, talented capitalists, utilizing the experience and expertise gained over the years, can often exercise effective control over the operation of state enterprises and manipulate these to their own advantage. When this happens, the vast majority of less talented people find themselves at a relative disadvantage. This sort of thing does happen, no matter how watertight the theory. There seems to be no way around it.

At this point we need to look at another school of socialism which we can examine under two subheadings, guild socialism and syndicalism. Russia's new constitution seems to draw heavily on these two types of socialism. A fundamental characteristic here is reluctance to organize on a truly nationwide scale, and a general distrust of the efficiency of a highly centralized government. Both guild socialism and syndicalism shy away from too great dependence on government as such; for example, both trade unions in the United States and syndicates in Europe are so organized as to constitute groupings based on common advantages and interests, depending less on government than on the members of the groups. This is the more traditional syndicalism. Guild socialism, a more recent phenomenon, is based upon the common interests of a number of people engaged in the same trade. These people form voluntary associations which govern their own economic activities. Each is, in effect, a smaller society. A number of such groups with related interests may constitute an associated society, with each separate group having its own plan and standard of organization, and administering its own internal affairs, without depending on the government.

In Europe, from medieval times until the industrial revolution, each trade had its own guild which assumed responsibility for the economic practices and affairs of all those engaged in that trade. Most of these guilds operated quite successfully over a period of several centuries. They governed the discipline of apprentices as well as prescribing their wages and working conditions. In preindustrial Europe many of the trade guilds enjoyed high status, founded and endowed schools, and both directly and indirectly wielded influence on the governments of the nations in which they were located, until the development of individualism which attended the industrial revolution. The guild system came to be regarded as a hindrance to the free development of individuals; and by the time of the French Revolution fell into desuetude. But now contemporary socialists advocate a return to the guild system, arguing that by taking each trade as a unit it should be possible to form groups to administer common enterprises in a democratic spirit, instead of depending so much on government. It is possible, with this idea in mind, to refer to the guild system as a sort of industrial democracy.

There are today in China commercial guilds which, it seems to me, could be exceedingly useful during this period when China is undergoing the transition between cottage industry and full-scale industrial production. It is important for us to determine which aspects of the guild system ought to be preserved, and to discover ways in which we may cultivate professional self-respect by promoting more effective communication among people who are engaged in the same or similar trades. After all, it is those who practice a trade who have the most intimate knowledge of what is needed, and wherein their own and their colleagues' interests lie.

Chinese scholars should engage in research on the guild system, to the end that those aspects of it which can effectively contribute to progress can be conserved.

From the very beginning of this series of lectures I have maintained that the proper function of social and political philosophy is to deal with concrete problems, and not merely to attack existing institutions by means of sweeping generalizations on the one hand, nor to offer doctrinaire solutions to problems in general on the other. My purpose is to draw attention to apparently discrete problems, and to suggest methods of dealing with them. Today I conclude my lecture by directing your attention to two problems which should be of direct and immediate interest to an audience composed of Chinese scholars and students.

First, the problem of the ways in which China can develop its important economic resources—its railroads, its highways, its mineral reserves, its forests, and its trade routes—so that they will not fall under the control of a minority who might yield to the temptation to develop them to its own advantage. These resources are intimately related to the public welfare, and, especially at a time when China is undergoing transformation from a handcraft to an industrial economy, play a strategic role in the total development of the nation.

Second, the problem of the means by which China may preserve the desirable aspects of the guild system, and of ways in which she can make these common-interest groups the central units of political organization. If she can do this, and if she can make satisfactory provisions for such groups to participate directly, as groups, in her elections, there is that much greater hope that popular government will contribute the more rapidly to the nation's total development. Because the Chinese version of the guild system is unique and distinctive, only China can find the answer to this problem—but when she does find it, the result may redound to the advantage of other developing nations of the world.

To sum up all we have said today in one sentence—socialism, no matter what its shade, is centered on the one concept of the welfare of the total society, and this, rather than individual profit, should be the criterion according to which economic organization and economic enterprises are judged. This same concept should be our criterion as we deal with the concrete problems which confront China today.

THE STATE

I n my introduction to this series of lectures I enumerated the problems of social and political philosophy and categorized them under three headings—economic problems, political problems, and the problems of knowledge and thought, or what we sometimes refer to as the spiritual side of life. We have already dealt with economics; today we begin our look at the second group of problems, those which fall under the heading of politics.

Broadly speaking the problems of politics fall into four divisions: (*a*) the problem of the state, its nature, the scope of its jurisdiction, and so on; (*b*) the problem of government, its nature, its function, the extent of its jurisdiction, along with questions about aristocratic or democratic governments, direct and indirect democracy, and even, for that matter, whether there need be government at all; (*c*) the problem of law, its nature and its function; and (*d*) the problem of the rights and obligations of persons, including questions of the protection of these rights and the enforcement of these obligations by law.

There would not be much profit in trying to deal with these problems seriatim as I have just enumerated them. Such a discussion would be both artificial and misleading, and unnecessarily complex. A better way is to look at a major idea which relates all these four concepts: the state, government, the law, and rights and obligations. Of these terms, law is the most nearly central, for people must of necessity act according to law of one sort or another. The unique significance of law lies in its effective enforcement by the state. When the state effectively enforces law, political problems become chiefly problems of law. In politics we ask whether something is legal or illegal, that is, whether it is in accord with or in violation of the law; we are concerned with the punishment of lawbreakers, the problem of criminal law; and we also concern ourselves with the processes by which laws are enacted and enforced; thus, cutting across all subdivisions of our second major set of problems, political problems, we find that law is the central concept.

Now, let us look for a moment at the problem of the state. A precise definition of the term is hardly possible, and even if it were, it would not serve our purposes very well. It will be more useful for us to talk about the state than to try to define it in a sentence.

A state must have people, and it must have territory—but an area of land containing people does not necessarily constitute a state. Look at India, for example—a territory so vast that it is referred to as a subcontinent, a population of hundreds of millions of people who have their own traditions and customs, but still India is not a state, merely a colony of Great Britain. For there to be a state, there must be political organization or government in addition to territory and population. But government is not the state; it is only an organization or instrumentality of the state.

Sometimes people say that the state is a social organization which has the power to control the behavior of its people. But the historian knows full well that there are many controls other than the state. The paterfamilias, the head of the clan, the chief of the tribe—all these are examples of agents of social control which preceded the state as we know it. Even in the contemporary world behavior is controlled by all sorts of organizations—voluntary associations, churches, business and industrial corporations, and so on. The state is, in one sense, more or less analogous to these organizations. Perhaps we can get a better understanding of the nature of the state if, instead of examining it directly, we take an indirect approach.

When we do this, we find that whenever people come together in any sort of associated living they face the necessity for organization, and they formulate regulations and rules to govern the behavior of the members of the group. Some form of restriction is inescapable—not in the state alone, but even in an anarchy. Although anarchists refuse to recognize the state's authority to govern, or to impose any restrictions on the conduct of the individual, they do acknowledge that there must, of necessity, be some kind of regulation of human behavior. The anarchist movement in America requires applicants for membership to signify their willingness to observe regulations which forbid members to be government officials, to vote, or to be candidates for political office or civil service positions, or to have any other association with formal institutionalized government. This restriction is no different, qualitatively, from restrictions imposed by the state in the form of laws which prohibit certain behavior.

Anarchists are opposed to the very existence of the state. Advocating a society constituted by freely consenting individuals in voluntary association, they repudiate the authority of the state. In their eyes the enforcement of law by the state, particularly when force is exercised in the process, is an unwarranted interference with individual freedom.

The problem of the use of force by the state to control the conduct of its people is of importance to others than anarchists, however. Count Leo Tolstoy of Russia, for example, held that the employment of force for any purpose at any time is never justified. But if the state could not employ police and military forces, it would lose its reason for existence. Thus, before we can deal with other phases of the problem, we must dispose of the issue of whether the use of force is or is not ever justifiable.

Even those who unequivocally oppose the use of physical or legal force admit the inescapability of moral or psychological forces such as persuasion, instruction, or reprimand. But this raises the question of whether there is a valid distinction between psychological force and physical force. As I see it, no such clear-cut distinction can be made. Even the most despotic tyrant could not possibly rule all his people by physical force. He could not imprison the whole populace, nor manacle them, nor order them to do this and refrain from doing that against their will. He can rule successfully only when he exercises some sort of psychological control over his subjects. He can make people fear physical punishment and imprisonment, or he can persuade them that it is really to their own interests to follow his dictates, so that they want to do so—but this is psychological control, not the use of physical force. Still, this psychological control is related to the possibility that physical force may be invoked. You can see that it isn't easy to say where one leaves off and the other begins.

History provides us with innumerable examples of the evil consequences which have ensued from the employment of force by the state. But when we are analytical about it, we discover that the real problem is not that force is evil per se, nor is it the problem of whether force should or should not be employed, but rather the problem of determining when and how force may be employed appropriately and wisely—not the problem of whether, but of how. We oppose such punishments as mass imprisonment, manacling or beating people, or shooting them, not because we reject the use of force itself, but because we regard as evil the consequences of using this sort of force in these sorts of ways. The evil is twofold: on the one hand it contributes to insensitivity and cruelty of disposition on the part of those who employ it, and on the other hand, it causes those who are subject to punishment to try desperately to evade the punishment. The more cruel and unjust the law, the more artfully and determinedly the lawbreaker evades its penalties. Thus when we oppose particular uses of force because of undesirable consequences, we are not by any means repudiating the use of any force at all.

Mental force or psychological force can be given expression only through physical force. The thought in our mind, for example, can be expressed only through the physical act of speaking or writing, of gesturing, grimacing, and so on. How much would a thought be worth if it were kept forever in the mind, and not made known to others through the exercise of the muscles of the throat or the face or the hands? If I want to go downtown, I must express my wish by leaving the room, getting into the car, telling the driver where I want him to take me, and so on—but all these are physical actions. All I am saying is that the problem is not whether to use mental or physical force, but rather the problem of when and how to apply force—recognizing that both psychological and physical factors are involved in all instances.

Force ought to be employed wisely and economically, not wastefully or recklessly. It is quite possible, for example, for two well-disposed persons to find themselves at loggerheads simply because they are inept in the ways in which they bring force to bear in the undertaking in which they are involved. The function of law and politics is to direct the use of force into channels such that, when translated into physical manifestations, the possibility of conflict is reduced and the danger of wasted energies is obviated.

In the first lecture of this series, when discussing the function of political and social philosophy, I pointed out the futility of either defending or attacking existing institutions by sweeping generalizations, and insisted that the thing to do is to examine and judge each individual case as a concrete problem. We must keep this in mind as we deal with force— determine which methods of using force are good and humane and which are evil and nonhumane—rather than sticking to our guns and adopting an either-or attitude on the question of whether force should or should not be employed.

What are the criteria by which we can make such examination and render such judgment? I believe that for our present purposes, two such criteria will suffice.

The first criterion is the public welfare—if the use of force contributes to the public welfare, it is good; if it is for selfish ends, it is evil. As an example, we can say that when William the Conqueror used his military force to invade England, and to subjugate and exploit the Anglo-Saxons, he was resorting to a use of force which, according to this criterion, was evil. The same principle applies equally to the internal affairs of a nation and to international relations.

The second criterion is the degree to which the employment of force can lead to the maximum development of knowledge and thought. When force results in the destruction or suppression of knowledge, or when it makes people less willing and able to think, it is evil; just as force which promotes the development of knowledge and contributes to the capacity to think is good—and this is especially important, because it is the quality of people's knowledge and thought which determines whether further application of force will be wise and conducive to humane ends.

When applying these criteria, we need to remember that force can be employed on three levels. The first of these is simply the expenditure of physical energy—the sort of energy that is indispensable in any human activity. A cabinetmaker building a table, for example, must use a saw, a lathe, a hammer, a plane, sandpaper, and so on—and in using each of them, he expends energy. We use energy when we chew our food or when we talk. In fact, no matter what we do, we expend energy in doing it.

The second level in which we are interested is coercion and resistance. When someone interferes with another's freedom of action, the latter has to utilize some sort of force to resist the former. The problem here is when to use force, and how, and how much. When is a nation justified in employing military force against another? When is a government justified in employing police force to restrain people from the activities in which they are engaged? There are times, of course, when such force must be employed. But the kind and degree of the force of resistance must be determined by the nature and severity of the coercive or interfering force that has to be countered. The more violent and cruel the nature of the violating force, the more justifiable the resort to forcible measures to resist it.

The third level of force with which we are concerned is violence—a completely negative, destructive force, nearly always wasteful. Energy is force employed to reach a purpose; resistance is the force employed to counter violence; violence is force expended to accomplish nothing—or at best to accomplish something destructive and not worthwhile. Ancient criminal law, in resorting to cruel punishments such as decapitation or maiming—the lex talionis—really contributed to the depraved appetites of the authorities themselves. The results were both negative and wasteful for the authorities, while members of the victim's family plotted revenge, or became confirmed in their determination to evade the law. Violence is wasteful both in the internal affairs of a nation and in international relations. Our problem, then, as far as force is concerned is to find ways of employing it at the first level—energy, or the conscious use of force to achieve a purpose. The more constructive and economical the employment of force, the better for all concerned. We must find out how to avoid the third level—violence—so that we can escape the need for resorting to the second level—resistance. It is only as we keep these things in mind that we can make intelligent judgments about the employment of force.

We have just said that better results eventuate when force is employed constructively and economically; worse results, when it is used destructively and wastefully. These criteria of economy and constructiveness are applicable in family and business situations as in national affairs—but today we are discussing the state. It is good for the state to employ force for the development of education, for the exploitation of its mineral resources, for the construction of railroads and highways, and for the building of housing for its people; but it is evil for the state to employ force to kill people.

Why does the state become an organization that has supreme power? It is simply because human beings require justice. When two men come into conflict, they must find a third person to decide who is right. When they disagree, or when one finds that his interests are in opposition to those of his neighbor, they have to depend on someone else to mediate the affair and find a solution to their problem, for it is difficult for people to be fair in their judgments when they are themselves involved in dispute. But not just any third party can render a judgment which both disputants will accept. People have a natural tendency to look to a power bigger than they are, a power which can render decisions in the justice of which they have confidence—and it is out of this tendency that they have evolved the institution of the state, and arranged it so that the power of the state is supreme.

You might ask why the third party who is necessary to pass judgments and bring a just solution to conflict might not be the family, the church, the business firm, or the voluntary organization. These lesser institutions do the same thing—but the scope of their power and authority is limited, and they therefore can do it only on a smaller scale. Moreover, sometimes one party to the dispute might be a member of one of these smaller groupings, and his adversary would not be likely to accept as just a decision handed down in such a case. This sort of situation creates the need for a more inclusive organization. The more complex a culture is, the more closely all the component organizations within it are interrelated, and the greater the need for a mediating power that is bigger than any of them—hence the need for the state with its supreme power.

Anarchists, who reject the idea of the state, hold that people must be free to make their own judgments. Some of them object particularly to intereference in such personal matters as love and marriage, holding that these are matters for individual judgment. Now, most of us agree that young people should have wide latitude in selecting their companions and in choosing the persons they wish to marry. But marriage is a social institution as well as a personal one. We certainly couldn't leave such things as divorce and the disposition of children to the independent judgment of the people involved. This is only one of the problems which must be handled in an orderly way; there are uncounted others. The more advanced a society becomes, the more disputes and conflicts of interests there are to be mediated by a third party. Eventually we get to the point at which this third party must be the all-inclusive and permanent institution known as the state.

Having seen how the state evolves and becomes the permanent organization of the supreme power of the society, we can return to the problem we posed at the beginning of this lecture, namely the criterion by which we evaluate the state. The reason a state can exercise supreme power is, as we have seen, that it is the most effective means to the welfare of the whole public. The smaller organization cannot exercise supreme power, nor can it be looked to for final judgments, because each such organization represents only a segment of the total public.

To sum up what we have said, the state is judged to be good when it represents the general public welfare; but it is not good, no matter whether it be called a democracy or something else, if it represents the interests of a minority of its people, or of a monarch and his relatives, or of one political party, or of one economic class. The fundamental problem in politics is to build a state which consistently works for the welfare of all its people.

I n my preceding lecture I discussed the nature of the state, and pointed out that it is easy to confuse the problem of the state with the problem of government. In history, the problems of the state and of government have to be considered together, for although these two are separate concepts, every state, by definition, must have a political organization, that is to say a government, to conduct its affairs.

At the same time I drew a distinction between state and country. Land and people can constitute the latter, but a state must have, as we have just said, organization of political power in addition to area and population. This organized power defends against invasion from without, and enforces the law within the state. The state is also to be differentiated from the idea of nation. By nation we mean a group of people who speak a common language, use the same written characters, enjoy the same literature, behave according to similar customs and habits, and think in the same general patterns. But a nation is not necessarily a state; many European nations—a notable example is the Slavic nation of Poland—have striven unsuccessfully to become states. A nation may also be a state, but it remains true that many nations are not states. It is not until the nation achieves the power to guard its borders against invasion, and to enforce its own laws within its boundaries, that it can be considered a state.

Now that we have made this clear, let us turn to the problem of government. One factor that makes government a perplexing problem is the frequency with which we find inconsistency between the ends for which government is constituted and the means adopted for the realization of these ends. The end of government is to accomplish those things for which the state exists, to cause each part of the state to operate in relation to and with regard to all other parts, and to do what the component units of the state cannot do for themselves. We must not forget that a government is composed of persons—men and women who have ambitions and desires, and who are sometimes selfish. There is thus always the problem of making government an effective means of accomplishing the legitimate ends of the state and of forestalling the tendency to subvert it to the ambitions, desires, and selfish ends of the individuals who compose it. The basic problem is that of channeling the power of government so that it promotes rather than interferes with the public welfare. A Greek philosopher once compared the government to a shepherd and the people to sheep. The shepherd's business is to fend off attacks by wolves and to see to it that the sheep are fed and watered—to protect and care for the sheep. But we need not press the analogy so very far to come out with the conclusion that perhaps the reason the government cares for the sheep is that it wants the wool and mutton to be available when the sheep are grown.

The problem of government is a thorny one. Realization of the ends of government requires resort to force—else government may not be able to repel invasion from without or enforce its laws within. But the power rests in the hands of the officials who make up the government, and a major problem is to insure that these officials use the power of government in the interest of the public welfare rather than to their own selfish advantage. This is a practical problem, not just a bookish one. Students of government in the last three centuries have advocated responsible, representative constitutional government as the most effective safeguard against that malfeasance in office which abuses power and works against the public welfare.

In the West the problem of government must be examined in the light both of history and of human nature. Control of government by a limited group who ruled by hereditary right was characteristic of both Orient and Occident until comparatively recent times. People simply took it for granted that their monarch ruled by divine right, and the question of whether he deserved the power which heaven had granted him wasn't asked. The monarch held the most exalted position, enjoyed the greatest dignity, and wielded absolute power. He was responsible to God and his own conscience alone, but not to his subjects. It was precisely the fact that such governments were, in a literal sense, irresponsible, that gave rise to the demand for representative government which would be responsible to those who elected the officials to constitute the government. It is interesting to note that this movement first made headway in Great Britain, because there the king was less powerful than in other countries of Europe, and the feudal system less deeply rooted as an institution. The British people were, on the whole, less disposed to accede to the idea of the divine right of kings. Thus Britain saw the earliest emergence of constitutional government. On the mainland of Europe monarchs were more firmly entrenched, and constitutional governments were slower to emerge.

We have been talking about the facts of history; let us turn now to a discussion of human nature. When a man is granted unrestricted power, there is always the danger that he will misuse the power to his own selfish ends—and this danger exists no matter how good the man may be. The way Lord Acton put it, when discussing government by the consent of the governed, was: "Power tends to corrupt, and absolute power corrupts absolutely." He meant simply that no matter how good a man may appear to be, he runs the danger of doing evil when he wields power without any restriction being placed upon him.

In a book I read a few days ago, the author advances the thesis that Western political systems impose restrictions on government because of the assumption that human nature is inherently evil, while the older political system of China was based on the assumption that human nature is inherently good. On this assumption it was easy to grant that an emperor could rule virtuously, and that there was no need for a legislative body to circumscribe his power. The author may have something of a point, but he goes too far. As a matter of fact, Western political institutions are not based on the assumption of the inherently evil nature of man, but merely on recognition of the fact that whenever one man is granted unrestricted power he goes beyond justified use of that power— that even good men do, in fact, become evil when they have too much power and no restrictions upon it. This is not the same thing as assuming that human nature is inherently evil; it is merely recognition of the need of restraints to prevent good men from becoming evil.

It is not true that all Western political theorists advocate a strong system of restrictions on government. There are two schools of thought on this matter in the West: one school advocates absolute power for the government, the other favors restriction of power. The first school prevails in Germany, where theorists speak out in favor of absolute power for the government; the second is exemplified in Britain, where political scientists favor a variety of restrictions on the government in the interest of preserving greater individual freedom for citizens.

Today we shall discuss the first of these two schools of thought—that which advocates unrestricted power for the government. In order to understand this position we must first know something about the age which gave it birth. The sixteenth and seventeenth centuries were an age of great change; prior to this time, the Holy Roman Empire and the Roman Catholic Church provided a sort of political unity for most of the continent of Europe. In the seventeenth and early eighteenth centuries, rapid economic change had as one of its results the emergence of a number of small independent nations in the northern part of Europe; the development of commerce created a propertied class distinct from the hereditary nobility; and even though the steam engine was yet to be invented, there were the beginnings of the factory system of industrial production. The influence of the Roman Catholic Church declined, and Protestantism became a feature of northern European life. The combination of these factors—religious, political, commercial, industrial—brought an end to the political unity of Europe, and introduced disorder which, in one degree or another, has continued to the present. While this transition was under way, many people looked with nostalgic longing on the unity that had existed in earlier ages, and in an effort to recapture the security of the Middle Ages, some of them formulated absolutistic political theories.

In a time of confusion people crave peace, and because they do, many of them are willing to accept any theory that promises peace. If a government that wielded absolute power could guarantee peace and security, many people would be willing to pay the price at which such a government could be had. The Italian theorist Niccolò Machiavelli was the first man in modern times to construct a coherent political theory on this basis and, in *The Prince,* he developed the theory that a monarch should rule with absolute authority. So long as a monarch could protect his people and his state from external attack and from internal rebellion, Machiavelli argued that he was justified in resorting to whatever means made these ends possible—even that force and deceit were honorable, and that the ordinary rules of morality could not and should not apply to rulers. All decisions and actions of a monarch are aimed, he said, to the end that his people might dwell in peace; and so long as he could achieve this end, no restrictions should be placed upon him.

Following Machiavelli in Italy came Thomas Hobbes in England.

Hobbes, living in a time of revolution, came to advocate supreme power for the government to an even more extreme extent than Machiavelli, and spelled out his theories in greater detail. He held that from the beginning of time men had lived in what was virtually a state of war, one with the other, largely because of three innate characteristics:

1. Acquisitiveness and competition. Normal man wants material wealth, and the more he gets, the more he wants; he has a natural desire to outstrip his fellows in possessions.

2. Distrust and suspicion. Men by nature mistrust each other, and constantly suspect others of trying to get the better of them.

3. Ambition. Man by nature is greedy for glory, and will go to any lengths to enhance his reputation.

As far as Hobbes could see, these three factors could have only one result: constant conflict. His solution was to organize the state so that only a very small number of men would have the power to rule and preserve order; and the state, once so organized with supreme power, should demand absolute and unquestioning obedience of all its subjects, under whatever circumstances. Hobbes was the first major philosopher to advocate a systematic political philosophy which granted supreme power to the state. He saw no alternative to the people's granting absolute and unqualified power to the state; for him, this was the only way out of the confusion which he had observed during Cromwell's Commonwealth in the two decades following the execution of King Charles I.

Certain Hobbesian scholars carried his theories even further than had Hobbes himself. Some of them interpreted Hobbesian doctrine to mean that rather than permitting its citizens to do thus and so, the state, in effect, ordered their every action. They even went so far, for example, as to argue that when we walk back and forth in the street, it is not that the state permits us to do so, but rather that it orders us to walk in the street. For them, the state became something which permeates the whole life of the people and stands above the law. In their view it was absurd to speak of the law standing above the state, since the former is created by the latter, and, as a stream cannot rise above its source, so the law cannot be superior to the state whose creature it is.

The influence of Hobbes was slight and short-lived in his own country; his doctrines were obsolete almost before they were formulated. Barely a decade after his death, as a result of the Glorious Revolution, William and Mary came to the throne under a constitutional form of government which persists with relatively minor changes right down to the present. But on the mainland of Europe the story was different, and Hobbes' theories of absolute power for the state gained adherents and became very influential.

The next major figure in the tradition of Machiavelli and Hobbes was Baruch Spinoza. Spinoza took the essential elements of his predecessors' political theories and used them as bases upon which to construct a nobler and more moderate political theory of his own. He held that before human beings organized themselves into societies they were not essentially different from other classes in the animal kingdom. But human reason, he argued, made men conscious of the necessity for social organization as means of overcoming their animal inclinations, and of giving effect to the need to show consideration for others. This awareness resulted in the formation of simple societies—one stage in man's social evolution.

Spinoza saw the state as the next step in this evolutionary process—a more complex form of society in which law rather than untutored desire furnished the framework for human activity, and afforded a means by which the rational life of man might be developed. The most advanced stage of man's social evolution, according to Spinoza, will be the republic; but this stage must first follow the simple societies spontaneously created by primitive man, and then follow the state, which marks the second stage of his evolution. A republic cannot come into being until all people behave according to law; and until the time comes when a republic is possible, an authoritarian government is the only choice, since such an intermediate development can make people aware of the importance of the public welfare, and of the necessity of foregoing personal advantage in the interest of the public good.

Spinoza held that the power of the state is supreme, so that the people can only obey; rebellion or revolt being unthinkable—certainly a severe political doctrine. He would, however, impose a restriction on the power of the state, namely that it must not interfere with individual freedom of thought and of belief. This limitation inheres in the primary function of the state, in that it is the organization through which human beings achieve rationality; any interference with individual freedom of thought and belief would defeat the very purpose of the existence of the state.

Spinoza's political theory had small impact in his lifetime, and even after his death there was no general adoption of his point of view. This may have been because he was a Jew; Europeans generally held Jews in low esteem. But the indirect influence of his theory has been rather marked, especially when subsequent German scholars combined Spinoza's outlook with Aristotelianism and Platonism, creating a new political theory which has exercised a tremendous influence on the mainland of Europe.

This new political theory appeared early in the nineteenth century. The reaction to the French Revolution at the end of the eighteenth century, especially among German observers, was that it was a tragic result of extreme individualistic liberalism; and the result of this assessment was the emergence of the new political theory born of a union of Spinoza's ideas with those of Aristotle and Plato. Georg Wilhelm Friedrich Hegel, the foremost spokesman of the new position, interpreted the state as being representative of the divine will. He believed that the times bring forth the man, in the sense that when the occasion demanded it, the divine will would appoint a particular person to develop the *Kultur*. War, in this view, is an expression of divine will, with victory assured to the side favored by this divine will, defeat to the side it disfavors. Hegel mustered historical data to prove his assertion that the divine will is predetermined, and that as the German people were foreordained to develop the highest *Kultur,* they were entitled to a position of permanent preeminence.

Hegel, regarded as the official philosopher of the German state, wielded widespread influence. His observation of history caused him to regard the state as an organization through which the divine will expresses itself; consequently, he concluded, the individual must be wholly subject to the state. Hegelian political theory has had both good and bad effects. On the negative side, it supplied the rationale for the Prussian political dictatorship that eventuated in state militarism. It led the German people to an exaggerated regard for their own *Kultur,* which they saw as the only one having true value, the only one expressive of the divine will.

The positive contribution of Hegelian political thought, we will see the more clearly when in our next lecture we discuss individualistic liberalism. We will see that the chief defect in this individualistic liberalism is that it seeks to place too much restriction on government, holding as it does that the primary function of government is that of safeguarding the material welfare of its citizens—the classical conception that that government is best that governs least. Hegelian theory takes the opposite point of view—and, at least in some measure, we believe that this is good—that the state as an organization should safeguard not only the material welfare of the people, but also their spiritual life, with promotion of culture and education being major governmental enterprises.

I have heard the recent World War characterized as a struggle between antithetical political schools of thought—schools so different from each other that compromise between them was impossible—liberalism on the one hand, authoritarianism on the other. We know that authoritarianism was defeated this time—and we believe that the result will be the same if the issue must be re-joined in the future. There is one aspect of Hegelian political doctrine, however, which has prevailed, and which will continue to prevail in the future: this is the argument that the responsibility of the state must not be limited to the protection of private property and the enforcement of contracts, but that it must also be responsible for the development of spiritual values. I wish that the theorists of liberalism could improve their political theories by incorporating within them this contribution of Hegelian theory.

I n the discussion of politics the central problem is that of reconciling the moral viewpoint with the exercise of authority by the state. In other words, the problem is what should be the moral limit of the exercise of authority by the organ of the state—the government—in legislation, administration, and adjudication? There are two answers to this problem.

First, the answer given by German scholars, as I pointed out in my last lecture, is that the problem is really not a problem at all, inasmuch as morality has its source in the state, and the state furnishes the criteria by which moral questions are judged. Their position is that since there can be no social life without the state, and since the problem of right and wrong, good and evil, morality and immorality, can arise only within a social context, the state, as the source of moral life, does not require any moral limit.

The second answer, that of British liberalism, is that the authority of the state derives from the degree to which it contributes to individual freedom, because the purpose for which the state exists is to mediate when individual freedoms get in each other's way. It is with this answer to the question that we deal today.

Political liberalism is most intimately associated with the name of the English philosopher, John Locke. Locke's political writing came after the Glorious Revolution in England in 1688, which overthrew the despotic government of the Stuarts and substituted for it a constitutional monarchy. This government, hedged about with constitutional restrictions, so completely replaced the authoritarianism of monarchs who had claimed to rule by divine right that, from that day to this, there has been hardly a shadow of a threat of recrudescence of any form of absolutism. Locke's political writing formulated the rationale for the new constitutional monarchy, and justified the revolution which instituted it.

At the outset, Locke postulated two stages of human social development, namely life in the state of nature, and life in the state of political communities. Because men are rational creatures, Locke assumed that social life existed even before the political community came into being, and what is more, this socal life was not one of turmoil and war as Hobbes had assumed it to be. Locke did, however, predicate three deficiencies in primitive social life which called political communities into being: (1) the primitive social community had no organization to enact laws and regulations to give direction within the community or to regulate relations between different communities; (2) in the absence of law and regulation, there could be no third party to act as impartial judge when disputes occurred; each man was a judge to himself, and each tended to defend himself; there could be no objective judgment, right or wrong; and (3) there was no provision for an impartial third party to enforce the law; in the absence of judicial arrangements, revenge was sought by the party who believed himself to have been injured, or by his descendants, with such feuds sometimes continuing for generations.

These considerations brought people to recognize the need for social organization to discharge the functions of legislation, administration, and adjudication, and thus political communities came into being. As Locke saw it, individuals, recognizing the inconveniences imposed by the absence of government, willingly sacrificed some of their individual freedoms in order to have a political community, and thus to insure certain rights which they were unable to maintain as individuals. In other words, they instituted governments having legislative, executive, and judicial functions to provide greater security of life and fuller protection and enjoyment of their property than was possible in the earlier state of nature, even though such institution did entail forfeiture of some of the freedoms they had enjoyed in their earlier naïve stage of social development.

As a result of negotiations and understandings of this sort, a few persons were granted the right to organize a government. It was as though a contract had been set up between the people at large and the few who constituted the governing body. In fact, this is the so-called social contract theory of government. People delegate to the government the powers of legislation, execution, and adjudication so that they may more fully enjoy life and liberty, that is, they make a contract.

Locke hoped that his theory would serve two purposes. The first was to afford a rationale for the constitutional monarchy instituted after the Glorious Revolution, and to show that both the constitution and the government set up under it were for the protection of the rights of the people. His theory was to serve as an undergirding for government with the consent of the governed. The second purpose was to justify the revolution, and to show that the overthrow of the Stuarts was a legitimate revolution rather than an act of rebellion. When a government which is the trustee of the people abuses its trust, the people are justified in overthrowing it—thus the dethronement of James II was a moral, reasonable, and legitimate revolution.

Some people reject the social contract theory of government on the grounds that there are no historical accounts of even one instance of a government's having been instituted by an actual, literal social contract. This objection, though, is not really a telling one. Locke was not writing about history, and did not appeal to history as justification of his doctrine. He simply wanted to show that a government does not come into existence spontaneously and without cause, and that the purpose or function of a government can be likened to the performance of a contract. If the government fails in this regard, the people are always justified in overthrowing it and replacing it with another government. He also wanted to show the basis on which the people should put restrictions on the government and exert pressure by the constant threat of replacement. These two aspects of the theory of social contract can stand on their own, whether or not history affords actual instances of such a contract's having been formally instituted.

Locke's political theory called for a constitutional monarchy rather than for direct democracy. He did not advocate that the people should reserve political rights, but rather that they should delegate these rights and authorize the government to exercise them. The people should place certain restrictions on the powers of the government, and they should reserve the right to change the government when it does not exercise in the public interest the powers delegated to it. Locke's bias can be accounted for by the fact that he was a Whig, a member of a political party which favored constitutional monarchy.

The French Revolution, almost exactly a century after the Glorious

Revolution in Great Britain, was a thoroughgoing democratic movement. We may regard Jean-Jacques Rousseau as the philosophical spokesman of the French Revolution, just as Locke was the spokesman for the Glorious Revolution a century earlier. Rousseau's fundamental contention was that all governments, both those existing in his time and in all preceding times, were evil; that good government as such had never existed. All governments up to his time, he averred, were based in the bald exercise of power. A good government, as Rousseau saw the matter, theoretically at least could be instituted on the basis of general will, and represent the welfare of society as a whole, even though this might mean holding the will of some individuals temporarily in abeyance. A proper government would be one which would give effect to the general will throughout all the operations of the society.

Rousseau held that since law most directly represents this general will, legislative power should be reserved to the people. Locke had argued that the three powers of government—the legislative, the executive, and the federative [Locke's terms]—must be kept in balance, or that otherwise a dictator might seize control of the government. This view is deeply rooted in the Anglo-Saxon tradition. But Rousseau, regarding the legislative power as the central element in government, did not see legislation as a function which could be delegated to a representative body. He contended that the legislative power belongs essentially to all the people. He granted that the executive and the judicial functions, which he regarded as of secondary importance because they were nothing more than means of giving effect to the law, could be delegated and representative—and that the personnel to whom they were so delegated should be changed whenever they failed to function effectively. Rousseau's insistence that the legislative power must belong to the whole people makes him an advocate of the most extreme sort of direct democracy.

Just as Locke's theory provided the rationale for the revolution in Great Britain, Rousseau's theory afforded a philosophical basis for the French Revolution. The British did not find Rousseau's doctrine at all palatable; they treated it as present-day conservatives do the theories of the Bolsheviks. A great part of Bolshevik theory, as a matter of fact, is a heritage from Rousseau, except for the relatively minor difference that Rousseau referred to the general will of all the people, while the Bolsheviks are concerned with the general will only of the proletariat.

Let us glance now at the historical development of liberal political theory. Locke's theory underwent a number of alterations between the time he propounded it and 1832. During the eighteenth century the British people could note increasing political corruption and abuse of governmental power. Since Locke's political doctrine was that of a constitutional monarchy rather than of a thoroughgoing democracy, the restrictions placed on government proved insufficient to forestall abuse and corruption. Locke's theories, under the impact of Rousseauian doctrine, were called into doubt. The eventual result was a marked modification in the early nineteenth century by those who are called utilitarians. In the utilitarians' view, the government is an instrument to be used to achieve the maximum happiness for the greatest number of people. They predicated the equality of all men, and treated each individual as a unit. This concept has three consequences in political theory:

1. Each person knows his own needs better than anyone else can possibly know them. This idea is very important, because the concept of general election is derived from it. Each person expresses his individual will by his vote. The current trend toward general elections is an outgrowth of this theory of individualism. The utilitarians, aware of the fact that people are not equal in knowledge or ability, advocated a parliamentary representative system, with the people electing their representatives through general elections. But how to put restrictions on the representatives, and forestall their abuse of power? Hence the second consequence, as follows:

2. Elected representatives must be responsible to the people. The voters elect the persons they favor, but they also specify the term of office for them. When the representatives' terms expire, they must depend upon the people for reelection, and this fact serves to keep officials responsible to the public.

3. Legislators are also subject to the restrictions embodied in the law. At first glance this appears to be a superficial point, but actually it is extremely important. It means that all parts of the government, including the legislators, are subject to the restrictions embodied in the constitution, the fundamental law of the land, to which all other laws must conform.

These three points illustrate the ultimate development of the theory of political liberalism. After a variety of vicissitudes, this theory has been put into practice in England. The United States has embodied the theory in its constitution and in political practice from the beginning—a fact which I think helps to account for the preeminence it has enjoyed among nations. The nineteenth century found these points being adopted by many other countries, to the extent that one might characterize the century as the age in which liberalism became a dominant feature of the world political scene.

As we have seen, the basic concept of liberalism has been subject to a variety of interpretations depending on time and situation. I will try now to give you a general summary which embodies the views I have outlined: those of Locke, of Rousseau, and of the English utilitarians:

1. The authority of the government stems from the consent of the governed, and not from divine will or any other power that transcends human experience. And since government is based upon the consent of the people, the people have the right to impose restrictions upon, or to replace, the government. This idea is the keystone of democratic political philosophy.

2. The state exists for the sake of the people, and not the other way round, as some German theorists hold; and this is the case because the state is an organization devised to promote communication of feelings, emotion, and will among the people of different social communities.

3. The state should be responsible to the people, and not the other way round. This means that the government must be answerable to the people for its actions; and if the people disapprove, they have the right to restrict or alter the government. Many procedural problems hinge on this important point. The problem is that of practical means by which the people can insure that the government will, in fact, be responsible to them.

Political liberalism poses a host of down-to-earth problems—general elections, direct election, terms of office, revision of election procedures, and many others—and solutions to these problems vary from time to time and from place to place. However, treatment of such problems is fundamentally based on the theory we have been discussing. Even when solutions must be sought in our everyday experience and on the basis of political common sense, they are still important problems. We must not allow ourselves to forget that both the concept of a state that is responsible to the people and the methods by which the people may effectively control the government are the fruit of many years of laborious struggle. Even the everyday practicalities which we sometimes take as a matter of course represent the crystallized and accumulated political experience of many generations.

THE RIGHTS OF INDIVIDUALS

A t the beginning of this series of lectures I grouped the problems of social and political philosophy under three headings: problems in economics, problems in politics, and problems in the cultural and intellectual life of man. We have finished with the first group, and in the last few lectures we have been discussing problems in the second, placing our emphasis on the application of law in the control of society. However, the law we are talking about is not law promulgated by one person, or even that enacted by a small group of persons, but rather, law which expresses the general will of the majority of people as this applies to the maintenance of public life. The history of political democracy is the story of continuing struggle to achieve this goal. The process has been one in which politics representing the will of a minority has gradually been replaced by politics representing the general will of the majority.

Political democracy means more, however, than the substitution of the general will of the majority for that of a minority; it involves also a radical change in outlook, namely that rational legislation should replace the "legislation" of tradition, custom, and habit. Even today there are still laws which are no more than the accumulation of traditions, and which do not embody rationality reached through discussion. Ideally, in a democracy, there is legislative organization, and law comes into being as a result of public investigation, discussion, and amendment. This is what we ought to mean when we speak of legislation. Democracy has gradually broadened its base so that nowadays people can at least elect representatives of their choice to do their legislating for them, even though we cannot always so directly choose the administrative officers of our government. We sometimes forget what an important change in outlook this is, and how recently it has come about.

The problem for discussion at this point is that of the practical function of law in society. Briefly, we may say that there are two main functions of law: first, people are granted a number of rights by law; and second, law imposes upon people a number of obligations.

What do we mean by rights? A right means the power which the individual has been granted to do something according to the law. He can do what he does because he has been granted the power by the law—by law which is supported and maintained by the power of the whole society. In other words, society buttresses the law and thus supports the power which the law grants to the individual person. When a man's legal power is abridged, both the law and the whole society come to his support. Thus, a right is the individual power granted to a man by the power of the whole society, which stands behind and supports the law. And since individual rights are publicly recognized by society, through the agency of law, we may say that the individual's freedom in law and in politics is the sum total of his various rights.

As a corollary to the rights which the law confers, it also imposes obligations upon the individual. This is true because one of the primary functions of law is to maintain order in society and to facilitate the operations of associated living. Negatively, the law must stipulate what behaviors the society forbids or finds unacceptable; positively, it must also stipulate that the individual is permitted to act only in this way, but not in that. This is to say that the law prescribes the scope or range of behavior—the things a person may do, those he must do, and those he must not do. Maintenance of social order and the smooth operation of associated living would be impossible without this sort of prescription.

Every right enjoyed by an individual has as its obverse an obligation. For example, a person has the right to own property, but his right imposes upon him the obligation to respect the same right for each of his fellow men. When he buys or sells property, he must have a contract; frequently he must pay a tax on the transaction, must have the contract witnessed by a disinterested party, must have the deed recorded in the appropriate government office, and so on. This is only one example of the obligations which go along with the right of ownership.

I think we see now that by individual rights we do not mean letting a man do exactly as he pleases; we mean specific powers granted to him and supported by the power of the whole society which stands behind the law. We can now proceed to discuss three categories of rights which the law confers: personal or natural rights, civil rights, and political rights.

Personal rights are those which belong to an individual as a person, and taken concretely, include four fundamental powers: (1) the right to life—a man has the right to live in safety and peace, and this right may not be abridged unless he forfeits it as a result of a crime, and then only after having been judged guilty under due process of law—on the surface this seems to be a commonplace, yet it is a right won by people in general only after centuries of bitter struggle; (2) the right of movement—this is also a very important right, because one cannot live as a man without freedom to move about; (3) the right of property ownership—mere possession of material goods is not enough; a man must have the right to acquire, to possess, and to dispose of property, and this right must be guaranteed to him by society through law; and (4) the right to make contracts, since contractual arrangements are indispensible to common enterprise and the complexities of associated living. These, then, are the four basic rights which belong to a man as an individual.

Civil rights are derived from personal rights. The four kinds of personal rights enumerated above must be stipulated by law and publicly recognized by society. They cannot stand merely on the moral and ideal concept of freedom of action. But when these rights become social and legal ones, various organizations within the society can be employed to protect them and pass judgment on them—notably the courts, and the police acting as agents of the courts.

Civil rights in the West are largely identified with the right to bring suit against another when a wrong has been committed, and the right to a fair and just trial when one is sued or charged with a crime himself. Is it a right, then, to be charged with a criminal offense, or to be sued for alleged breach of contract? The answer is affirmative. If one did not have the right to a fair trial after being formally charged with having committed a specified offense, the disputants in each case would be their own police, judge, and jury, and each his own executioner—and, of course, chaos would result. In a civilized society, an individual must have both the right to bring suit or to make charges, and the right to be sued or accused, and to defend himself in a court of law when so sued or accused. In a society or a state where democratic politics is still undeveloped and the concept of law is wanting, people often take unto themselves the punishment of criminals, and deny them the due process of law. The right to a fair trial according to law is thus a fundamental civil right.

Civil rights define relations which exist among people in a given society, but they also define the relationships between the people and their government. Political democracy stipulates that the law must protect individual rights from infringement by other people, but it also sets up safeguards against infringement of these rights by the government itself. One of the explanations for the preeminence of Great Britain among nations is that it was among the first to have constitutional law, and also because the British people have been so fiercely jealous of the rights conferred upon them by their constitution. Their freedom of life and movement, as well as freedoms of many other sorts, is protected by the government strictly according to the law. Even taxation procedures, as well as protection of property, are legislated by elected representatives. This level of democracy was achieved by the British people only as a result of long struggle with the government, and it is necessary to know the story of this struggle in order to understand the emergence of political democracy as it has come to exist and operate in the twentieth century.

We come now to the matter of political rights. Political rights are basic to the first and second rights—personal rights and civil rights—because these two kinds of rights cannot be maintained without political rights. It is only when people are granted their political rights that their enjoyment of the other two can be guaranteed. This is why people demand the right to participate in the government. Even if they cannot always elect administrative officers, they at least demand to elect legislators—and often these elected legislators have the right to confirm or reject appointed officials. Political rights are the most basic of all rights; they constitute the guarantee of enjoyment of other rights.

Ideally, of course, it would be possible to have an enlightened despotism without the people's participation in the government—given a wise and virtuous monarch, honest and well-disposed officials, and a good body of consistent law. I say it would be possible, but it never has happened. Virtuous monarchs and wise officials have existed, but as we look at history, we note that they seem not to have remained virtuous and wise. As we have said before, no matter how good a man may seem to be, he tends to yield to the temptations of corruption and to abuse the power that has been granted to him, whenever the grant is made without restrictions or qualifications. This seems to be a universal defect of human character. It is for this, among other reasons, that the whole people must insist upon their political rights, in order to insure their enjoyment of their other rights.

The most important single one of man's political rights is the right of suffrage. Until comparatively recent times suffrage was limited to a very small number of people, but gradually it was extended to all male citizens, and most recently it has been further extended to include women as well. Through popular suffrage the people can elect both legislative and executive officials. People also have the right to run for office, and when elected, to serve as government officials in charge of government affairs. In earlier ages only a sharply limited number of people were concerned with public affairs, but nowadays all citizens, both men and women, are entitled to their say-so through the ballot. Viewed superficially—and there are those who do so view it—this may seem to be a thing of small moment; but in actual fact, it is of vital importance, not so much as an end in itself as an instrumentality by means of which to preserve and guarantee individuals' civil rights.

It is worthwhile to emphasize again the point I have already made a number of times, namely that the rights and powers we are discussing have no meaning if we choose to consider the individual apart from the society and the state. The individual can have these rights only so long as he is a member of his society and his state; there are no such things as individual rights until and unless they are supported and maintained by society, through law. It is absolutely fundamental that the concept of individual rights be considered with reference to the society which grants them and to the state, which, through the agency of law, enforces them. Even anarchism gives implicit recognition to this fact at the very time it advocates the abolition of governments. In the anarchists' eyes all governments are suppressive; suppression is evil per se; ergo, governments must be abolished and people must assume the risk of seeking their freedoms without the agency of law to maintain and guarantee them. But the anarchist advances the second proposition that social organization has existed for a long enough time for people to have become habituated in social discipline to the point at which the restraints of government are no longer necessary, so that social order can still exist even after the abolition of government and law. It is clear that both these propositions are advanced within the context of social organization, and even were there some among us who find themselves in agreement with anarchist arguments, what we have said about the social matrix within which individual rights are embedded would still stand.

The concept of rights has been advanced by political individualism, which, as we have repeatedly pointed out, is the culmination of a long struggle to obtain and preserve human rights. Too frequently, however, there is talk of rights as though these stood apart from, rather than being based in, a social context. I feel that I must run the risk of overemphasizing this point, because so often political individualism is confused with self-seeking individualism.

In an earlier lecture in this series we indicated that philosophy—social and political—is not absolute, but relative to existing social situations. A given political theory grows out of the facts and situations in a given society at a given time. The quest for the granting of individual rights is not really a matter for concern in countries of the West today. A few hundred years ago it was the important problem, but by and large, these rights have been established by this time so that the crux of the problem lies elsewhere.

Historically speaking, the movement to seek rights for individuals has been in reaction to suppression of individuals by despotic governments. But the number of such despotic governments has been so sharply reduced in the West that to all intents we might say that this particular problem doesn't really exist any longer. Most Western states have governments which represent the will of the people, and most have adopted constitutions and enacted laws which protect the people. For these reasons the political problem of the moment, as far as the Western world is concerned, has become one of finding ways to give effect to the rights which the law has conferred on individuals, and of finding means by which these rights may be exercised effectively, to the advancement and facilitation of the public welfare.

Another way of saying the same thing is that the problem has changed from that of seeking individual rights themselves to one of seeking the opportunity to exercise these rights; the goal is no longer stated as "a person should have such and such a right," but rather, "he should be provided with such and such an opportunity to exercise his rights." How, for example, can one exercise the right of property ownership without any property? Thus, political theory has to be reoriented to inquire into ways in which the individual can get property, so that he can exercise his right of property ownership, instead of continuing to theorize in empty abstractions about the need for every man to be granted the right to own property.

A French wit once ridiculed the absurdity of finding satisfaction in merely getting laws on the statute books and in writing statements that all men have certain rights, by pointing out that the law prohibits both the rich and the poor from stealing bread, and from sleeping in the streets. This sarcasm is right to the point. It reminds us that it is not enough to put a statement about rights on paper; we must also provide individuals with the opportunity to exercise these rights, to put them into practice.

There are already a number of indications that social and political thinkers of the West are responding to this need for a change of focus. Society employs law and political organization not only to reduce injustice and to produce justice; it is beginning more and more to bring into play the concept of social justice and to remedy some of the injustices that were taken as matters of course, to be regarded with indifference.

Let us return to an example that we have already used to illustrate another point. Almost all industrialized countries have in recent years enacted laws which specify working conditions and safety provisions in factories. These laws also proscribe certain sorts of work for children and women, and set limits on the number of hours per week for which they can be employed. The law now prescribes a minimum wage, below which industry may not employ workers—a provision which has resulted in a higher standard of living for working people. Society also uses tax money to assist the old, the ill, the disabled, and the handicapped. These are not actions seeking rights for individuals—all persons in these countries theoretically possess these rights already—but they are efforts to employ political organization to enable individuals to exercise the rights which they theoretically have.

The most conspicuous example of this sort of thing is the graduated income tax, which tends to equalize the right of property ownership on the one hand, while at the same time increasing the income of the national treasury on the other hand. The percentage of a man's income tax is in direct proportion to his income; the more money he makes, the higher percentage of the total he must pay in taxes. A man who earns barely enough to make ends meet may have his entire income tax forgiven, while the man who makes a million dollars must hand over the major portion of it to the government in the form of taxes. The percentage of the inheritance tax is also in direct proportion to the amount of property inherited. This is a device not nearly so much for increasing the tax receipts of the government as it is for the achievement of justice and equality through political power. It is in line with the tendency to broaden the scope and definition of rights, so as to provide people with the opportunity to develop themselves.

To what extent should the state employ its power to equalize the right of ownership of property and to achieve equality for its people? This is the most pressing problem with which Western politics finds itself confronted. It has stimulated serious discussion both by socialists and by political individualists. Individualism takes the stand that the state should restrict itself to the very minimum use of its power, and should refrain as much as possible from interfering in the natural operation of the laws of economics. But both socialism and individualism have many ramifications. No matter what one's political orientation, he must grant that this is a basic problem. I see it as being of fundamental importance both in the West and in China. But the problem, as it concerns China, has facets which are different from those we see when we look at the same problem as it confronts the West. The problem as it exists in China can be stated as follows: assuming that we agree that our ultimate goal is the fullest possible development of individuals, should China, as the West did, first go through an age of self-seeking individualism, and then employ the power of the state to equalize society as the West has had to do; or should it amalgamate these two steps and achieve social equality at one stroke?

It seems to me that there are grounds for hoping that China can achieve social equality in one operation. There are three reasons why I say this:

1. The first basis for hope that China can achieve social equality without repeating the sequence of events followed in the West, amalgamating two steps into one, is that she already enjoys the traditional concept of the state's obligation to protect its people, as this was propounded by Mencius. Political individualism has not made headway in China, so that the tradition of the state's obligation to protect its people, which may be likened to the parents' obligation to protect their children, or the emperor's to protect his subjects, can readily be modified into the concept of the protection of its citizens by a democratic government.

2. Modern China can achieve equality of opportunity for her people by popularizing education. Popular education is not intended to satisfy the self-seeking urges of individuals, but to provide all men with equal opportunities for self-development. Education in the West became universal long after the begining of the industrial revolution. But the indus-

trialization of China is just now beginning; there is thus the chance for China to universalize education now, so that by the time it reaches full-scale industrialization it will also have achieved social equality.

3. Another basis for hope is that there is still time for Chinese scholars and scientists to pursue specialized knowledge and devote their research activities to special problems. One of the shortcomings of political individualism in the West lies in the fact that it tends to deprecate specialization, and to hold that any reasonably well-educated person can pretty well take care of himself. It ignores the extreme complexities of modern society and politics, and fails to see that even in a small district the problems of education, taxation, and government as well as those of industry, can be dealt with effectively only by those who have mastered a great deal of highly specialized knowledge. If China can begin now to develop appropriate degrees of specialization, her rewards in the future will assuredly be great.

These remarks about China are no more than a few random suggestions of my own. The problem, though, is one of extreme importance, and worthy of the most careful study. Although at the moment China is confronted with particular and exacerbating problems, these are temporary. China is certain to be faced with more lasting and more fundamental problems in the near future, and the two which are of the most far-reaching import are the inevitability of industrialization, and its concomitant problem of self-seeking individualism. The problem thus becomes one of conserving the positive aspects of individualism while at the same time avoiding its negative aspects, which are certain to introduce disorder into your society.

NATIONALISM

AND INTERNATIONALISM

This is the last lecture in which we will deal with the political problems that are included in the second of the three headings under which we have grouped the problems of social and political philosophy. In the last few lectures we have discussed the problems of the state. Today we will discuss political problems on the international level and their relationships with the state.

At the beginning of this lecture series, I suggested that all social and political philosophy is an effort to understand and provide a theoretical framework for the study of the conflicts which arise when different groups within a society, or different societies, seek incompatible goals. The conflicts with which we are concerned today are those which arise when people exhibit hostility toward those who come from another area, and refuse to make the necessary effort to communicate with them. When we extend this concept, we see people of one state treating those who come from another state with even greater suspicion and hostility. All these conflicts are psychological in nature, both those among different groups within a given society and those between people of different nations. There is a widespread tendency for human beings to fear strangers, and the more unlike themselves the strangers are, the more likely that people will treat them with contempt. They even speak of them as savages or barbarians. And because different peoples sometimes have differing standards of morality, people tend to look upon those who differ from them as morally inferior, or even immoral. These facts, and others like them, account for the incidence of conflict among peoples. When one group feels the urge to extend the range of its power and influence, it often invades the territory of another group, and hence conflict—or, if the action is on the international level, war. In its ultimate simplification this is the source of international problems.

The problem is so obvious as not to call for further comment. We all know that everyone has, to one degree or another, loyalties based on geographical relationships. People living in the same village, or even in the same province, more or less naturally feel loyalties based on geographical factors. Logical extension of this idea gives us the concept of national loyalties. This concept of geographical loyalties finds two sorts of expression: on the one hand, people tend to cooperate with and give assistance to others within their own group; on the other hand, there is the tendency to look with suspicion or hostility on members of other geographical groupings. When trouble erupts, people unite with their neighbors or fellow nationals in open conflict against those whose loyalties lie elsewhere.

The idea of the nation-state is so familiar to us nowadays that we are likely to forget what a relatively recent historical development it is. With a few important exceptions it might be said to be a creation of the nineteenth century. Prior to the emergence of the nation-state as a unit, geographical loyalty was largely limited to the level of the village, township, or province.

Although, as we have just noted, the nation-state did not become the typical unit of political organization until the nineteenth century, there were, of course, nation-states before that time. The fact that the islands which make up Great Britain are physically isolated from the mainland of Europe was undoubtedly one of the influences responsible for Britain's becoming the first of the nation-states in the modern sense. Spain, Holland, and France next emerged as nation-states, but the number of such units remained small until the nineteenth century. Germany was composed of more than a hundred small principalities, and Italy was also made up of a host of duchies, republics, and principalities, some of them frequently at war with others. It was not until the middle of the nineteenth century that Germany and Italy became united into nation-states, and, in the sense in which we are speaking, it was not until the Meiji restoration in 1869 that Japan actually achieved this status. Many other countries are, even now, seeking to become nation-states and take their places in the family of nations—Poland, Bohemia, Armenia, India, Ireland, and a host of others. We see that the nation-state is, to all intents and purposes, something new under the sun.

The development of nationalism has had both good and bad effects. On the positive side is the fact that it has extended the concept of geographical loyalty to the national level. The emergence of the nation-state has helped to obviate, or at least to mitigate, conflicts between small groups, to bring people into the more inclusive community of the state, and to create the concept of national loyalty and sympathy. The other side of the coin is that it has also resulted in hostility toward other states. Before the emergence of the nation-state, warfare rarely involved men's feelings, and soldiers were enlisted on a mercenary basis, fighting as readily for one employer as for his enemy. Now, however, each state has its *Geist,* and war involves the entire society and all its members, as well as its institutions—industrial, commercial, and educational. Just before the recent World War broke out, Europe had become a veritable armed camp, with all nations keeping their armies in a ready-for-war condition. And when war came, it was total war; nobody was exempted from the suffering it imposed. Yes, the price of nationalism has been a high one.

A concomitant of the concept of the nation-state is the concept of sovereignty, the idea that the state is the supreme authority in the governance of the people within its borders, and that it is answerable to no higher authority. It has the power to legislate, to administer, and to judge—and it will brook no interference from without in its discharge of these powers. The logical outcome of the application of this concept of sovereignty to each of the nation-states of the world is, of course, international anarchy. The historical development of international politics, and that of internal political arrangements are diametrically opposed, the one to the other. When we discussed the internal politics of a given state in an earlier lecture, we noted that the virtually universal trend was from authoritarianism toward democracy, from irresponsible government toward government answerable to the people, from despotism toward government with sharply restricted powers. But on the international scene, the story is just the opposite; each state is a law unto itself, answerable to no institution superior to it, and the result is international anarchy.

At such a time of international anarchy, there is a crying need for international law which at its best might be expected to maintain a modicum of order among nations. But it is extremely doubtful that even what little international law we now have on the books can work that way. The effectiveness of law depends upon the existence of an executive branch which is publicly recognized. However, such international law as now exists has neither a tribunal to render judgments nor an executive authority to give effect to such judgments. When the world is at peace, international law works fairly well, but as soon as trouble erupts it loses its effectiveness. For example, in the recent World War, each side accused the other of having violated international law—and as a matter of fact, both were correct in their accusations, because both sides did violate international law. This is hardly to be wondered at, though, as international law itself has not become law in the sense that law cannot recognize the legality of war. The internal laws within the state do not recognize the legitimacy of war. But international law does accord such recognition, and even promulgates a minimum number of regulations which are supposed to be adhered to (but which, as we have seen, are not) by nations at war with each other. It has thus lost its effectiveness, and does nothing to relieve the scene of international anarchy. Treaties between nations may supplement international law, but in actual practice they aren't very effective either. Treaties are based on the balance of power between or among the contracting nations; as each party seeks to augment its power, sooner or later things get out of balance, tensions arise, and wars begin—treaty provisions to the contrary notwithstanding.

But people are becoming impatient with international anarchy, and in spite of the development of nationalism, they are cultivating other forces to unite the separated nations of the world. These are the transnational forces, such as science, the fine arts, literature, religion, travel, postal services, commerce, finance, and a growing number of other activities which must ignore national borders. All these are, in one or another degree, forces which counteract the separateness of nations. Developments in science in one country are reported and applied in all nations. Religion is also very markedly one of these unifying factors. Christianity has penetrated the farthest corners of the earth; Buddhism is popular throughout China, Japan, India, and Korea, as well as in southeast Asia. We could multiply examples which demonstrate man's impatience with international anarchy, and his development of transnational forces which tend to unite rather than to divide the world.

The unifying function of economic activity has proved to be more significant than efforts to seek unification of the world through the spiritual and religious life of man. The development of international trade has already united the world in one sense of the term. A shift in the price of gold, silver, cotton, barley, or rice in one nation will necessarily influence the price structure in others. As the world becomes more united in economic and spiritual matters, people become increasingly impatient with the sort of polities that tries to keep them isolated in separate camps.

There are two opposing forces operating in the world today: on the one hand, trends toward unification in the spiritual and economic spheres have caused increasing impatience with international anarchy; on the other hand, governments of the various nation-states seem committed to policies that must inevitably lead to war. And war today is far more serious than it was in ages past. There are two reasons which account for the destructiveness and disruptiveness of modern warfare. First, technology has produced new instruments of warfare, of which the submarine and the airplane are two examples. Historically destructive weapons, such as the bow and arrow, the gun, the cannon, and so on, seem not to have been invented for the purpose of warfare; but in the desperation of war, people have resorted to their use, and they have come to be regarded primarily as military weapons. Since contemporary technology has produced so many devices of unspeakably destructive power, any war that breaks out henceforth will make all former wars, including the horrible World War so recently concluded, pale into insignificance. The second factor is that, merely because war has become so much a matter of applied technology, it no longer involves just armies and navies, but the whole economy of the nations engaged in war. When war breaks out, the productive capacity of the nation must immediately be retooled to military production; the production of civilian goods is curtailed, and the entire national economy must be managed with reference to military ends. Then, when the war is over, years of time, unmeasured energy, and great ingenuity, are required to retool industry to the requirements of peacetime production, and to reconstruct and rebuild the facilities destroyed in the devastation of war.

For these reasons more and more people are becoming determined that something must be done to replace the international anarchy which is so inordinately costly in terms of human welfare. More people now believe that the principles which operate in the internal democratic political system within the state can be extended to the international level, and that it must be possible for us to have a responsible and effective international organization. This isn't going to be an easy goal to achieve. What is called for is a fundamental reconstruction of the world—a reconstruction that will be possible only through the cooperation of the internal governments of the various nation-states. A necessary first step will be the development of cooperation, within the framework of law, between and among the various governments.

Up to the present, the people as such have had no voice whatever in setting foreign policy, and hence it has not been possible to extend the principles of internal democratic politics into international relations. Even in those cases in which the internal politics of a state are of the most completely democratic nature, the state's diplomatic policies are still under the control of a few government officials. This is something that must be changed. People must take an interest in, become informed about, and demand to have a voice in, the foreign policies of their government, for certainly there is no basis for hope that we can have a responsible international organization unless there are democratic foreign policies within the nation-states that will make up the international organization.

The impatience of so many people with international anarchy was the chief reason for the enthusiasm with which so many nations greeted the proposal by President Woodrow Wilson of the United States for the formation of a League of Nations. Here was a suggestion that would change the world situation from one of anarchy to one of responsible international government. Here were concrete provisions for international legislation, administration, and adjudication—provisions which would put an end to absolute sovereignty, and which would render needless offensive and defensive alliances and other similar treaties between pairs of nations. Here was a proposal for an arrangement in which all powers in international legislation, administration, and adjudication would be exercised by one competent international organization. We need not go further into detail, but only note that impatience with international anarchy caused millions of people to hail with gratitude and relief President Wilson's proposal for a League of Nations.

I don't need to tell you how disappointed and discouraged so many of us have been during the past year at the failure of some of President Wilson's other suggestions for international organizations to materialize. Some short-sighted nations have pursued their own advantage, and have benefited at the expense of the nations defeated in the war. These things are matters of common knowledge. But the disappointment is of the moment, not permanent. I am confident that the trends of which I have been speaking are, in fact, in operation, and that the world situation is bound to improve.

It is difficult to foresee just how the League of Nations can successfully discharge the functions for which it is being set up, but there are already certain developments which warrant optimism. The first of these is the development of a means of arbitration. The importance of this lies not only in the fact that it can render fair judgments in cases in dispute, but even more important, that it can delay the outbreak of war. When a member of the League of Nations is involved, the Court of Arbitration must first make an investigation of the situation before the member nation can go to war. And it may well be that while this investigation is going on, the people of the nations involved may get better control of their tempers, and be less disposed to engage in the wasteful and devastating business of war. In this way the number of wars will certainly be sharply reduced, because in actual fact, there are very few people in the world who actually want war.

The second area in which we find warrant for optimism is in the reduction of armaments. Until very recently people have entertained the false belief that the best way to insure peace is to prepare for war, to enjoy a sort of permanent armed truce; but fortunately this belief is disappearing. People are beginning to recognize that they are going to use the things on which they spend their money and their efforts. When the housewife gets a new knife, she wants to put it to use as soon as she can, and keep it bright and sharp as long as she can. The same thing is true when a state supports huge armies and navies—the temptation to use them, or at least to threaten to use them, becomes too strong to be borne. But starting a war is one thing; stopping it, another. Nobody wins a war nowadays; the burden on the victors is as great as that on the vanquished. I hope with all my heart that the time will come soon—and when I say soon, I mean within the next year or two—when there will be a truly irresistible demand for reduction of armaments and for the formation of a genuine world government.

The third warrant for optimism is the demonstration we have had in the past couple of years that open diplomacy is at least a possibility. Traditionally, diplomatic policies have been secret; in fact, certain agreements reached among diplomats more than a century ago are still not matters of public knowledge. But the day of secret diplomacy is passing; people are better informed than ever before, and public opinion is becoming more influential. When we have truly open diplomacy, as it seems to me we must have, we will have taken a long stride toward effective international organization.

Allied to this, but also enumerable as a fourth warrant for optimism, is the possibility of public intervention in diplomatic policy. Public participation in diplomatic decisions will mark a drastic change in longstanding policy, according to which foreign policy was not only secret, but was in the hands of a very small number of diplomats and other government officials. Now, however, we know that it is not true that diplomatic decisions are no concern of the people, and we know that people as a whole have as much at stake in the diplomatic relationships of their state as do the diplomats and government officials whose signatures appear on the documents. I hope to see a growing demand on the part of the public that it have an effective voice in determination of the foreign policies of its government. Such a movement will reduce the possibility of war, since people as a whole are opposed to war, now that they have learned what a tremendous stake each separate person has in it.

To conclude, I am not speaking of a peace that is merely the absence of armed conflict—a passive conception which we encounter all too frequently. Even unpatriotic men, cowards, and rich men who want to keep from losing their money, can want this negative kind of peace. But we must work for a positive peace, a peace built upon common constructive enterprises undertaken on an international scale. Just as a nation grows strong by engaging its people in large-scale constructive activities, the world will grow stronger and the danger of war will disappear when the nations engage together in constructive enterprises that contribute to their common welfare. I believe that at last we can look forward to a time when there will be associated living on a world-wide scale, with mankind living in a society which transcends all national and linguistic barriers.

A
t the beginning of this series of lectures, I grouped the problems of social and political philosophy under three headings—economic problems, political problems, and problems of the intellectual and cultural life of men. We have now dealt with the problems which fall under the first two headings, and in the final two lectures we will deal with those which fall under the third.

The problems of the cultural, intellectual, and spiritual life of men are closely related with the problems of economics and politics. In fact, the solutions to these latter cannot be sought independently of the solution to cultural and intellectual problems. We can offer two propositions, discussion of which will throw light on what I mean: (1) the intellectual and spiritual aspects of life enhance the values of associated living, and (2) these aspects are in themselves the very foundations of civilization.

With regard to the first of these propositions, we know very well that human beings are something more than mere animals. As is the case with other animals, they must enjoy the satisfaction of the basic needs for food and sex, but as is not the case with lower orders of life, these satisfactions are not enough. Men must engage in intellectual and spiritual activities, and through them metamorphose their animal appetites and elevate them to the level of civilization.

Let us look for a moment at the phenomenon of the labor strike as an illustration of the fact that man requires more than the mere gratification of animal appetites if he is to find satisfaction in life. Why do we see

laborers striking all over the world? Many people—most people, in fact—
assume that labor strikes are means by which laborers seek a more equita-
ble distribution of the profits of industry, and that if the wage structure
were such as to guarantee this, there would be no more strikes. Now
certainly the economic motive is a major one in strikes, but there is another factor for us to consider, and one that is of great importance. I am
convinced that even when labor is assured an adequate wage, there will
still be dissatisfaction, because something more fundamental than mere
wages is involved. This something is the fact that, up to the present,
capital has monopolized not only the material and economic aspects of
industry, often exploiting the workers, but has also followed policies
which inhibit the intellectual and moral development of the laboring
classes. Matters of policy—those activities which call for the exercise of
imagination and intelligence—are the monopoly of management, with
labor being systematically excluded from any participation.

As laborers become better educated and more sophisticated, they tend
to resent this exclusion, and to demand a voice in the determination of
policy. Already a few—a very few, I might add—enlightened industrial
leaders are making matters of company policy subject to negotiation with
labor unions; where this happens, and labor thus has a voice in the determination of policy, morale has risen, the workers show a spirit of identification with the industrial enterprise with which they are associated,
production has increased, and costs have gone down. This is a good example of one of the ways in which concerns of the intellect and the spirit
can enhance the values of economic and political life.

Let us look at politics as another example. Why do men work for democratic governments? Is it just because under a democratic government
they pay less in taxes, or enjoy a higher standard of living? Quite the
contrary. Measured by these yardsticks democracy is often less "efficient"
than the more authoritarian governments it displaces. Men struggle to
achieve democratic government because they want to have a voice in the
determination of their own destiny, and democracy calls for general participation in decision making. It thus opens the way for fuller development and utilization of the intellectual and emotional potentialities of
greater numbers of people. Under these circumstances, economic interests
which may originally be selfish in character become broadened; dedication to public welfare may replace the urge of self-aggrandizement. In
one sense, therefore, we can say that the greatest single advantage of dem-

ocratic government is that it is, by its nature, educative; under it the material goods of life are relegated to a secondary level of importance.

We could educe additional illustrations, but these are enough to illustrate the proposition that intellectual, cultural, and spiritual activities and drives can enhance the values of the political and economic life of mankind. Such activity increases not only the sum total of the culture, but also the number of people who participate in and profit from the cultural life.

Now we come to the second proposition, namely that the intellectual, cultural, and spiritual life of man is the very foundation of associated living. It becomes obvious as soon as we think about it that those aspects of living which we designate as intellectual, cultural, and spiritual are indispensable and fundamental to associated living on any level. All of us know that the industrial revolution has introduced countless machines, and that the factory production which these machines make possible has produced a civilization markedly different from that which our ancestors knew only a few centuries ago. But what we sometimes forget is that the machines of the industrial revolution were only the agents of change; what is vastly more important than the machines themselves is the development of modern science in the two centuries preceding the industrial revolution—a development which produced the knowledge which produced the machines which produced the industrial revolution, as it were.

The industrial revolution did more than change our methods of production and enable us to substitute the power of steam and electricity for the muscle power of man and beast which had earlier produced the material goods of life. It also stemmed from profound changes in the intellectual and spiritual life of mankind. Contemplation of recent history thus underscores the fact that intellectual and spiritual drives and activities form the very foundations upon which we erect the structure of our social life. I don't believe that there can be any argument about the statement that a viable civilization must be based on a consistent system of thought and a commitment to a consistent set of moral principles, any more than there can be about the corollary statement that significant social changes and reforms go along with changes and improvements in our ways of thinking. These are things which we all recognize.

Today the whole world stands at the crossroads of change. Our knowledge is expanding, and our ways of thinking are changing. Dozens of nations are undergoing political revolution, but change is not limited to politics. People everywhere are calling into doubt the traditions and beliefs upon which their whole social structure has been built. Ideas that have been unquestioningly accepted for countless generations are being reexamined, often doubted, sometimes discarded. But new ways of thinking and new commitments are not yet evolved to replace the ones that are being discarded. In this generation we must formulate new ways of thinking, and make decisions about principles to which we will give our loyalty; this is why we say that the world stands at the crossroads of change, with regard both to knowledge and to modes of thought.

The most pressing social problem in the modern world is that of replacing the authority of tradition with the authority of science. What do we mean by authority? Basically we mean any thought or belief which directs human behavior. We cannot dispense with authority, nor can we exchange one sort of authority for another all of a sudden. Authority—the system of ideas according to which we make our decisions and which controls the ways in which we act—can be shifted only gradually, and by the combined efforts of many people. The problem is, therefore, one of finding ways by which we can substitute the authority of science for that of tradition, and of evolving means by which we can make the scientific method as authoritative for the future as tradition has been for the past, and still is for much of the present.

People everywhere are subject to two sorts of forces, the forces exerted by the material environment on the one hand, and thinking and psychological forces on the other. It is the fact that man has the ability to control both external environmental forces and the inner psychological forces that has made civilization possible. Brutes such as pigs and dogs do not have this ability, and are thus almost completely under the control of the material forces of their environment; this control is the essential difference between man and other animals. The more effectively man can exercise this control over both the outer and the inner forces which impinge upon him, the more advanced is his civilization. It is through taking thought and utilizing knowledge that man exercises this control—control that is effective, in one degree or another, in every facet of society. But it isn't enough that man merely exercise control over the forces that impinge upon him; he must also be able to use his knowledge and his power of thought to change and modify his systems of traditions and beliefs if his civilization is to advance to new levels.

Anthropologists tell us that at a conservative estimate the present race of man has inhabited the earth for some 300,000 years. During these 300,000 years there have probably been no significant alterations in his anatomy or physiology, but certainly his social life has been immeasurably enriched. Even within the relatively brief period for which we have a recorded history, man has developed, used, modified, and discarded systems of beliefs; he has evolved a host of cultural and educational activities, and he has grown in his desire for and skill in cultural interaction.

Thus modern civilized man is not very different physically from his ancestors who lived 300,000 years ago, but he is vastly different in terms of cultural development. Ever since man first appeared on earth, he has been subject to some sort of authority. At different stages of his development he evolved different ways of thinking, but always his system of thought, whatever it might have been at a given time, the organization of his knowledge, primitive or sophisticated, his habits and his traditions, incorporated into institutions—all these dictated and controlled his behavior. Times came, of course, when men doubted the authority to which they had been subject, and when this happened, all other aspects of their lives were immediately affected. The strands that make up the social life of a group are so closely interwoven that a change in any one of them is ultimately reflected in changes in all the others.

Let us get back now to the authority of knowledge and thought which we were discussing. From the moment of our birth we absorb innumerable bits of knowledge; we are trained to think in certain ways; we form habits, all in response to forces in our cultural environment; and the pattern of response which enable us to live comfortably in that environment is the authority which controls our behavior. The absence of some sort of authority is utterly unthinkable; behavior must be subject to some sort of control. But one can expect to be able to change the nature of the authority to which he responds, or to alter the methods of its exercise.

What is the nature of the authority of science which we have said must replace the authority of tradition? In what direction are we to reconstruct our thinking so as to render science authoritative in control of human behavior? What are the characteristics of the authority of science? We must examine these questions, for we can hope to reconstruct our thought in the proper direction only if we understand the characteristics of the authority of science. The first hallmark we note is that science substitutes realism for the old method of speculation, and naturalism for supernaturalism.

Again, though, what do we mean by replacing the old method of speculation with the method of realism, by replacing supernaturalism with naturalism? We oppose the authority of tradition because, for the most part, it is not the result of observation and analysis, but is dictated by history (often unfounded), myths, rituals, and so on. When supernatural mysteries of this sort accumulate day by day without being examined or questioned, they become more mysterious than ever, and people, without taking thought, move into deeper thralldom to rules which are essentially absurd.

The scientific method that we advocate is the antithesis of this method based in supernatural mystery. The scientific attitude places emphasis on fact, and follows observation and investigation of fact with a judgment about its value. Realism recognizes only fact and judgments based in fact; it is loyal to fact, no matter where such loyalty leads. Thus, the first reconstruction in our ways of thinking calls on us to recognize only facts. Authority which cannot be justified on the basis of fact must be rejected, even if it has been operative for thousands of years. Speculation cannot provide authority of the sort needed in the modern world; observation and analysis of fact can.

Some people argue that this emphasis on fact and opposition to speculation will result in a crass materialism and a denial of values of the human spirit. They could hardly be more mistaken. Actually, the emphasis on fact and the rejection of the method of speculation involve man's spiritual life. It is true, of course, that human beings live in a material environment; but if they can understand this environment, cope with it, and control it, they have mastered and risen above the level of the material and achieved a life which nourishes the spirit.

The second characteristic of the new authority is its accessibility to public examination, and its dependence upon public cooperation for the spread of culture. The progress of culture is facilitated and expedited by the publication of truth; the more freely new knowledge comes into the public domain, the more rapidly the culture advances. On the other hand, when new discoveries are kept secret or revealed only to a select coterie, progress is retarded. Accessibility to public examination, whether of knowledge or of the basis on which authority is claimed, can be said to be a precondition of progress.

Probably the chief reason that tradition has maintained its authority so long is that it is so often rendered esoteric, with its real meaning accessible only to a small number of persons. Exactly the opposite is the case with science: when a scientist in one country formulates a new theory or advances a new hypothesis, it is published in journals around the world, and is subject to testing, challenge, or application, by his fellow scientists in other countries as well as in his own. One of the reasons that scientists have been so enormously successful is that they publish their findings internationally, and are in constant communication and collaboration. But in business and in diplomacy, rather than laying things out and making them accessible to public examination, the practice is to keep everything as secret as possible. The result is less progress, and oftentimes the multiplication of error.

One reason why we see less progress in business than we do in science is that people so often want to keep their trade secrets to give them advantage over their competitors, or to profit from royalties on their patents. There would be little progress in science if scientists were to behave like this. Many diplomats keep their negotiations secret, alleging that publicity would render their policies less effective, or even reveal the purposes underlying some of their deals. But when we compare the practices of publicity and of secrecy, weighing their merits and demerits the one against the other, we find that the balance regularly shows up in favor of publicity.

Right now we have a good opportunity to engage in the enterprise of cooperative publicity. We must first systematically collect and organize our materials, then communicate them to others through publication, just as has been done in the case of scientific discovery. The developments of modern technology make this easier for us to do than ever in the past. We have all sorts of instruments of communication—the telephone, the telegraph, the radio, transoceanic cables, and so on. Our printing presses can turn out thousands upon thousands of copies in an hour. The fact that there are so many newspapers indicates that there is a great demand by the public. We must confess that much of what comes out in newspapers is not as well organized or as thoroughly thought through as are the articles in scientific journals. The speed with which current commentary must be prepared and presented results in publication of material which leaves something to be desired in terms of style, and frequently even in accuracy. Some publications are even manipulated by political parties, by industrialists, or by others, to achieve their own selfish purposes. When this happens, we call the result propaganda, which is the antithesis of what we're talking about, the free publication of truth.

It borders on the ridiculous for us to have to admit that we have not mastered the art of making our thoughts accessible to public examination through publication, and there is irony in the fact that we fall so far short of fully exploiting the means of public communication which modern science has placed at our disposal. Still, we have no choice but to admit that we have not yet learned to publish our thoughts in other fields with anything like the accuracy and precision that scientists have achieved. In areas of social concern we just cannot collect our materials, arrange them, investigate them, make judgments about them, and communicate the results to others as systematically as we manage to do in scientific research. We still have a long way to go before we can do an adequate job of laying out and making accessible to public examination and appraisal our claims for authority of the scientific method in economics, politics, and the intellectual and cultural problems of man.

If someone were to ask me what method would guarantee smooth and systematic progress for society, my answer would be that our best hope lies in proper and effective publicity. This means the collection and recording of materials, making judgments and interpretations, and communicating them through publication just as honestly and as objectively as possible. When this level of scientific publicity on social and political matters has been achieved, we will have taken a huge forward step. People can have faith only in the facts that are available to them. If they are presented with the facts exactly as they are, they will respond properly. But if the facts are concealed, or distorted, or presented partially and in a biased manner, how can the people respond properly? In a democratic nation, honest publicity is an extremely important means of social progress.

Let us go on to the third characteristic of the new authority—the reform and popularization of education. The biggest need here is to replace traditional methods of schooling with scientific methods. This means that youth must be brought into effective contact with the real facts of life, which contact will enable them to understand the intellectual and spiritual aspects of life, as well as their material environment. All that we have been saying is applicable here; further discussion at this juncture would be beside the point. We must never allow ourselves to forget that education is the instrument—the only instrument—that will enable us to find solutions to the problems in the intellectual and spiritual life of men, which problems form the third grouping of social and political philosophy that we have discussed in this series of lectures.

The traditional method of education is mere pouring in of instruction. The authority of tradition is simply inculcated into the child, so that he can be expected to preserve it. But today we look upon education as a means, and the school as an institution, for reconstructing our ways of thinking. We must develop the innate potentialities of the child from within, rather than pouring in subject matter from the outside, as was done under the traditional method. We must make full use of the child's potentialities and develop his ability to think and to judge. This sort of education must not be bound by tradition, but must rather be seen as means to the emancipation of human ability.

The function of education as a means of preserving the culture has been recognized since time out of mind. However, it is only recently that very many people have come to look upon education as a means of promoting social progress. And now that social progress has become the aim of education, the process must take place within the context of the present society in such a way that the quality of our social life in the future will be enhanced.

INTELLECTUAL FREEDOM

I n our previous lecture we pointed out that the value of social life is a function of the cultural and intellectual life of man. This is what distinguishes human group life from that of a herd of sheep. Sheep gather in herds simply for warmth and protection, but the life of human groups involves cultural and intellectual interaction. The life of the human group is characterized by a spiritual quality which is lacking in a herd of sheep.

While the material aspects cannot be ignored when we consider associated living, they are not nearly so important in value as is education, which ranks above all other values. We must emphasize here our disagreement with those who narrowly define education as that which occurs in schools, and we must insist that every facet of associated living has a potentially educative influence. When associated living becomes static and when interaction is minimized, it has just that much less educative potential. When it is active, when it promotes communication of knowledge, thought, and emotion between and among people, its educative value is naturally thereby enhanced. Thus, while the material life of man is a valid concern of society, the development of the spiritual life of each individual is far more important, because it is in the spiritual realm that we locate the ultimate values of associated human living.

These remarks are only an introduction to the problem of freedom of intellectual life with which we will deal today. We have already discussed personal rights, civil rights, and political rights, but have postponed to the last, discussion of the right to intellectual freedom. We might say that the underlying purpose of other rights is to insure the right to intellectual freedom, for it is only when we have these other rights that we can hope for the opportunity for full and free development of the right to think, to believe, to express opinions, to explore, and to publish. We will look today at the reasons why this intellectual freedom is so basically important.

Without exception, dictatorial governments deny to their citizens freedom of thought and expression, because they rightly fear the consequences of such freedom. This very fear is justification for our assertion of the importance of intellectual freedom. A dictatorship can endure only when its people are denied the freedom to think, to speak, and to publish freely; to state the converse, the enjoyment of intellectual freedom would guarantee the overthrow of the dictatorship. This is what in mathematics we might call an indirect or negative proof of the importance of intellectual freedom.

Thus we see that freedom of intellectual life is not only indispensable to a democratic society, but is also the most greatly feared threat to a dictatorial government. In fact, we can say that this freedom is a necessary condition to human progress. The progress of civilization depends largely upon free communication of knowledge and thought; so when we strive for intellectual freedom we are fighting for more than mere personal satisfaction, as important as that may be—we are also working for the advancement of civilization itself.

Some people argue that it is impossible for a government to interfere with the freedom to think, since thinking is an interior process which cannot be known to anyone else. They admit that the authority of government can be brought to bear to restrict freedom of overt expression—speech or publication. But this distinction really is not valid; thinking and expression are two sides of the same coin. An idea is useless unless it can be given some sort of expression. Ideas do not occur in a vacuum; they are caused by something. A man thinks only when he is dissatisfied with the state of affairs, when he undertakes to identify his dissatisfaction, and to postulate alternatives. It doesn't mean much for a man to think by himself without communicating the results of his thinking to others. Further than this, the very quality and extent of our thinking depends on the opportunity we have to express it, to share it with others. Ideas remain obscure and shallow when they are unexpressed. The systematization of ideas in both Christianity and Confucianism can be attributed to innumerable public lectures and disputations, and by publications by unnumbered authors over the centuries. Ideas cannot be systematized without being expressed, and it is obvious that freedom to express one's ideas is part and parcel of freedom to think one's thoughts. If the expression of ideas is forbidden, freedom of thinking is interfered with at the same time.

To put the matter in a slightly different way, we can say that there is a double reason why we attach so much importance to the freedom of speech, to the right of assembly, and to unhindered publication. In the first place, the value of an idea lies in its expression, and interference with freedom of expression inhibits freedom of thinking. In the second place, society cannot benefit from unexpressed ideas, and if an idea cannot bear fruit, why have it? The value of an idea grows from its being discussed and compared with other ideas; it is only through these processes of discussion and comparison that ideas can become organized into systems and give rise to other ideas. These facts demonstrate the importance of freedom of speech.

Freedom of speech is not absolute, any more than is freedom of action. The latter does not provide warrant for inflicting harm on others, nor does the former provide license for one to incite others to do so. Even in the family, as in the more inclusive society, each man must accept the responsibility for the consequences of his thoughts, his speech, and his actions.

Historically, freedom of speech has been justified on two grounds. In the first, analogy with the steam engine is instructive. Every steam engine must have a safety valve through which excess steam can escape, otherwise there would be an explosion which could destroy the engine. Just so, when one has a consuming idea in mind, he must be provided with opportunity to express it, lest he become carried away and, so to speak, burst into flame. In Hyde Park in London anyone may say publicly, to as many people as will listen to him, whatever he wants to say, no matter how misled or even crazy he may be. Great Britain, as the first major country to allow freedom of speech, seems to be aware that suppression of opinion might cause grave danger, but she has discovered that there is virtually no danger at all in allowing freedom of expression to all shades of opinion.

Second, there are two general types of politics and government—rule by coercion and rule by persuasion. We advocate freedom of speech because we have found that persuasion is more effective than coercion. This is the positive aspect of freedom of speech. Whenever an idea is advanced, some people favor it, others oppose it. When both proponents and opponents are free to voice their opinions and to engage in discussion, governmental politics can be evolved on the basis of such discussion. At first glance this looks like a risky business, but our confidence in human nature is such as to make the risk more apparent than real. If I may paraphrase Abraham Lincoln, some people are absurd all of the time, and all people are absurd some of the time, but not all of the people are absurd all of the time. No matter how absurd people may become, they never all become absurd at the same time. When some people are absurd, there are always others who are normal and who can counteract their absurdities. Full and free discussion of an idea will serve to bring to light and rectify any absurd elements which it may contain. When an idea is totally absurd it will be discarded with a minimum of discussion. This is our basis for asserting that freedom of speech is essential in a democratic government which rules by persuasion.

In times of rapid social change there is always the temptation for the government to adopt a policy of suppression. But in a time of social ferment such as the present, it would be short-sighted indeed to try to muzzle those who advocate social reform. When such persons are silenced they often undertake to achieve their purposes through conspiracy, assassination, or rebellion. Strong convictions, when dammed by suppressive measures, find other outlets. When there is as much instability as marks the present scene, reorientation of thought is what is called for, not suppression. We must have confidence that the majority of the people will never accept an idea that is wholly absurd. In all the millennia of history we have no record of a single idea's being eliminated by force. When ideas are openly expressed and published, they can be modified and corrected; when they are suppressed they erupt in some other form, frequently in violence. The more rigid the efforts to suppress ideas, the greater the danger.

What assurance can we have, then, against the general adoption of an idea that is too radical? Two characteristics which are shared by the vast majority of the populace give us reasonable assurance in this regard. In the first place, most people prefer to lead peaceful lives, and this fact causes them to look askance at any idea which is so radical as to threaten disorder. In the second place, most of us are creatures of habit, and habit is often more effective than thought in dictating action. Most people prefer to follow existing habits and customs; they dislike change, because change nearly always involves some degree of inconvenience. These two characteristics serve as brakes on the spread of radical ideas. Nevertheless, there have been a number of times in history when new and radical ideas have spread like wildfire; it behooves us to look at the reasons why and the circumstances under which such phenomena have occurred.

The basic reason why a radical idea can gain acceptance quickly lies not in the idea itself, but in the circumstances under which it is advanced. For example, the recent Bolshevist revolution led by Lenin received wide support from the Russian people within a very brief time; but we can be pretty sure that very few among the Russian masses have any understanding of Leninism. It wasn't, as we have just said, the idea itself that accounted for its ready acceptance, but rather the circumstances that the Russian populace was suffering from shortages of food, clothing, and housing. Prior to the World War, the wealth of Russia was concentrated in the hands of a small number of aristocrats and capitalists, and the devastation of the war itself accentuated the situation to the point at which the people were desperate enough to support any proposal which promised betterment of their lot. Thus only a few slogans, rather than any real understanding, were enough to enlist millions of people among the ranks of the revolutionaries.

It is still true that, by and large, people are predisposed to follow existing habits, customs, and institutions; but there are numerous occasions when history shows us the spectacle of rapid disintegration of established ways of doing things in response to radical ideas propounded by one person or a few people. In every such case, however, the phenomenon can be accounted for by factors in the socio-politico-economic situation in which the radical idea was advanced, rather than in the idea itself. Governmental attempts to fend off rebellion or revolution by suppressing ideas because of fear of their results have been self-defeating, because the ideas themselves are not the fundamental cause of revolt. The real cause is nearly always shortage of food and clothing, feelings of being abused and mistreated, or animus generated from some other source, with the radical idea playing the role of the fuse that sets off the explosion or the trigger that fires the gun.

Some philosophers and many politicians have advocated unity in the thoughts, aspirations, and beliefs of an entire population, and have even undertaken to stamp out opinions which differ from what they want the consensus to be. This, of course, they cannot do. Society is always changing—the very facts of death and birth mean change. When the rate of change is accelerated and things become markedly different from what they have been, it is utterly impossible to design a single outlook that can control the behavior of people in a whole society or an entire nation. If people are prevented from legal expression of their ideas and opinions, they will sooner or later resort to illegal or extralegal modes of expression. For these reasons the far-sighted leader will tolerate differing ideas, and support freedom of thought and expression. He will recognize that there is a built-in safety factor in the universal psychological tendency to prefer the existing social order and to live in the comfort and security provided by the familiar; he will count on this factor to keep in check those elements of society which actually do constitute a danger to it, and to promote positive proposals for desirable changes. If he knows his history, he will know that attempts to achieve unity of opinion and conviction by force are virtually certain guarantees of trouble and disorder.

Ideally, of course, it is a good thing to have the people of a nation thinking about the same problems and moving in the direction of agreement. But—and this is especially true of a time like the present—this sort of consensus can be achieved only through gradual development, as the result of free discussion and evaluation of conflicting ideas and claims; it can never be achieved by force. The reason this is true is that free discussion brings to light the irrelevance, the inconsistency, or the contrariety of ideas that are inimical to the development of associated living, and thus serves to eliminate these ideas through the action of human reason instead of by governmental suppression. True unification is the result of free communication and interaction, never of force. The more determined the effort to achieve unity through force, the more alluring the invitation to conspiracy, assassination, rebellion, or other forms of violence—"remedies" all too likely to result in a state of affairs worse than the conditions they set out to cure.

We can understand why some members of the privileged classes oppose socialism in the realm of economics—it is simply that they don't like the idea that their possessions will be shared with others. But the same objection does not apply to what we might call socialism of knowledge. Where material possessions are concerned, the more people who share them, the less each will have; but just the opposite is true of knowledge. The store of knowledge is increased by the number of people who come to share in it. Knowledge can be shared and increased at the same time—in fact, it is increased by being shared. This is the soundest argument for freedom of intellectual life: the more people who share in ideas, the more they are refined and improved. Thus, socialism of knowledge is acceptable to all of us.

In earlier lectures in this series I have reiterated my conviction that there is one ultimate criterion by which we judge the goodness or badness of any socio-political institution: it is good when it contributes positively to the free exchange of ideas, feelings, and will; it is bad when it impedes progress toward this goal. The same criterion can be applied to man's intellectual activities. Intellectual endeavor is good when it contributes to free exchange of ideas and improvement in the quality of associated living; bad when it hampers the achievement of this goal.

The ideal of democratic government has had its harsh critics. One of these was the Scottish essayist, Thomas Carlyle, who derided democracy as "government by talk," and who acidly raised the question of how we can take seriously as politics gatherings of hundreds of people engaged in idle chatter (since "parliament" is derived from French *parler* 'to talk'). Carlyle's mistake lies in the fact that he underestimated the value of discourse. The importance of discourse is that ideas are clarified and refined through public discussion; the more an idea is discussed, the more clearly it is possible to judge its merits and demerits. The greater the number of people who engage in the discussion, the greater the likelihood that the idea will be improved, or reformulated into a better idea. Carlyle's dim view of the value of discussion is a result of his ignoring its fundamental function.

As a matter of fact, the greater the extent to which a government undertakes wisely to reorient the intellectual life of its people, the more it has to be a government of talk.* Basically there are two types of government—rule by force, and rule by persuasion. Those governments that have ruled by persuasion rather than by force have had the greater success in promoting effective associated living. The function of public discourse is the use of intellectual and spiritual power to achieve the goals of associated living by persuasion rather than by force.

Finally, this series of lectures can be concluded by returning to the rela-

---

* A literal translation of the sentence which appears at this point in the Chinese text reads, "As a matter of fact, the greater the extent to which a government undertakes to suppress freedom of knowledge and thought, the more it will become a government by talk." This rendering is so obviously contradictory to the context in which the sentence occurs that we can only deduce that the amanuensis made a mistake in transcription, or that there was a misprint; we have therefore taken the liberty of rendering the sentence as we believe Dewey said it.

tionship between democracy and education. Education is basic to democracy, because democracy, by definition, is based on the conviction that most people have the capacity to be educated, and that they are capable of learning. In fact, democracy means education; it is, itself, a process of continuing education of all the people. A democratic society provides schooling, but it also calls for those who have had the privilege of schooling to dedicate themselves to public service, and at the same time, to continue learning as they did while in school. Each person is called upon to make his contribution to his own society, and ultimately to the whole of humanity. If we had effective education, we would have a world in which each person would recognize that his own welfare is intimately interrelated with that of his fellow men. The entire world would benefit from this sort of education, not just one nation or a single society.

Emancipation of human spiritual forces will be the result of the general recognition by each of us that his welfare is bound up with that of everybody else in the world. This is the most important goal toward which we can strive, for with this recognition will come a common-mindedness of all mankind. As we move toward the achievement of this goal, as advocates of the democratic way of life, we can take comfort and satisfaction in the fact that we are not merely creating a sociopolitical institution, but are also contributing to the emancipation of the spiritual forces of man.

PART II A PHILOSOPHY
OF EDUCATION

THE NEED FOR

A PHILOSOPHY OF EDUCATION

At the outset of this series of lectures on a philosophy of education there are two problems which I want to explore with you. The first of these is the question of why there must be education, or, to push further than this, to determine why education is indispensable to human life. The second question is whether there must be a philosophy of education, or, to go further, how important and how nearly indispensable is a philosophy of education?

The answer to the first of these questions is obvious as soon as we think about it. The human infant cannot grow up and become an adult without the help and teaching of parents or parent surrogates, and later, without learning many things about his environment from other associates. In the lower orders of life the difference between a newborn animal and a mature one is largely physical. But in man, physical development must be accompanied by growth in the psychological, intellectual, and moral aspects of his being. Each of us goes through the gradual processes of infancy, childhood, and adolescence before reaching maturity; education is the means of the qualitative improvement of this process, the means by which development in each phase of maturation is facilitated and enhanced. It follows that in a human society education, rather than being a luxury, is a necessity.

Two ineluctable events—birth, without which no man comes into being, and death, which no man can escape—account for the indispensability of education for human beings. Without the care and tutelage of adults the infant could not survive, hence education of one or another sort is indispensable. At the other end of the scale of life, when a man dies, all his experience and all the meanings he has accumulated from this experience cease to be. It would indeed by uneconomical, even were it theoretically possible, for his descendants to have to undergo the same experiences and derive the same meanings anew in each generation. All that we call culture would disappear if we did not have education as a means to transmit it to oncoming generations. The fact, then, that death is the common end of man accounts for the indispensability of education.

Regarding the second question, we do not say that a philosophy of education is absolutely indispensable, but we do say that it is very important. The enterprise of education does not become a subject for thinking and inquiry where a philosophy of education does not flourish. When this state of affairs prevails teachers either copy what others do, or use the methods that always have been used. Sometimes a particular method achieves popularity without much thought being given to it; at other times teachers work out methods based on their own prejudices and biases. Generally in these circumstances, teaching becomes a recurring process or a routine rather than a progressive process—a defect that follows inevitably when active attention is not devoted to education theory. The office of a philosophy of education is to create an awareness of the reasons why one mode of teaching is preferred to another, to guard against the danger of blind subservience to custom or of slavish imitation. A philosophy of education produces conscious criticism and evaluation of educational endeavor, creates a desire for improvement, and affords criteria by which improvement may be assessed.

A philosophy of education is of minor importance in a conservative society, as we can see when we examine various societies of the past. Fortunately there has been some change in people's attitudes in the last two or three hundred years. Anthropologists have a joke about a man in the Stone Age, when all axes were made of stone, who discovered that a better axe could be made of iron. His people killed him with his own iron axe. Even though this is a joke, it does illustrate a common phenomenon of evolution. People appear to be inherently conservative; they do not like change even when it means progress. They don't want to progress themselves, and they tend to dislike others who make innovations.

But there are societies which regard change as desirable rather than as something to be guarded against—and in such societies theory is indispensable. Such a society welcomes change, tries to foresee the results of each change, and helps its members to improve their lot in the process of change. In a time such as the present when change is so rapid, when so many things are changing from day to day, it is imperative that we be able to judge which trends move us in the direction of the goals we want, and which others interfere with the achievement of these goals. We have to be able to distinguish between that which is primary and that which is of secondary importance. But we can't do this without a philosophy of education. Only a sound and consistent philosophy of education will enable us to choose among the trends which compete, conflict, and contradict each other, to select those we really want to foster, and to discourage those which threaten to hamper our progress.

Education and growth go hand in hand. Education means growth. Without it there can be no growth, except in the purely physical sense. Social progress is dependent upon educational progress. We have already referred to the fact that among lower animals the young are not essentially different from the old except in physical size; but as we come higher in the scale of evolution, there is a lengthening period of infancy. When we get to man, we see that infants and adults are essentially different in nearly every respect. Sometimes we are disturbed by the prolonged infancy in the human species, the highest order in the animal kingdom. Wouldn't it be better, we ask, if the period of infancy could be abbreviated, so that we could get about the business of educating the child more quickly, and thus save time? But the prolongation of human infancy has profound social and psychological implications. It is directly related to the capacity to become educated, and for this reason it is an important factor in the evolution of the human species.

In human societies we also find the gradual prolongation of the education of the young. Life in an undeveloped social group is rather simple, and education in it is correspondingly simple, consisting for the most part in imitation by the young of the activities of their elders. The same thing is true, to a degree, in some segments of modern, civilized societies, where children grow up without formal schooling, learning what they need to know by imitation and emulation. The whole range of activities which they can observe and in which they participate constitutes their education; in some cases this sort of education is productive of a surprising degree of common sense. Even though such children do not have formal schooling, there is no warrant for our saying that they do not have education. For all that it is on the nonliterate level, it is still education; and, as a matter of fact, such nonliterate education was all that was available to the greater proportion of mankind until relatively recent generations. It was when men became aware of the necessity of conserving experience and knowledge, so that the culture might be more fully transmitted from generation to generation, that written language assumed importance and began to form the basis of school instruction. As time went on, more and more people recognized the written word as the key with which they might unlock the store of experience and knowledge accumulated by earlier generations. The written word remains one of the most effective and economical means of achieving knowledge.

However, after schools became preoccupied with education for literacy there was a tendency for education to become more and more remote from ordinary everyday human activities. While formal schooling and education for literacy are certainly necessary, since without them we could not conserve the culture and pass it along to oncoming generations, there are still conspicuous dangers which stem from the alienation and isolation of educational efforts from our daily interests and activities. These dangers fall, generally speaking, into three categories.

The first of these is the danger that formal schooling, with its emphasis on the literary aspects of education, will produce an elite, a special social class enjoying unusual prerogatives—the so-called intellectuals, literary men and scholars, who are too frequently out of touch and out of sympathy with the great mass of the people. Where this sort of education prevails, of course, it does so because of the values that are cherished in the society which supports it. The chief beneficiaries of this sort of education tend to be first, the clergy and educational leaders, second, members of the ruling class, and third, the propertied classes.

The second of these dangers is that education will become overly preoccupied with the conservation and transmission of the cultural heritage, to the exclusion of other matters with which it ought also to be concerned. It is true that traditional culture represents the best part of the experience of former generations, but when educators put so much emphasis on it that they denigrate the daily activities of life and regard them as something irrelevant to formal education, they end up with programs that are actually not educative in the proper sense of the term.

Let us look at the word *culture* as an example of what I mean. Originally culture referred to the nurturing of plants. The parallel with daily human activities is obvious. But later the word took on new connotations, and now we have people who have learned a number of languages referred to as persons of culture, or cultivated persons. This is only one example of the many ways in which humanism has replaced realism in education; history shows us many others. Modern science, to take another example, reached a high level of development in Europe in the sixteenth and seventeenth centuries; but even today science is frequently not included in the curriculum of the schools, or when it is, it occupies an inferior status in the hierarchy of school subjects, subordinated to literary or humanistic education. This tendency can be traced to the influence of classical Greece, where education was well-developed, but where natural science was not emphasized.

The third danger is that the view of education which we are discussing often results in the school's becoming an independent institution, isolated from the real needs and interests of the society which supports it. How many times do we witness the spectacle of things being emphasized in the school long after they have ceased to be relevant to social needs. And, conversely, how often is it the case that something sorely needed by society is totally neglected by schools. People seem to look on education as a simple matter; they fail to see that it must provide for thinking and inquiry. They seem to think that wherever there's a teacher, a book, and a group of children, education is taking place. Because so many people take this attitude, the school has become one of the most archaic and conservative institutions in society.

Let us take an example from the history of Western education to illustrate what we are saying. Two or three hundred years ago—long before the invention of the steamship—commerce reached a high level of development in Europe. Commodities were shipped all over the world on small sailing vessels, and commercial and accounting procedures were developed which were appropriate to this sort of trade. Eventually accounting and other commercial subjects found their way into school curricula. But by the time this happened, the steamship had come onto the scene, and the whole system of commercial enterprise was revolutionized. Did the schools change their textbooks and their curricular practices to conform to the revolution in commerce? No, they continued to teach about the navigation of sailing vessels, to drill their students in accounting practices that were no longer applicable to the situation which actually prevailed. The old subject matter had acquired a sort of sanctity of age; it had become part of the tradition that must be conserved and transmitted, despite its irrelevance to the needs of the time. Because it had been handed down from the past, it must be passed along to the future.

Consideration of these three dangers enables us to formulate some of the problems which must be discussed as we consider a philosophy of education.

First: How can we provide for the majority of people to have access to education, rather than having it restricted to an elite? That is, how can we popularize education, and make it universal?

Second: How can we bring about a balance between literary education and education for ordinary human activities?

Third: How can we make school truly conservative—that is, on the one hand, enable it to conserve and transmit the best of our traditional cultural heritage, and, on the other, to cultivate personalities which can successfully cope with their environment?

The third of these is the most important problem confronting us. We are modern men living in the twentieth century, and the culture handed down to us from our past is not sufficient for our needs. We must reconstruct the traditional aims, methods, and subject matter of education so that it may adequately serve the needs of our age. Guiding such a reconstruction of education is a task not unlike that of steering a ship. The cargo (that is to say, the cultural heritage) must be so arranged that the ship can maintain an even keel and not sink to the bottom of the ocean. On the other hand, the ship must also be able to go forward and deliver its cargo where it is needed and can be used, rather than remaining tied to the dock so long that the cargo desiccates or decays. If the cargo is the heritage of our culture, the winds into which we tack are the trends of the current age. We must make sure that our ship is well laden with a cargo made up of the best that our traditions have to offer; the cargo must be well stowed so that we can get at what we need when we need it, and we must also make sure that the navigation of the ship takes the fullest advantage of the winds and currents which flow from today's and tomorrow's trends and needs.

I started this lecture by talking about growth; I want to conclude it on the same note. The young of lower animals are not markedly different from older members of their species; the kitten looks like the cat, the puppy like the dog. But the development of the human organism is a complex process, with many and significant changes taking place between infancy and adulthood. We can be pretty sure that two thousand years from now cats will look and behave very much as they do today, but we have no way of predicting what human beings will be doing and wanting and needing two thousand years hence.

We must organize our guiding principles into a philosophy of education which will help us make our lives what we want them to be—unless we are willing to walk in the dark and submit to whatever fate brings our way. But it is just because we cannot predict the course of human evolution that we dare not walk in the dark and submit ourselves to the vagaries of fate. We value education because it is the means by which we can avoid this danger. And for this reason we cannot allow education to be a private enterprise; it is the business of the public, of the whole society; and the public, through its government, must assume responsibility for it, inasmuch as it is the indispensable basis of all social progress.

THE MISUSE OF SUBJECT MATTER

Let me first summarize what I said in my previous lecture: education is necessary because a child cannot survive without the guidance and help of others. The gap between the capacities of a child and those of an adult is so wide that nature has prolonged human infancy so that the former can be nurtured, educated, and trained. The very nature of the human being creates the necessity for education.

Three important reference points are implied in the foregoing summary: (1) the child, (2) the society into which the child is to be introduced, and (3) the subject matter by means of which the child is to be introduced into his society. The third of these is the focus for today's discussion. One function of the science of education is that of organizing subject matter in such a way that the child will be appropriately introduced into and made a functioning member of his society.

Since the process of education must always take account of all three reference points, it obviously is not a simple matter. First, in order to set up viable goals for education, we must know a great deal about the society into which we plan to induct the child, and must also possess a reasonably well articulated social philosophy. This means that we must have insight into social situations and problems, as well as an appreciation of changing trends in and the needs of the society; and, in addition, we need a depth of vision which can enable us to postulate the changes that ought to be wrought if the society is to become the sort in which we want our children to participate as they grow older.

Sensitiveness to the complexities and needs of social life enables us to formulate goals for education. This is the remote term of the problem; the proximate term is the child himself: what is he? what does he want? what does he need? This means that child psychology is the second thing we must know. When navigating, the captain of a ship must not only know where he is going, but must also be aquainted with the ship itself and its cargo. In the same way, productive membership in society is the destination toward which education aims—the remote term of the problem of education—while the child who is being educated is the proximate term, and as such should be emphasized and studied.

These two terms do not constitute the whole of education. There are the factors which mediate between the child and his society—the school, the subject matter of instruction, and so on. Of course it is important for teachers to know their subject matter—subjects such as history, geography, the sciences, and so on are important for all of us. But it is not enough to know subject matter alone; we must also be aware of its possible significance to the development of the child, and of his society. To be effective, teachers must have considerable knowledge about the child, about the subject matter they use, and about the society in which they operate.

Education becomes a complicated and difficult enterprise when we consider that relevancy to so many factors must be maintained. At the same time it is an interesting and challenging enterprise precisely because so many things are relevant to it. No other profession offers such rich demands and opportunities—acquaintance with the evolution of society and its institutions, knowledge of the development of the child, and continuing improvement in the teacher's own grasp of the many fields of human knowledge. The variety of experience enjoyed by the professional educator is not paralleled in any other occupation. When you look at it in this light, does not education appear to be an interesting enterprise indeed?

With this in mind, we can understand that many times in the past teaching methods have failed and philosophies of education have proved inadequate because, at one time or another, the child, the society, or the subject matter, has occupied too much attention, throwing the other two reference points into eclipse. We are going to talk today about the difficulties that have ensued when people have emphasized subject matter to such an extent that they have lost sight of the development of the child and of his social context, society.

Subject matter is more likely than the other two reference points to usurp the center of the stage and to be treated as though it were independent both of the child and of the society. It happens not infrequently that the things with which we have daily intimate contact monopolize our attention, and that we consequently neglect other things to which we should pay equal attention. A small object held immediately before the eyes can block off the view of a much larger one some distance away; if you hold even the smallest coin near enough to your eye, it can prevent your seeing the sun. This is what we have done with subject matter— held it so close in front of us that we cannot see either the child or the society. When used properly, subject matter is, so to speak, a bridge which connects the two banks of the river; but in our preoccupation with subject matter for its own sake, we have detached the bridge from both banks, and erected it into an independent entity which doesn't connect anything with anything!

When subject matter is treated as though it were independent of the practical activities of the child's life, three ill-effects can be observed. The first of these occurs in three steps: (1) subject matter and practical living become separated, each being treated as though it were an entity; (2) then the subject matter tends to become superficial, with no correspondence to life situations; (3) until finally the subject matter becomes so remote that there is not even the possibility of applying it to our living. The most obvious example is the method under which the child is told to memorize and recite the summarized knowledge and experience of the adult world. Sometimes, to make material more palatable, or to aid the child in recalling it, it is put into verse or a catechism such as some churches use. Both these examples illustrate the general tendency of people to conserve a given body of subject matter, once it has been formulated, regardless of what changes may have occurred in living habits, in moral concepts, or in use of language. But society does change, and formulations of subject matter made with reference to earlier conditions will inevitably, sooner or later, become outdated and lose their significance for day-by-day living.

Those who try to defend the use of this kind of subject matter argue that even though the child cannot grasp the significance of the material at the time he "learns" it, he will come to understand it and apply it in the future. All too often the bald fact is that the child cannot, and never will, understand material so learned, let alone make use of it. Such subject matter makes little sense to the child, even though it may be regarded by adults as unassailable knowledge or incontrovertible truth. It is easy enough to understand why the child does not grasp subject matter which is irrelevant to, and does not occur in, the experiences he has in life. And it follows that what he cannot understand he is not likely to use; consequently the subject matter cannot have the desired effect on his behavior.

Before he enters school, the child enjoys playing with his mother and his playmates. His play activity is rich with significance to him; he understands it, and is able to grasp its meaning for his living, then and there. But when he enters school the situation is different; he is confronted with things he has never seen or heard before; and because his activities in school bear so little discernible relationship to those he carries on outside, he comes to look upon them as irrelevant to his real interests and upon school as a routine of doing meaningless tasks to keep the teacher happy. We expend our time and money to build a school, hire a teacher, and enroll pupils—yet we countenance methods which yield almost nothing in the way of practical results. Isn't this clearly a case of wasting our time and money?

This fault is not confined to seventeenth century schools where children learned to read the Bible and recite the catechism; it can also be observed even in some modern systems of education where the subjects of science, history, geography, physics, chemistry, and so on, are taught apart from activities of human life. The student who merely studies his chemistry without making any reference to other subjects, concentrating on memorizing symbols and formulas, repeating the "experiments" which appear in his textbook, is not likely to be able to apply what he has learned. He probably doesn't even know what soap actually is, or how it acts to clean the dirt off his hands or out of his clothes. The same thing happens with botany, or zoology—or any other subject. You can't blame the students for not being aware of relationships between what they learn in such schools on the one hand and the ordinary business of living on the other. Educators must recognize that it is their job to help the learner become conscious of such interrelationships, and unless the practical affairs of human daily living continue to concern them as the matrix and background out of which the subject matter of the school takes its meaning, their educational system will be just about on the same level of efficacy as the old dame-schools in which children memorized passages of scripture and learned to recite the catechism.

This shortcoming springs from a disposition to treat knowing as though it were entirely separate from doing. Sometimes a person who has learned a great deal is referred to as a highbrow—but the term is more often an insult than a compliment, since the implication is that the highbrow doesn't know much about the practical affairs of living, that his knowledge does not take effect in his behavior, and that he does not act on the basis of what he knows. Hence the public distrust of erudition. When we look at it this way we can see that the practical aspects of education take on considerable importance. Some people understand practical aspects of education as referring to those activities designed to prepare students to earn a living, but what we are talking about is really something quite different and much broader. To be sure, making a living is important, and if the school does help the student in this regard, the function of education has been partially fulfilled. But we must go beyond this; when we speak of practical aspects we mean that learning in school should be managed in such ways that both teacher and student are sensitive to the social connotations of the subject, so that what is learned takes effect in behavior.

The second shortcoming is related to the first one. You will recall that the first fault is observed in three steps: first the subject matter and practical living become separated; then the subject matter becomes superficial and trivial, with no correspondence to living situations; and finally the subject matter becomes so remote that it is not in any degree applicable to life. Even when so handled, though, subject matter could be of use to those students who persisted long enough and concentrated hard enough. But, precisely because the subject matter is so isolated from life, most students try to escape from it. They become afraid of learning. School work becomes even more just a matter of doing things to keep their teachers happy, and when students lose interest in learning, they come to look upon it as a chore. It is small wonder that so many of them play truant to escape from the drudgery of meaningless memorization.

When pupils lack interest in learning they naturally come to regard study as hardship. Many people, including not a few educators, ignorant of the facts of the case, hold to the opinion that lack of interest in studies is inherent in human nature. But, since living in the modern world requires that we study, these people would force or entice pupils to study— and they show considerable ingenuity in the range of tricks and procedures which they devise to this end. But these methods don't work, because the pupils do not understand what they are supposed to be learning; and the fact that they don't understand stems from the circumstance that the material to which they are required to apply themselves has so little to do with their actual living. But lack of interest in learning is not inherent; in fact, the case is just the opposite. When we organize subject matter in such a way that it is closely related to the social activities in which the child normally engages, he will become interested in learning. It is a characteristic of human nature—and more especially so in the period of childhood—to be interested in learning.

Let us glance at the activities of the child before he enters school. He plays with his parents, his brothers and sisters, and his playmates with great enthusiasm. He asks questions—hundreds of them, incessantly and spontaneously. He has a natural disposition to learn; an inherent interest in learning. The only children who are exceptions to this rule are those who are idiots or otherwise psychologically abnormal. Thus, when mismanagement of our schools makes pupils lose interest in learning, dread and fear it, and look upon it as hardship and drudgery, we are, in a sense, producing groups of man-made idiots.

In a certain Western country there is a course called ethics for which the textbook is in catchechism form. In the section dealing with the pupil's obligations to his school, one of the questions asks why a pupil should not play truant. The answer is in the form of an analogy: If one has a toothache, he must visit a dentist; and if he can stand the pain which the dentist may inflict on him, he will soon recover from the toothache; but if he doesn't risk the painful visit, his tooth will keep on aching. The implication of this answer is that the school accepts the interpretation that learning is an inherently painful activity.

Of course, we do sometimes have toothaches, and we do have to visit the dentist; but a toothache is a pathological condition, a negative aspect of life, and not a universal experience. The pupil's lack of interest, or his dislike of learning, is also a pathological condition, a negative aspect of life. Study will assuredly become interesting to pupils if we can pay more attention to the positive aspects of life by improving our teaching methods and our organization and utilization of subject matter.

The importance of the pupil's interest in learning should not be underestimated; it actually has great significance for society. When a student isn't interested in learning, and therefore cannot apply what he learns in school, society gets small return on the expenditure it has made on his education. Ineffective schooling is an extravagance from the viewpoint of society. We must improve our methods of teaching, and our organization and utilization of subject matter so that we can arouse pupils' interest in learning, and help them face up to whatever difficulties they may encounter. If this could be done, teachers would save much of their energy, society would realize greater gains from its investment in education, and pupils would no longer lack interest in learning.

The third fault is that there can be no equality of opportunity for education so long as the school and society are considered separate entities, which is largely the case at present. As long as the school puts such a disproportionate emphasis on humanistic studies, it caters to the interests of a minority of the population—the relatively small class which engages in endeavor that is primarily intellectual. The great majority, who must earn their living by the sweat of their brows, find the content of such schooling far from their interests and needs. But society fosters the intellectual tradition, and accords to intellectuals a privileged position. Our present schools cater to the interests of this class, and thus serve to perpetuate privilege, while neglecting the needs and interests of those to whom intellectual studies are largely irrelevant. Is this not unequal treatment of groups within the society?

The fact that the majority of people lack any interest in intellectual learning can eventually be corrected by improving the schools and making more effective use of subject matter, so that all can benefit from education. The importance of education for everyone is critical in nations which have democratic governments. In such nations everyone—workers, artisans, farmers, as well as intellectuals—must be educated, so that each can make his own contribution to his society.

Today I have dwelled on the negative aspects of the present educational picture. In my next lecture I will talk about positive factors in the educational scene.

WORK AND PLAY IN EDUCATION

As we begin today, let us summarize the first and second lectures in this series. In the first, we saw that the process of education must be adapted to the development of the child, as he moves from childhood to adulthood through the gradual development of his psychological and physical potentials. In the second, we advanced the proposition that education should take account of the innate capacities and the experiences of the child on the one side, and of the needs of society on the other. Otherwise education fails to achieve its end. We also commented on the difficulties which have arisen when the subject matter of the school is isolated from the child on the one hand, and from the society on the other.

Exaltation of subject matter to the center of the educational process is the most serious fault of contemporary education. Effort and ingenuity are exercised to pour into the child's mind those things which adults value, while little attention is paid either to the capacities and the experiences of the child or to the needs of society. But now we know that preoccupation with subject matter for its own sake is inimical to the ends that we want education to serve. This malfunctioning can be corrected only when we shift the focus of education from subject matter to the child. To do this we must base our practice on the psychological and physical development of the child, adapting to the stages of his development until he is in a position to take over the continuance of his education as his own responsibility. When we say that a person is educated, we do not mean to imply that he has ceased to grow, but rather that he has been educated to the stage at which he can and will take the initiative in the further development of his capacities and interests.

As we have already said, fruitful and creative participation in society is the end at which we aim in education; the child as he is when he comes to us is the point from which we start; and the school is the bridge linking the child and his society. The business of education is to help the child walk across this bridge and become a useful, contributing member of his society.

We must not ignore the fundamental fact that before a child enters school he has innate capacities, dispositions, and impulses, without which it would be impossible to educate him. Education must be devised on the foundation of these natural resources. Some time ago when I was lecturing at the National Peking Academy of Fine Arts on "Modern Trends in Education," I used the example of a child's learning to talk. When a child is born, he already has the latent capacity to talk and to listen. All the adult can do is to see that he learns to listen to and speak Chinese, for example, rather than English. Our most assiduous educational efforts would be in vain if it were not for these innate drives. The child's development is a matter of having these natural capacities developed and channeled through the assistance first of his parents, and then of his teachers, to the end that he may be able to satisfy the demands which society imposes upon him. The business of education is to utilize the inborn drives of the child and the opportunities for their exercise offered by the environment to achieve the end of a fruitfully and creatively functioning member of the society.

The child does not only possess the capacity to listen and to pronounce words; he also has a natural desire to do so. Parents, when teaching a child to speak, make use of these capacities and desires, and provide the environment which necessitates that the child, to achieve satisfaction, must speak the same language and use the same grammar as his parents do. This stage of education in infancy is universal in character; at this stage parents everywhere, consciously or otherwise, base their procedures on the innate drives and desires of the infant, providing the sort of environment in which the child will develop in the directions they desire.

The reason I put so much emphasis on the importance of recognizing the child's own powers is that many educators tend to slight these innate capacities. They know that a child cannot automatically become an adult overnight; but they seem to believe that the best way to shorten the period of dependency is to impart to the child the knowledge and experience of the adult world. They look on infancy as wasted time; they fail to recognize that it is an important stage of development—one on which the whole system of sound education must be based.

I suggest that an education designed with reference to the natural powers of the child is of particular importance to present-day China—for two reasons. First, in an authoritarian country with a class society, mere pouring in of instruction could conceivably constitute an adequate education, because the child is merely being trained to occupy a predetermined position and role, and this sort of education can condition him to this end. But in a democratic country there must be equal opportunity for each person to develop all his potentialities, so that he may become a contributing member of his democratic society and a good citizen of his country. The second reason is that when a society is static, pouring in instruction may work fairly well; but when things are in flux as they are in China today, when everything is in motion and undergoing change, education of the child's natural capacities takes on a particular importance. The adult's character is fixed, and is not easy to change, but the child's reactions are more plastic and flexible, more susceptible of direction toward a new and more suitable orientation.

So much by way of introduction. Today I am going to talk about play and work, and their function in the disciplining of innate capacities. Play and work are both matters having to do with the functioning of our bodies. Oriental peoples have typically paid little attention to the body. The same thing was true in an earlier day in the West, when theologians held that the body was the enemy of the soul, and that the flesh should be subjugated in order that the soul might flourish. It is this concept that underlies teachers' insistence that their pupils remain quiet, so that the subject matter which the teachers regard as important can be inculcated in the pupils. The spirit of the new education is a complete reversal of this old concept. Once when I was lecturing in the United States on the subject of education, I said that in China pupils are required by their teachers to recite in unison and in a loud voice. I told my audience that even though this wasn't an ideal method of education, it at least allowed the pupils to have a modicum of physical movement, while in the West pupils are required to sit quietly and are not allowed to make the least noise. Education is fruitless when bodily functions are inhibited. And, as I have said, play and work are both matters of bodily function. Play is the name we give those activities in which a child freely and spontaneously takes part because he likes them and derives enjoyment from them. There is nothing wrong with this. When a child is allowed to play freely, he engages in a range of activities, many of which are imitations of the activities of adults around him. Anthropologists tell us that this is true even in primitive societies. Among the more popular play activities of Western children are tea parties, make-believe dinner parties, pretending to cook, and so on. Little girls dress and undress their dolls; little boys play with toy automobiles and trains; both boys and girls play house. In general, these activities are largely imitations of activities engaged in by adults.

The fact that children are born with a tendency to imitate social activities provides us with opportunity to devise a variety of meaningful play situations and to utilize them to develop children's practical knowledge of their society. This is exactly the method employed by Friedrich Froebel, who originated the kindergarten. Here I shall repeat what I have said so many times before: the present offers an excellent opportunity for China to make use of what has been invented by others. It makes sense for China to adapt the general methods which have been devised as a result of other people's efforts and investigations, though of course the method must, in each case, be appropriately modified in its details when it is practically applied.

The kindergarten makes good use of the child's natural propensity for imitation by devising a variety of meaningful activities. It is interesting that almost without exception kindergarten teachers are women; neither very old people nor careless and giddy men can be good teachers of very young children. Women are better suited to this work because they can show tenderness toward the children; they can be, in effect, substitute mothers, so that transition from the home to school is easier for the children. Properly prepared, young women of China can apply Froebel's theories here, and create a new kind of kindergarten, with activities based in Chinese customs and using Chinese subject matter. But whether the kindergarten is in Germany or America or China, the children play and sing and move about. I expect to see considerable development of the kindergarten movement before I leave China to return to the United States.

It goes without saying that organized activities and play on the playground contribute to the physical development of the child; but what is even more important is that they also contribute to the development of his social insights and understanding. Play provides for both leadership and followership; but most important of all, in a democracy, it affords the opportunity to experience and gain satisfaction from teamwork.

Other moral qualities are also developed on the playground, notably sportsmanship. A sportsman values fairness and justice, despises cunning and subterfuge and cheating. Children can also develop an abiding interest in sport for itself, rather than for the money or fame that preeminence sometimes brings. Wellington remarked that his victory over Napoleon at Waterloo was won on the playing fields of Eton, rather than by the brilliance of his military maneuvers. Of course, this story may have been invented by a football player, but even so, there is a point to it. Look at the recent World War as an example: both Great Britain and the United States had less, and less strict, military training than was the case in the countries of mainland Europe, but still they won the war. I am sure that the sportsmanship cultivated in the various kinds of ball games that are so tremendously popular in both countries was a factor in our victory. During the war, playing fields were constructed in France for the use of British and American soldiers, because the French knew of our fondness for sports. The idea caught on, and now the French are building playgrounds and ball fields for themselves, and going in for sports more than they ever did before the war.

We've been talking of play; now let us go on to work. All valuable manual work involves many of the same elements that play involves. Children not only like to imitate adults; they also like to make things. We must use construction activities for at least three main purposes: first, to cultivate the senses; second, to develop the ability to cope with changing environments; and third, and most important, as an avenue to intellectual education and acquisition of knowledge.

Perhaps you wonder what I mean when I say that manual work and construction activities are a necessary part of intellectual education. But I'm sure that you've noticed—and any child in school can have his attention directed to the fact—that when a saw or a hammer or a plane is used continuously in the carpenter shop, it gets hot. Men have known this for uncounted thousands of years, but only fairly recently did they formulate the law of conservation of energy. This principle of physics is somewhat abstract, and difficult for a child to grasp when presented in words isolated from experience; but when it is offered as an explanation of the fact that his tools heat up in use, he's much more likely to comprehend it. We can also introduce him to the basic principles of chemistry through cooking; of botany through growing a garden, and so on. This is why we argue that work is a necessary condition to the acquisition of real knowledge.

I shall conclude with an example. When I first went to Nanking in May, the children in the Nanking Teachers College Kindergarten were raising silkworms. They started by collecting silkworm eggs and arranging for their protection; then, when the eggs hatched, the children fed the tiny worms with mulberry leaves. This continued until the silkworms spun their cocoons. At the time I was there, the children were unreeling the silk from the cocoons. At first glance one might think that this business of raising silkworms in the schoolroom might fascinate the children (and it did, of course), but that there wasn't anything to it other than the mere fact of fascination. But as the situation was actually being handled, the children were also gaining knowledge. They watched the eggs hatch into larvae, the larvae become chrysalises, and then a few days later, they watched the mature moths emerge from their cocoons. In their firsthand experience with the development of the silkworms, the children were laying a basis for understanding many of the facts and principles of biology. Even in the area of industrial production the experience was profitable; the children learned about the selection and collection of eggs; they had experience in distinguishing good silk from poor; and they took the first steps toward an appreciation of the whole process of silk production. Silk is a major product of this part of southern China, so the child who has a basic understanding and appreciation of some of the chief factors in silk production has, by this token, a better understanding of the society in which he lives. Wouldn't you agree that this sounds like an effective way to pursue knowledge?

One final caution: please do not take what I have said today to suggest that play, sports, and manual work are to be used merely as means to capture the fancy of children. When we want a child to take a bitter pill, we sugar-coat it, and some teachers sugar-coat bitter studies with layers of play, sports, and handwork. But this is not what we mean when we speak of the importance of play and work in education. What we really want is a method of education which is based upon the innate capacities and interests of children, so that their development, both physical and intellectual, will be enhanced.

CREATIVE DRAMATICS AND WORK

I
n the earlier lectures of this series I pointed out that education involves three major points of reference: first, society, the pattern
and values of which are the source of our aims in education; second, the
school and the subject matter, which constitute a bridge between society
and the child; and third, the experience and innate capacities of the child,
whence we take our point of departure in the educative process. We have
seen that many teachers tend to attach undue importance to subject matter, and to depreciate the importance of society and of the experience and
capacities of the child. We have also seen how this tendency has resulted
in the isolation of subject matter both from the society into which the
child is being inducted and from the experiences and capacities which
give meaning to the life the child is leading. In the lecture before this
one I proposed two methods for counteracting this tendency to overemphasize subject matter—play and organized games, and construction activities, or what we used to call at the University of Chicago laboratory
school, *occupations*. These two instrumentalities of education can be employed to help the child to develop in line with his interests and capacities. Today I will discuss a third and a fourth approach, creative dramatics and work, and will indicate how these methods can be applied
in the school.*

* The phrase "creative dramatics" was not current at the time these lectures were
delivered (the first use of the phrase which the translators have been able to locate
was in the early 1930s), and we do not imply that Dewey actually employed these

Let us first talk about creative dramatics, a method about which I am enthusiastic because of what I know about child psychology. There is a tendency common to all human beings—even adults are not exceptions—to give expression to their feelings and their imagination. When we are happy we laugh, and when we are sad we weep—and all of us do this except when we hold our emotions under strict control. Now most of the child's feelings, concepts, and images are about concrete things; and since they are concrete, they can easily be expressed in words, gestures, and attitudes. In unstructured play a child expresses his feelings and images through bodily action only, but in creative dramatics he can express them in a more ordered way. Since the child in his daily life expresses his feelings and images through words, gestures, and attitudes, we can make use of these natural tendencies and devise situations in which the child can systematically express his knowledge, his will, and his emotions.

There are many areas from which we can select materials for creative dramatics: literature, history, human geography—all of which are closely related to society. Novels and short stories from literature can be dramatized easily; the personalities, customs, and habits described in human geography lend themselves to the medium; and there is virtually nothing in history that cannot be dramatized. I am almost afraid that the word *drama* may appear too serious for me to use in this context; people usually think of drama as consisting of formally structured plays with elaborate scenery, costumes, and settings. Originally, though, in Greek *drama* simply meant "doing something." I have no objection to children's taking part in formal drama when they can, and have the opportunity, but the creative dramatics of which I speak denotes something broader, and is closer to the meaning of the word as the Greeks used it than it is to the drama of the theatre as we know it. I do not suggest that we write plays for children to perform, but rather that we present historical events, stories, novels, personalities, or customs in such a way that children are stimulated to create and to play different roles. In short, the point here is that we must let children express the subject matter through their own words, their own actions, and their own attitudes, as though they themselves were involved in it—and, in fact, if we do this, they will be in-

words. But the concept he advances in this lecture is so precisely what later educators denoted by the phrase that we have presumed to use it rather than resort to cumbersome circumlocution to get a literal translation. Sixteen years before this lecture the pupils in the Dewey School at Chicago had engaged in the activity which subsequently became known as creative dramatics.

volved in it. As far as the traditional and professional theatre is concerned, that is another matter altogether, and at the moment we are not concerned with it.

The interest that creative dramatics generates in studies is its most obvious advantage. As I've already pointed out, this is something quite different from sugar-coating bitter pills to get children to take their medicine without a fuss. The fact that children develop genuine interests when they participate in creative dramatics results in their learning being more effective. It does this in four ways:

1. In this activity children feel as though they are actually involved in the subject matter, and that they are characters in the play with which they are working. In this they are no different from us adults—when we enjoy a good play we tend to identify ourselves with the characters on the stage. In the same way, when children act out a story, both the children who perform and those who make up the audience are involved in the development of the play; historical persons come alive; historical events take on reality. This kind of teaching is naturally more interesting to children than just talking about things in an abstract way. In moral education, inculcation of moral doctrines into children's minds seldom succeeds. When creative dramatics is utilized in moral education, the results are much better than outright moral instruction. I have already pointed out that moral education must be a matter of behavior. But oftentimes we must deal with ideas and concepts which do not operate in the immediate environment, and in such cases moral insights and moral behavior can be cultivated through the acting out of stories.

2. Creative dramatics gives children opportunity to select the subject matter for their acting, and to arrange and organize their plays. Not all parts of all stories can be performed, hence the children must develop the ability to select the most suitable parts of a story. Again, it is not true that any child can perform any role in a play, so it becomes necessary for children to decide which roles are to be played by which children. Then when this has been done, the next step is to decide such matters as the arrangement of the play, how to talk and how to act, what words are necessary, what needs to be added, and what can be eliminated—and then the play is ready to be performed. You can see how this sort of teaching can cultivate pupils' ability to exercise discrimination and to arrange events for performance. It also promotes the spirit of and provides practice in cooperation, because all the pupils together are responsi-

ble for a satisfying performance. This is the antithesis of pouring in instruction; it is a way of teaching in which pupils can actively make their own plans and select their own materials.

3. The third function of creative dramatics is to make pupils' images more clear and precise, their knowledge more accurate. In traditional instruction the teacher asks questions and the pupils answer them according to the text. This is a relatively easy task, but even when the answers are correct, the teacher has no way of knowing whether they represent anything more than mere rote learning. But when the method is that of creative dramatics, the pupils cannot act out the material they have read unless they understand it clearly. They have an incentive to grasp the meaning of the words used, the nouns, the verbs, and the qualifiers. They must know—or find out—what sort of thing each noun represents, and what kind of action each verb denotes.

4. The fourth function of creative dramatics is to cultivate and provide practice in the habits of associated living. Traditional class work is assigned on an individual basis, but in creative dramatics pupils need to cooperate with each other, so that class work becomes team work. Thus, while creative dramatics does increase pupils' interest in learning and provide the stimulus to investigation, it is probably even more to be valued because it promotes the spirit of cooperation.

Let us leave creative dramatics now, and go on to talk about work—for work also brings learning into closer relationship with the living experiences of the child than pouring in instruction can ever do. But first we must ask what we mean by work, and try to establish the difference between work and play. The critical difference between work and play is that work is activity directed toward a purpose or end beyond the activity itself, while play is activity engaged in for its own sake, for no other reason than that the pupil is enjoying what he is doing. Thus, when the child aims at results consequential to but beyond the activities in which he engages, he is at work, even though he may enjoy what he is doing just as much as he did the play which had no end external to itself. Thus, from a child's point of view, there is no sharp line of demarcation between play and work. We are all familiar with situations in which children get fun out of such tasks as cooking and cleaning which adults tend to regard as drudgery. This is worth remembering.

We have been talking about the difference between work and play; we need also to note the difference between work, in the sense in which

I am using it, and doing lessons. There is a difference, albeit a slight one. Doing lessons involves an expenditure of effort, but the ends toward which the activity is directed are frequently not evident to the child; and even more infrequently are they of any particular importance to him. Doing lessons implies a kind of instruction in which the subject matter is somehow or other to be inculcated in the child's mind by the authority of the teacher or of the text-writer. The work that I'm talking about is much more spontaneous, and is directed toward ends which the child can both recognize and appreciate; it consists of activities appropriate to the physical and psychological development of the child. It must be distinguished both from doing lessons and from tasks imposed on the child by adult authority—tasks which the child regards as drudgery.

There are many educational advantages in work which is interesting, active, and which leads to discernible and satisfying results. First, because work produces results external to the activity, we can help the child who is working to become aware of the importance of having a purpose in his activities, and to develop his skill in formulating purposes, and thus to decrease the amount of purposeless behavior in which he engages. In the second place, work helps the child to recognize the importance of selecting means appropriate to the ends he has in view, and to learn that a means is effective only in relation to the ends sought. Through work of this sort, the child's ability to judge can be developed. As things are at present, schools turn out large numbers of incompetent graduates— people who have not developed and exercised the ability to make judgments, and who cannot bring about the exact correspondence of ends and means. This sort of failure would be obviated if work were more widely recognized as an instrumentality of teaching.

However, what I am most concerned with is that through work the child can gain a great deal of useful knowledge in all fields, and especially in the fields of science. Botany is a good example. What high schools teach is chiefly the final results of investigations that were carried on long ago, not the method of investigation itself. Students learn long lists of scientific names, and can sometimes identify a number of trees by genera and species, but they rarely learn anything about the methods of taxonomy. This sort of uninteresting teaching cannot be used in the elementary school—or if it is, the result is at best rote learning and not understanding. But the interests of pupils in learning will be enhanced if we use work as a means to teaching. Children like to plant trees and flowers, and to watch the growth, the budding, the blossoming, and the maturation of plants they have tended and worked with. They learn a great deal in this way; they build up a body of firsthand experience which will stand them in good stead when the time comes for them to be concerned with scientific principles.

In some classrooms children plant flower seeds in soil, other seeds of the same sort on wet cotton, and still others on damp blotting paper. When the seeds sprout, the ones on the wet cotton have shorter shoots than the ones planted in soil, and the seeds planted on the blotting paper have even shorter shoots than the ones planted on cotton. Very soon the seedlings on the cotton and the blotting paper begin to wither, but the plant growing in soil keeps on growing until it blossoms and fruits. The teacher watches with the children, guides them in their questioning, until they come to explanations that relate plant growth to sunlight, water, temperature, and fertility of the soil. The teacher may carry the demonstration even further, so that the children can observe the effects of different kinds and amounts of fertilizer. The children are learning things that at the same time are intimately related to their daily life and form the experiential basis on which, when the time comes, they can understand more highly theoretical matters. Pupils in schools below the secondary level seldom grasp theory when it is presented to them directly in words; but they can, through directed activity, not only grasp, but begin to derive, theory.

Or, take an example appropriate for children a little older than those we have been talking about: a few years ago a scientist who was investigating the energy exerted by growing plants devised a demonstration in which he placed a little wooden box over the tip of a pumpkin vine, with a meter attached to measure the energy expended by the plant to push out of the box as it grew. From a demonstration such as this, the child can be helped to deduce that fertilizer contributes to the energy produced by the plant, and can draw parallels between that and the fact that the energy output of his own body is related to nutrition. His interest can be extended in any number of directions—to learn about the importance of plants to animal life; to find out how plants absorb fertilizer; and eventually to come to the realization that in the ultimate analysis all the energy of which man makes use derives from plants. But these are theoretical matters which the child is not likely to grasp except when he approaches them through involvement in activities—or what we have been referring to as work.

With the introduction of the laboratory there has been a revolution in high school science teaching in the last few decades. Many areas of science, including physics, chemistry, and biology, are now taught by the laboratory method, so that students can put to practical test the theories they are learning. This laboratory teaching in high schools is not essentially different from the work method in the elementary schools that we have been talking about. Both have the common purpose of combining knowing and doing. It is not enough for a student merely to memorize facts from a textbook; he must also do something. He must test his theory in the laboratory to see whether it will hold water, and in doing so, he begins to learn the experimental method which is applicable to many fields of knowledge. The fact that the laboratories in high schools have produced such good results should remind us of the necessity for developing the spirit of experimentation in elementary schools and kindergartens.

I used to wonder why the natural sciences had not developed until so recently in our history, since men have been surrounded by a natural environment from the very beginning. I suppose that it is because men are too easily satisfied; they have been willing to take common sense interpretations of the phenomena of nature instead of observing carefully and formulating theories to account for what they see. They have used their ears for listening to others, rather than their eyes for seeing for themselves. Often they even closed their eyes altogether, leaned back, and speculated. This tendency can be counteracted by the laboratory method we have been talking about, using it as means to the cultivation of the habit of checking a theory by the physical changes it produces. I am convinced that wider application of this method will bring rapid improvement in the teaching of science, will produce more men and women who understand science and who have the scientific attitude, and thus ultimately contribute to acceleration in the growth of the sum total of scientific knowledge.

I have spoken of four methods of teaching: the method of play and organized games; the method of construction activities; the method of creative dramatics; and the method of work, or the laboratory method. Thus, we have said all that needs to be said at this time about teaching methods which capitalize on the child's interest and living experience.

At this time let us remind ourselves once more that education involves three reference points: the child, the subject matter, and the society. We have just finished talking about one of these reference points. In the next few lectures we will talk about society and about subject matter.

THE CULTURAL HERITAGE

AND SOCIAL RECONSTRUCTION

We have pointed out in earlier lectures in this series that education involves three major reference points: first, the child, the beginning point of education; second, the school and the subject matter, which form a bridge between the child and his society; and third, the living society, from which we derive the aims of education. We have dealt with the first of these points, and have touched briefly on the second; today, and in the next lecture, we shall talk about the third reference point, society.

In a nutshell, the aim of education, especially in democratic countries, is to create good citizens. A more detailed way of saying the same thing is to say that education must enable every individual both to benefit from the past and present culture of his society, and to contribute to the development of the emerging culture by initiating new experiences of his own which may influence others to participate in new kinds of social action.

The phrase "being a good citizen" seems to have a sort of political flavor. A good citizen is usually thought of as a person who conscientiously votes in elections, and who is patriotic. Such things are, of course, important aspects of good citizenship, but there are others that are more important, especially in a democratic country, where a citizen not only should not cheat or use base means to achieve his ends but also should encourage others to be good citizens through mutual supervision and mutual criticism.

The political aspects of citizenship are obvious and superficial in comparison with the nonpolitical, which can be enumerated as follows:

1. A good citizen must be a good neighbor, a good friend. All men share in associated living in a democratic society, and all important human activities and institutions, ranging from recreation to libraries and museums, are social in character.

2. A good citizen must be as able to contribute to others as to benefit from others' contributions.

3. A good citizen, in an economic sense, must be one who produces rather than one who merely shares in the production of others.

4. A good citizen must also be a good consumer. To be a good consumer is as important as, and as difficult as, being a good producer. It isn't always easy to detect adulteration in the commodities we buy, but in the interests of the total society, all of us should learn how to be cautious customers and wise consumers. This is one of the reasons why it is so important for women to be educated, since women, not men, are responsible for most households, and therefore do much more shopping than men do. If a woman is educated, she will be more likely to detect adulteration and to know the actual value of the commodities she buys, and will thus be a better consumer than her uneducated sister. Western women have made great progress in this respect in recent years.

5. A good citizen must be a creative contributor to his culture.

I have enumerated these conditions of good citizenship because I want to emphasize the fact that the end of education is not just the cultivation of scholars or bookworms who are satisfied to spend all their time reading, but rather it is to cultivate useful members of society. Ability to read is not enough to make a good citizen, if by good citizen we mean one who must make real contribution to his society. The school must observe three conditions if it is to cultivate the kind of good citizens we have described. First, the school must make students want to fulfil their duties to society, not from compulsion, but interestedly and willingly, and out of love for their fellow men. Second, the school must acquaint students with the nature of social life, and with the needs of society. And third, the school should not merely acquaint students with the needs of society, but must also prepare them to meet these needs. This means that the school must, among other things, equip students with a knowledge of technology, and develop familiarity with at least its major processes.

What are the means by which we can achieve the ends of society in school? There are many, but I shall mention only those which are the most important. The first, if we are to utilize and build upon the achievements and experience of the past, is language, both spoken and written. By the time a child learns how to speak, he has already absorbed a lot of adult experience, but such experience is necessarily limited. Through the use of writing, the human experience of many centuries can be conserved and drawn upon.

The conservation of human culture through spoken and written language is a very important aspect of education, but we have put too exclusive an emphasis on it; in fact, all too often, we have regarded it as the only end of school instruction. I believe that this is a familiar enough fact not to require further elucidation. I should like to emphasize the social function of language, something to which we have as yet paid far too little attention. The social interests of the child are sacrificed when the social function of language is neglected by the school. The traditional, impractical literary education, still more influential in our schools than it ought to be, can be immeasurably improved if new methods of teaching, such as creative dramatics, of which we spoke in our preceding lecture, are introduced.

I was pleased to read in the newspaper the other day that the Chinese National Education Conference had passed a resolution favoring the adoption of textbooks written in the spoken language of China. Although I am not as familiar with conditions in China as I should like to be, I believe that the use of the spoken language of the people in textbooks should prove to be one of the greatest steps forward that you could take. As I pointed out a moment ago, the end of education is not the production of more specialists than society needs—the use of the spoken language in school textbooks is a step in the direction in which education must go, that is, toward emphasis on the social functions. Many people have wrongly identified the conservation and teaching of traditional culture with blind and unquestioning acceptance of that culture. They forget that though the materials to be taught and thus conserved may remain the same, their forms and the uses to which they are put can be changed whenever it is necessary or desirable. They make this mistake because they tend to regard the process of history as mechanical repetition, rather than as forward progress. We must not forget that the main reason we want to conserve and teach the culture of the past is that we need to relive it, to infuse life into it, to use it, and make it applicable to present-day social situations and conditions.

There is a parable in the New Testament which illustrates what I mean. A wealthy man who was going into another country divided his money among three of his servants. One servant invested his money in business and doubled the amount of his investment; the second also increased his holdings many times over. But the third servant, afraid that he might lose the money, hoarded it, so that when his master returned he had exactly the amount he had been given, but no more. The master praised the first two servants, but punished the third because he had made no use of the wealth that had been entrusted to him. The same thing can be said about our cultural heritage—if we do not use it to enrich our life in the present, we are not only getting nothing out of our ancestors' investment, but we are also likely to lose sight of the meanings which these customs and traditions had when they were first instituted.

So much for the first means; now for the second, which is the selection of those aspects of the total social environment which best meet the needs of the child. The total social environment is extremely complex; some of its factors contribute to the development of the child; many do not so contribute, or have a negative effect. Our business is to prevent, in the school, the unworthy features of the existing social environment from influencing the child, and to establish a simplified and purified environment which will promote his wholesome development. It is not enough for the child to be able to pass judgment on and make use of his cultural heritage; he must also learn to pass valid judgments on and make constructive use of the environment in which he lives. This is the only way that society can develop and be reconstructed.

The reconstruction of society depends, to a very great extent, upon the school. The school is the instrument by which a new society can be built, and through which the unworthy features of the existing society can be modified. In the school, new elements of thought and new strength of purpose, the basic instruments of social reconstruction, continue to come into being. Other institutions such as agencies of law enforcement, the courts, political parties, and so on, do contribute to social reconstruction; but none of them is as effective as the school, because they are constantly confronted with obstacles which can be overcome only by education.

I will mention two reasons why other institutions are less effective than the school in bringing about social reconstruction. The first is that these institutions exist to control or channel the behavior of adults, whose patterns of behavior are relatively fixed and not easily changed. We know that adults can be educated, but we must also admit that efforts to educate them are frequently nullified by the adverse environment in which they live. It follows, then, that the second reason is that so many adults live in adverse social environments which hamper them or prevent them from taking an active role in social reconstruction. For these reasons, efforts to bring about fundamental changes in the character, outlook, and behavior of adults have all too often ended in tragedy. But the case is quite different with children in school. Their characters have not yet become fixed; their habits of thinking and feeling are still in the stage of formation; they are more malleable and flexible, and are more receptive to education. In addition, even though the school is a kind of social life, it is different from the total social environment because we deliberately make it a simplified and purified medium, from which unworthy features have been excluded, and in which the positive factors which contribute to the wholesome development of the child are emphasized. But the environment of adults cannot be so readily manipulated, and institutions which deal chiefly with adults cannot be as effective in social reconstruction as can the school.

So much for the importance of environment; now let us talk about the importance of habits. I suppose that you think at once of "bad" habits, such as smoking and drinking—and you are well aware of the difficulty of breaking such habits, once they have been formed. Another familiar example is that it is always difficult for an adult to learn to speak a foreign language correctly, especially when the new language contains sounds which are different from those in his native tongue. He has difficulty in producing these new sounds because he has never formed the speech habits requisite for making them. But the child is different; he is just beginning to form his habits. Before he becomes the victim of bad habits, we can, through education, cultivate good habits in him. The early cultivation of good habits may enable him to resist the temptation to slip into bad ones.

We have every reason to believe that in this possibility of forming good habits in children lies the greatest hope for the future of mankind. If it weren't for this possibility, life would be a matter of laborious work and dull routine, a treadmill from which there would be no hope of escape. In a very real sense, we can say that children represent the future of mankind, while adults represent the past. Man has made uncounted mistakes and encountered unnumbered failures—but these are now part of the past. Where there are children, there is hope for social reconstruction. This is what we mean when we say that children represent the hope of mankind.

A frequently used quotation from one of the ancient Hebrew prophets says that "a little child shall lead them." This is a prophecy of man's ultimate success in reordering his world. Not long ago the great French novelist and historian, Anatole France, told a gathering of teachers:

> I have great hopes for you, and great aspirations, since the hopes and achievements of the world of the future are in your hands. All nations, both victors and vanquished, have undergone tribulation in the World War. The restoration and reconstruction of the world depend on you. I trust that you will not hesitate to shoulder this responsibility, because if Europe is not to fall into a state of madness and savagery again, it is you who must cultivate a new generation of mankind. There are those who say that man is inherently evil, and beyond redemption, but they are wrong. Man has already been redeemed from some of the worst of his errors and failures, and this has been largely the result of education. Education is as essential to civilized life as are air and food.

Having said this much about the first two means, conserving and utilizing the cultural heritage, and selecting for incorporation into the school those elements of the social environment which meet the needs of the child and give promise of promoting social reconstruction, let us go on to talk about the third means, which is extending the limits of the child's environment. Before he enters school, the child lives in the limited environment of his family; when he comes to school, his environment is immediately extended. Now, the business of the school is to continue to extend the limits of the environment, and to promote its integrity. To do this it calls upon all subjects and all areas of man's knowledge.

This matter of extending the limits of the child's environment is the most important among the three that we have talked about. As he learns history, geography, and literature, the child will learn about the people who lived in the world in past ages; he will learn that just as he has his own country, China, there are other countries and other peoples in other parts of the world, with different languages, different cultures, and different customs. As he studies biology, chemistry, physics, and astronomy, he gains a broader and clearer view of the physical world in which he lives. The child's environment must be continually broadened, and the child must grow in his power to cope with his environment as it widens. The traditions of the past, the realities of the present, and the possibilities of the future are eventually embraced in this concept of an environment of always receding horizons. That is why we say that broadening the environment is the most important undertaking of the school.

One of the reasons that this function takes on such urgency at the present time is that we are moving into an era of cultural contact between the East and the West on a scale unprecedented in history. I have often pondered on the loss involved in the fact that so much of the contact between civilizations in the past has been military in character, on how much we have missed by our failure to make effective contact with other authentic civilizations. But if there is to be effective contact among authentic civilizations, the teacher must develop a clear understanding of other cultures, so that he can help his students develop a world outlook. Only in this way can we develop mutual understanding among nations, and reduce the possibility of misunderstanding and conflict. This is why I say that the broadening of the child's environment is a matter of greater urgency now than it has been in the past.

Of course it is not just in China that there is such a need; it exists everywhere. But I do believe that China faces an unprecedented and unparalleled opportunity to do this sort of thing in her schools. It is perhaps true that up to now contact with the West has brought China more disadvantages than advantages, more ill than good. But it is also true that the chaos and confusion in morality and economy have reached a point in China at which it would be ill advised, if not fatal, for China to isolate herself from the influences of Western culture. The only method by which China can remedy the present sad state of affairs is to speed up cultural exchange between East and West, and to select from Western culture for adaptation to Chinese conditions those aspects which give promise of compensating for the disadvantages which accrued from earlier contacts. This is a task which calls for men and women of wide knowledge and creative ability. The men and women who will do this are now children in our schools, and this is why the matter of broadening the child's environment is of such great urgency in China today.

DISCIPLINE

FOR ASSOCIATED LIVING

I n the fifth lecture of this series we discussed three objectives of education. But we cannot achieve objectives without methods for doing so; therefore, today I want to talk about ways in which these objectives can be realized. I refer to the objectives of conserving and utilizing the cultural heritage, of selecting appropriate parts of the total social environment for incorporation into the school, and of extending the child's horizons; or, in summary, of socializing students, making them into contributing members of their society, and causing them to be interested in social endeavor. We have already said in an earlier lecture that the socialization of the school environment takes place in three steps. The first has to do with the emotional development of the child, and the cultivation of his social interests and concepts through direct or indirect contact with his own and other societies. The second is a matter of knowledge, skills, and attitudes which make him willing and able to work to meet the needs of his society. The third is the development of practical skills and habits which will enable him to become a contributing member of his society.

So much for general principles. We will now talk about something concrete. First of all, we must understand that school life is, by definition, a kind of social life. Students may come from different social environments, from different family backgrounds, and from different religious sects—but in school they study and play together. Some of them even live in school dormitories, and thus spend virtually all their time on campus. We must bear this in mind as we go into detail and cite illustrations.

Since the school is a kind of social life, we must make full use of its social environment. Students share the universal tendency to drift into cliques; it is easy for those who come from the same town, the same province, or the same social class, to form small and exclusive groups, in which they are friendly with other members, but often reluctant to establish contact with students who don't belong. They may become preoccupied with the advantages and interests of their own group, sometimes even to the point of conflict with other groups. When this happens they are likely to lose sight of the public interest of the whole school. Such behavior, of course, defeats the very purpose of education. Teachers must counteract such tendencies, and concentrate on making the school an instrumentality for developing students' social interests on an ever more inclusive scale. In life outside school, when people become overly concerned about the interests of the small and exclusive groups to which they belong, the result is isolation of their feelings and emotions from those of outsiders.

There are many ways of integrating these small groups into a more inclusive school life based on common interests. One of these, common in the West, and beginning to be tried in the East, is coeducation. This is an effective means for overcoming difficulties in communication among students and for constructing a school environment characterized by a full social life. There are two places where we can begin coeducation with a minimum of difficulty: one is kindergarten, where the children are not yet concerned with the differences between the sexes; the other is college, where students are relatively mature and have developed the power of self-control and their own interests, from which they are not likely to be diverted.

The establishment of a system of public schools is also tremendously important. The existence of a system of public schools exercises marked influence on the life of the total society. In earlier times, schools were mostly private. Some families employed tutors for their children; or sometimes several families would pool their resources to secure a teacher for their children. Until relatively recent times the idea that education was a social affair, or that it was the business of the state, would have struck most people as strange. At the most, the government exercised a modicum of supervision, and sometimes conducted public examinations once or twice a year. In most of the countries of the world, however, and largely within the last century or so, public school systems have come into being. Most national governments have become aware of the fact that unification of the state is impossible without public education; this awareness has caused them to devote a great deal of effort and money to the construction and operation of public schools, so that now public schools are viewed as important and indispensable institutions.

The United States affords a good example of the value of public schools. The United States is a huge country, three thousand miles from east to west, and more than half that distance from north to south. Its population is increasing every year, with hundreds of thousands of immigrants coming from all over the world, bringing with them different customs, different traditions, different habits, and different languages. At first glance one might think that the United States could not possibly be a unified nation; but as a matter of fact it is, to a much greater extent than one might suppose. Even though the peoples of the United States have come from the four quarters of the globe and have brought with them a variety of customs and languages, they have, usually within a generation, altered their habits and ways of life, and have formed themselves into an integrated nation. It is true that they have not yet achieved the goal of complete integration, but they are constantly approaching it, and may well realize this goal within a relatively few years. This fact must be attributed to the existence of public schools which all children of all people may attend without charge. In these public schools, children from different lands study and play together, and this associated living in school contributes greatly to the ideal of national integration.

We have been talking about the informal discipline of the school—the absorption of cliques and exclusive groups into more inclusive groupings, the introduction of coeducation, the establishment of public school systems, and the subordination of class differences. Now we will move on to the topic of formal, or deliberate, discipline in the school. In a democracy, school regulations and discipline should invite and involve full participation by the children. Children should be taught to comply with school regulations because of their awareness of the meaning of and need for such regulations, rather than because the teachers have the authority to enforce the regulations. The maintenance of order should be a function of the whole body of students rather than of a few monitors. Only when we have children growing up in this kind of environment can we hope to produce truly law-abiding citizens of a democratic state.

It is a common mistake in school discipline to regard regulations as transcendent to children's experience, and to assume that children are not competent to discuss these regulations intelligently. When this mistake is made, discipline cannot have the effect we want, because it is enforced from the top down, and is compulsory rather than spontaneous. We must remember that the purpose of school regulations is not merely to maintain order in school, but to be instruments of education, the means by which we cultivate in children the habits, dispositions, and attitudes toward law which will carry over into their adult lives. It is not enough that children should be law-abiding; they must also be lawmakers in school, just as in adult life, as voting citizens or as officeholders, they will engage in lawmaking. Providing such experience for children, and cultivating such habits and attitudes in them, can contribute significantly to social reconstruction.

Of late, some schools have organized small cities within their walls. Some have even gone so far as to organize the entire school into a miniature republic, with the separate classes constituting municipalities, each with its local government, and with provision for legislation, adjudication, and administration. The students promulgate and enforce their own laws, and conduct elections for office. This is not just play—it is, indeed, a structured and semiformal way of cultivating useful citizens. In the case of elections, for example, the knowledge acquired, while immediately useful in the school, can also carry over into adult life and function in the elections in which the student will eventually take part as a citizen.

But this discipline for associated living is not limited to politics and law; we can apply the same principles in activities which we might designate as economic and industrial. Here we make a virtue of the necessity for keeping school buildings and grounds clean, for running the library, and for caring for classroom and laboratory equipment. Students can be encouraged to assume responsibility for these activities, and may carry out their tasks in ways which will cultivate and promote a generalized sense of responsibility which will then characterize them throughout life. Even in the lower grades the pupils can be divided into groups, with the groups taking turns at keeping the blackboard clean, sweeping the floor, distributing materials to the class, and so on. Teachers need not do all these things; they can make constructive use of the children's desire to compete, which might otherwise be directed into nonproductive or harmful channels. Perhaps you think that these examples are trifling and not worthy of mention, but they are examples which illustrate the theory that we need to grasp every opportunity for pupils in school to participate in practical activities and thus gain practical experience in social living. There is a Western proverb to the effect that an ounce of practice is worth a pound of theory. The suggestion here is that all too often theory ends up as nothing more than platitudes, while practice is more likely to produce results. We might change the proverb a bit to apply it to school situations, and say that an ounce of practice is worth more than a pound of memorized mottoes.

Other tasks in which children might be profitably engaged include arranging classroom furniture, or decorating the schoolroom, the hallways, or the assembly hall; care of laboratory equipment, and setting it up when needed; and collecting, arranging, and exhibiting specimens. They can make little things for classroom use, and take care of the more costly items purchased by the school. They can also collect zoological, botanical, entomological, and mineralogical specimens, label them, arrange them, and care for them. If the school lacks funds, pupils may earn money through a variety of activities, such as putting on a play, soliciting funds from their friends and relatives, selling theater tickets, or working at the theater as ushers. These are only a random sample of the innumerable activities in which children may learn the skills and acquire the habits necessary for associated living.

Now that we have talked about both informal discipline and planned and deliberate discipline, let us go on to the third method, which has to do with acquisition of social knowledge and experience on the intellectual level. Some children are quite bright; others are not. Frequently the brighter ones try to help the slower ones by giving them answers without the teacher's catching on. There really isn't much use in trying to stop this sort of thing; the bright students have the energy and enthusiasm, and one way or another they are going to use it. One good way to make use of this natural tendency is for the teacher to appoint the brighter pupils as his assistant teachers, and arrange for them openly to assist the slower pupils. The bright pupils enjoy giving help to others, and in doing so, they unconsciously help themselves, since the very best way to learn new material is to try to teach it to someone else. The slower pupils make better progress when this is done; and encouragement of this sort of co-operation among pupils helps to develop a group consciousness, and contributes toward the general enhancement of associated living.

One final admonition: teachers talk too much! I can't count the classrooms in which I've seen the teacher talk, and talk, and talk, without giving the poor pupils a chance to say a word. This sort of thing is, of course, terribly poor teaching, partly because it is ineffective for almost any purpose, but even more so because it runs exactly counter to our aim of cultivating the habits of associated living. A much better method is to have one pupil describe his general impression of the matter under discussion, with other children chiming in to correct, supplement, or offer alternative ideas. In this way children can share each other's ideas as well as the teacher's. It is better if pupils use a variety of sources instead of depending on a single text, because this makes it possible for a child to report on what he has learned and actually contribute something that the other children don't know. I'm sure that you can see how this sort of teaching and learning can better cultivate the habits of associated living than the sort of traditional teaching in which the teacher does all the talking.

When I lecture, I customarily propound a theoretical point, and then follow it with examples to illustrate what I mean. I am afraid, though, that at times the examples I use do not sufficiently illustrate my point, so, in closing, I am going to restate the theoretical position which I have tried to establish in this lecture: reading is not the only purpose of the school. The purpose of the school must also be to educate useful citizens for the total society, to cultivate habits of associated social living, to develop respect for social virtues and social welfare, to acquaint students with the structure and operation of government, in its legislative, administrative, and adjudicative functions. To do these things, the school has to be a living society itself, and the children in the school must become functioning members of the society, building an awareness of the needs of their society and developing their ability to participate in social living. If we do these things in the school now, the state which these children will build when they are adult will be a prosperous, social state.

THE FUTURE AND THE PRESENT

To repeat what we have said before, three reference points define education: the child, who is the point at which we begin; the school and the subject matter, which are the instrumentalities; and society, whose values provide us with our aims. In the last two lectures we have discussed the social matrix of the aims of education; and in the lecture just before this one, we indicated ways in which school organization, discipline, and the contrived environment of the school can serve as means for achieving the social aims of education.

The main point of the last lecture was that school environment is a kind of social life, and that school must be organized as a society if it is to produce people who can contribute to the qualitative improvement of social living in the future. The most serious weakness of school is that it so often sets for its pupils aims that are remote from their present experience, and tends to look upon education as preparation for the future. Defenders of this view argue that even though what pupils are required to learn in school may have nothing to do with their present living, it will eventually become useful to them at some time in the indeterminate future. When this theory is applied, the result is that learning is isolated from living, and pupils have no opportunity to apply what they learn in school. We should know by this time that school environment must be closely related to the larger social environment, and that only when this is the case are pupils likely to be interested enough to participate actively in classroom matters.

When education is oriented to the future and ignores the present, one of two equally disastrous outcomes is almost certain. First, very probably most of the pupils will waste their time. Since learning that is primarily preparation for the future has so little discernible relationship to present living and present interests, pupils will tend to dillydally about their studies, and to enjoy the insistent present by indulging in play or random activities which appeal to them on the spur of the moment. Children are, of necessity, shortsighted; they know only the present, and it is unrealistic to ask them to attend to the demands of a future which is still far off. Second, a minority of the pupils, however, responsive to adult demands, will yield to the pressures exerted upon them and become more interested in a hypothetical future than in the real present. This response is equally as dangerous as, if not more dangerous than, that of ignoring the demands of the school and frittering away time in dawdling and idle play.

Some religions and life philosophies exhibit the same tendency to rely on a future state of bliss, a heaven, a nirvana, or a paradise, making this the highest good, while ignoring the exigencies of living. The followers of such religions and life philosophies seem to me to be indulging in escapism; historically they have been responsible for retarding the progress of civilization. Otherworldiness in religion and philosophy, the dependence on the promised solace of a future existence, is somewhat understandable in the case of adults who have lived a long time and experienced a great deal of suffering. For such people this hope of an afterlife may represent salvation—but there is no justification for otherworldiness in education. Children are naturally interested in the present; aims of education oriented toward a dim future can only be imposed by adult authority, never derived from the interests of children. This sort of emphasis on the future is obviously against nature and contrary to common sense. The fact that teachers must resort to examinations, penalties, and other such methods to "motivate" their pupils is evidence of the weakness that inheres in a plan of education which puts a premium on supposed future utility and which ignores the demands and the significance of present experience.

We are shocked when we read accounts of the cruelty shown by teachers in the past toward their pupils—and we find far too many examples of such cruelty, no matter what country we happen to be reading about. Knowing that there is a natural tendency for adults to be kind to children, to treat them with tenderness, we find these accounts of cruel treatment by teachers strange indeed, and difficult to comprehend. The only explanation that I can think of is that these teachers accepted the notion that they had to teach for future utility, while the children, constitutionally incapable of looking into a remote and unforeseeable future, simply could not be interested in the things which their teachers thought should interest them. To gain the ends for which they thought they had to work, the adults had no choice but to resort to force, punishment, and coercion in order to get the children to do their lessons.

Later, when people's consciences were revolted by the inhumane infliction of punishment on little children, they devised more humane methods of teaching, and enticed children to study by rewards. When a pupil did well on an examination the teacher would put a gold star by his name, or give him a prize. This was nothing more than another case of getting children to take their medicine by sugarcoating the pills. This method was obviously more humane, but scarcely more effective; pupils still couldn't sense the importance of the future, and could not, therefore, develop any genuine interest in their studies. The main difference was that bribery had been substituted for punishment.

Another difficulty that is inescapable when education is oriented to the future rather than to the present is that there is no valid criterion by which the pupils' achievement can be evaluated. A future which is remote and isolated from present experience simply does not afford any criterion for evaluation. The alternative is to resort to examination, and to gauge progress in terms of how much the pupil has learned—which isn't evaluation at all, in any real sense of the term. Real evaluation is finding out how much progress the pupil is making day by day, seeing how far he is remedying his weaknesses and how well he is developing his potentialities, how effectively he is discovering interests of which he was previously unaware. Real evaluation is determining what progress a pupil is making, not how many things he has memorized.

Please do not misunderstand me. I am not saying that education should not prepare for the future. What I am saying is that the methods of preparing for the future which the schools have traditionally followed simply do not make sense and cannot work. Preparation for the future should be the outcome—the by-product, if you will—rather than the aim of education. When pupils realize the significance of the present and develop active, vital interests in it, they will naturally grow in such ways that they will be better prepared to face the future when it comes. But if a future which is of necessity remote and isolated from the present is constituted the aim of education, we defeat our own purposes. The present is neglected, and the future is not, in any real sense, prepared for.

At this point our discussion impinges on a basic philosophical problem, the real meaning of human life. Should men live for the future, or should they concentrate on making the present as rich and as fulfilling as it can be? This problem goes far beyond education, but our answer to it determines what we do in our schools. If we believe, as I do, that the real meaning of life is found in the enrichment of present living, then the aim of education should be the cultivation of abilities and interests which enrich life now, which bring present fulfillment. Our emphasis should be on helping children to grow, and growth takes place now, not in some dim and distant future.

In his famous essay "What Knowledge Is of the Most Worth?" Herbert Spencer propounded the thesis that utility is the criterion by which we should select the materials which form the curriculum of the school. Even though his emphasis was still on preparation for the future, his insistence that the school should deal with usable knowledge marked an advance over the day when the materials dealt with by the school were all but completely isolated from any needs of life. But even Spencer fell into the error of making preparation for the future a preparation for a stage that was remote from present living. The only preparation for the future that actually works is preparation for the next step in living, which is continuous, which moves forward step by step in a progress in which the future is constantly becoming the present.

This much by way of introduction; now let us get down to the topic of this lecture, the sort of subject matter—one of the three reference points which define the educative process—that is most effective for the realization of the social function of education. Or, we can state the topic differently, by asking what the school subjects of reading, writing, geography, history, and so on really have to do with the child and his society. What is the justification for teaching these—or any other—subjects? What subjects should we teach, and how should we teach them, so that we can best achieve the aim of education? If school life is social living, it must exhibit the salient characteristics of the life of the larger society. The essential problem—and it is a difficult one—is that of devising ways in which pupils can get the sort of knowledge, experience, and abilities in social life which will enable them to participate actively and creatively in it.

This is far too big a problem for one single person to solve; even if one person could solve it, he could not do so in one lecture. The problem must be attacked cooperatively by many people as they experiment, abandon or modify methods that don't work, and discover effective methods. But the problem is not one that will be solved by trial and error; rather its solution must be sought in relation to a general theory which will generate hypotheses to be tested, and which will afford a framework within which the results of experimentation can be checked.

It is true that I have had a good deal to say about ways in which subject matter can be related to the child and to present social living, but I have talked in terms of general principles. Devising concrete methods, and filling in their details, will take a great deal of effort by many people. I can, though, point to two errors that we must avoid. First, we must not allow ourselves to take as our standards for judging our experimental efforts the traditional practices of instruction. Whether the tradition is that of our own or of another country, it is not necessarily suited to the task before us. And second, we must resolutely abandon the traditional regard for the bookworm. The traditional view of learning as a prerogative of privilege, as a luxury to be enjoyed by the few, must be changed.

We could go into classrooms selected at random and ask the teachers why they were teaching the particular subject matter they were dealing with at the moment, and if were to get any answer at all, it would probably be that this was something that had always been taught in schools. A British educator raised the question of why schools put so much more emphasis on the humanities than on the sciences; the only answer he could get was that this was a tradition which came down to us from the Greeks more than two thousand years ago. Thus, the answer to the question about what goes on in English schools today can be found only by looking at life in ancient Greece, and not in the society in which British schoolboys are living.

A somewhat parallel case is afforded by the eagerness with which many countries copied the revolution in German education in the last century. They noted that Germany was prosperous, and assumed that her educational practices had made her so; what they failed to see was that the revolution in German education was a reflection of the situation which prevailed in Germany at that time. There was a blind rush to copy German methods and organization, without questioning whether these methods were in actuality applicable to the situations in the countries which adopted them. We must never forget that methods to meet an evolving situation must be derived from experimentation, and this experimentation must be carried on by people who are themselves involved in and part of the changing social scene. Mere imitation of what some other country does is not very likely to give us a workable scheme of education.

I repeat that we must rid ourselves of the idea that tradition is a source of valid authority, as well as of the concept that education is a badge of prestige, or a luxury to be enjoyed by the few. People who think in this framework tend to equate education with social class; when this idea prevails, we find that education caters only to those who have an interest in erudition, while ignoring the interests of the great masses of people. Under these circumstances, the minority who have studied literature, rhetoric, and grammar have become respected scholars, while people in general also come to suppose that learning means the mastery of those few subjects, and that there is no learning besides them. The result was that the minority controlled education and perpetuated their position of privilege which accrued from traditional erudition. People who held this view of education argued that it would be cheapened if it were extended to deal with the affairs of day-by-day living. They contended that including in the subject matter of education the sorts of things which the masses of people are interested in would be lowering standards. This sort of intellectual arrogance has been an important factor in maintaining traditional teaching methods, and in making education a matter of prestige and privilege, a permanent possession of a minority of the population. There is not much point in bringing an end to hereditary political and economic aristocracy if we continue to countenance an aristocratic attitude about knowledge and learning.

There is one more aspect of the problem to which I wish to address myself. In earlier times the range of subject matter available for use in school was relatively limited, so it was hardly to be wondered at that schools in all nations concentrated on literature, grammar, and rhetoric. But this situation has changed radically, and the time is past when we could appropriately limit ourselves to so few subjects. We live in an age in which the boundaries of knowledge are being extended at an unprecedented rate. Scientific discoveries and the extension of other knowledge which takes place in a single year now is greater than the sum total of knowledge available to our ancestors of three hundred years ago.

The trouble with education in the past was that there were too few subjects from which to choose, while now the trouble is that there are too many subjects. We are surrounded by such a wealth of subject matter that it is difficult to decide what to teach and what to omit; this is a difficulty which can be dealt with only by formulating a theory which will provide us with guiding principles. Otherwise, we will try to learn everything, and end up knowing nothing.

One of the serious weaknesses of present education is that it tries to keep the curriculum up to date by adding all sorts of subjects to it. The idea that the curriculum can embrace all knowledge is a tragic illusion; when we keep on adding subjects, the whole thing becomes thin and superficial. It is another case of making education into aristocratic privilege by ostentatious pansophism on the one hand, and by misinterpreting the meaning of true learning on the other.

But the increase in new knowledge and the progress of scientific discovery have also made two contributions to education. First, it has increased the number of subjects from which we can choose the materials of instruction; and second, it has extended the subject matter of the school to include fields other than the humanities.

How can we choose from among so many subjects those that are meaningfully related to the child's actual living? This will be the topic for the next lecture. We will close this one by observing once more the necessity for us to do something about the outmoded view of education which depreciates the immediate environment of the child. We must persevere in our determination that the living environment of the child—including his needs, his interests, and his physical surroundings—must be employed as the starting point of the educative process. We can understand, without accepting, the two reasons why earlier educators tended to take such a dim view of the native environment in which the child lived: first, the fact that earlier education was designed to prepare for a future which was so far away from the child, both in time and in space, that his native environment was deemed to be all but completely irrelevant; and second, the fact that education was regarded as an instrument for the unification of the total state, a goal to which the child's present environment did not appear relevant.

THE DEVELOPMENT

OF MODERN SCIENCE

I n the preceding lecture we talked about the relationship between the subject matter of school and social life. We also talked about the way in which the goals of social living can be achieved through the teaching of this subject matter. We will continue to address ourselves to the same problem. But since we cannot take time to deal with all subjects, one by one, I would rather give you a general introduction. Obviously changes in our knowledge and ways of thinking have an inevitable influence upon subject matter. Today I want to talk about the influence of the development of science in recent centuries upon education.

I will be talking primarily about theoretical aspects of the problem, and I fear that some of you may feel that what I say does not have any direct bearing upon the problem of subject matter—or you may even feel that what I say is too difficult to understand. However, since we are talking about the philosophy of education, which is one application of general philosophy, we must broaden the scope of our inquiry to include some of the historical background of the problem. All social life and social organization at a given time will inevitably influence education and its development at that time. The development of scientific method and its application has had its influence on society, on human thought, and on our way of looking at life. I will elaborate on this idea under three headings.

First, the significance of the development of science lies not in the fact that it has quantitatively increased the amount of our knowledge nor in the fact that it has substituted new knowledge for old, and replaced in-accurate and speculative facts with accurate and verifiable ones. Mere in-crease in the amount of knowledge and improvement in its quality are not enough to bring about a revolution in knowledge and thought. The development of science is not merely a matter of increase in the amount of knowledge available, or even of its nature; much more significant is the change in our method of knowing. The older methods were incapable of producing reliable new knowledge, because they lacked the character-istic of accuracy. Our ways of thinking have undergone fundamental changes as a result of the development of science. The new method of science has exercised tremendous influence upon civilization, since it is applicable in every area of our experience. This is the essential point.

If you were to ask me to put into one sentence what I mean by the method of science, I would say that it is the method of induction; it starts with observed facts, and continues into controlled experimentation. Since the development of modern science, human ways of thinking have undergone profound changes, so much so that we can speak of an intel-lectual revolution. This intellectual revolution occurred only about three hundred years ago. In the early years of the sixteenth century, European thinking was not fundamentally different from what it had been a thou-sands years earlier, except that there had been a scant increase in the amount of knowledge in the Medieval Ages and later. It was not until the sixteenth and seventeenth centuries that progressive reformers inaugu-rated the new method that has brought such great changes in the fields of industry, politics, religion, and morality.

We have been talking about the first point, which is the influence of scientific method on our ways of thinking and knowing; now we come to the second. In addition to changes in method, the development of modern science also introduced two concepts which have fundamentally changed our way of looking at life. The first is the concept of law in nature. The development of modern science has made man aware of the fact that, despite ostensible disorder, nature does operate according to laws. For example, knowledge that celestial bodies move in predictable orbits enables man to infer that nature follows regular laws of operation in other realms. This concept of the uniformity of nature has had great impact, and among other things, has resulted in marked changes in the way in which we look at human life.

The second contribution is the concept of energy. Our ancestors paid more attention to the static aspects of the universe, such as its substance.

The development of modern science has made explicit the concept of energy, and has enabled us to investigate the phenomena of light, heat, and electricity. This concept, basically different from the concept of static substance entertained by the ancients, has markedly changed our way of looking at human life. The significance of this concept lies in its emphasis on the dynamic aspects of the universe rather than on its static aspects. This concept, in its earlier phases, was limited to the mentioned light, heat, and electricity; but it was subsequently expanded to account for changes which occur in living creatures. It has thus brought into being not only a new astronomy, a new physics, and a new chemistry, but has also created a new biology, and a host of other new sciences such as anthropology, ethnology, sociology, and linguistics. All these have come into existence as a result of man's awareness of the dynamic aspects of the universe, in addition to its static aspects.

The development of this new way of thinking undermined superstition in old traditions and beliefs. The traditional way of thinking was based on the false premise that the world was constituted on some sort of permanent principle or substance that was not subject to change. Under the influence of this premise, men followed traditional religions and traditional institutions, convinced that they were not liable to change; and consequently the majority were subjected to the authority of the wise and the virtuous minority. But since the development of new ways of thinking, men have come to recognize the fact of change in human life, and to perceive the relationship between cause and effect; they have begun to question traditional authority, and to discard the traditional concept of the eternal verities.

In the West, the eternal verities were the domain of a minority of the people, among whom the medieval church was a representative organization. But since people have begun to abandon the concept of eternal truths, they have cultivated a spirit of inquiry and experimentation which is bringing an end to the monopoly of knowledge by the few. Conflict occurred, and a revolution in thinking was started when the privileged few rallied to the defense of the eternal verities. There was widespread and long-lasting contention in Europe between the new camp of the majority and the old camp of the minority. Among the more cogent of the new concepts was evolution, the theory that all species of plants and animals evolved from lower forms into higher ones in the process of adapting to changing environments. It was this concept of evolution that finally dealt the deathblow to the idea of the eternal verities. Because the theory of evolution posed such a threat to the traditional beliefs that were deeply rooted in the existing society, the conflict for the last sixty years or so between those who supported the new concept and those who clung to the traditional concept of fixed truths has involved vast numbers of people.

Here I must digress and say something about the history of the development of knowledge and thought in Europe. This may seem to have nothing to do with education, but since there is a fundamental difference between Europe and China as far as the history of the development of knowledge and thought is concerned, I find it necessary to sketch in the European development so that you can better understand my lecture. Greece was the cradle of European culture. The Greeks were interested in the study of nature, and collected and classified materials and derived knowledge which they organized into the sciences of astronomy, geography, biology, and physics.

During the period of the Roman Empire, Christianity became the common religion of people who had already absorbed the science handed down from the Greek tradition. These people incorporated their outlook on the world, inherited from the Greeks, as well as other aspects of their social life, into their religious life. And just as the science of classical times became closely interrelated with all aspects of the social life of the time, so when modern science developed and was substituted for traditional concepts, it also brought in its train new social outlooks which displaced the older traditional ones. It is in this regard that Chinese culture is so markedly different from European culture.

We have said that traditional science in Europe was woven in with religion and other aspects of social life, but religion was also interwoven with politics. In the Medieval Ages, religion and politics, the state and the church, so interpenetrated that they were all but identified the one with the other. Ways of thinking were therefore subject to the authority of the traditional state. The development of modern science has outmoded the traditional concept of the state and of politics. When we know these things about the history of European culture, it is not hard to understand why the conflict between modern science and traditional ways of thinking caused tension in Europe which lasted for three hundred years. This is where the history of Western culture is basically different from that of Eastern culture. The cultural origins of Western culture were in Greece, and Christianity incorporated Greek culture into the fabric of society, politics, and religion. But there was no parallel to this in the East. Although I do not know a great deal about the history of the development of Chinese culture, I do know that traditional Chinese culture was more concerned with a philosophy of life than with the natural sciences, so that science never developed enough to be incorporated into the general pattern of politics, religion, and other aspects of social life. Since this is true, there could not be the same reaction in China against the introduction of new thought that there was in the West. The introduction of modern science caused deep-seated conflict in the West, conflict which lasted hundreds of years; but when the same ways of thinking were introduced into China, Chinese society did not see them as revolutionary at all.

We must not underestimate the significance of this difference. The fact that the introduction of new ways of thinking did not provoke a strong reaction in the East was a disadvantage rather than an advantage to Oriental society. Since traditional science permeated all areas of social life in Europe, and since the development of modern science therefore caused dislocations throughout the length and breadth of life, as it were, the people of Europe could not remain unaware of or insensitive to the impact of this new way of thinking. Since all people were affected, they gave attention to the arguments and disputations of the opponents and proponents of modern science, and upon listening to them, understood much of the significance of the intellectual revolution, and discovered new ideas. But in the East, where science was not developed to a degree that had any marked effect on social outlooks, the introduction of new ways of thinking did not provoke any marked reaction, because people did not comprehend the significance of what was happening, and had no reason to suppose that it applied in any real sense to the situations in which they lived. About the only thing that most people noticed was that the change brought new words into their vocabularies. Science does not develop when we are not conscious of its significance. The reaction to the introduction of modern science in Europe was a sign of progress; the stronger the reaction, the greater the progress. When people are indifferent to the introduction of new ways of thinking, this is evidence that the new thought does not have much influence on their lives. And when this is the case, the development of new thought is slowed down and narrowed.

The significance of the development of thought in Europe lies in the struggle for freedom. It is only when freedom of thought, freedom to write and publish, freedom of investigation, and freedom of belief have been established that we can hope to promote the development of science, which is the agency of the evolution of civilization. Freedom is so important that we stake our lives to secure it; it is gained only when we strive for it. Freedom has not been so greatly prized in the East as in the West. Perhaps this sounds strange to you, but I have noticed that the Chinese people still do not seem greatly interested in the import of the development of modern science and in the question of intellectual freedom which is part and parcel of this development It seems to me that the Chinese people equate science with mere technology, with building railroads, with improved methods of mining, with the construction of highways, with engineering. A few years ago when Ching Hua College sent students to study in the United States, eighty per cent of them chose enginering, and only twenty per cent majored in all the other subjects put together—an interesting commentary on the attitude of Chinese intellectuals toward Western culture. Of course technology is important, but the development of the scientific spirit and the cultivation of a new attitude toward life are far more important.

We have now talked about the first two ways in which the development of modern science has exerted influence; we now come to the third, which is that the development of modern science has introduced the concept of energy and has thus encouraged man to force nature into his service. Let us take an example: for thousands of years men have known that a wood table, such as this one before me, could be burned; but this same fact has been reinterpreted by modern science, which presents the table as being made up of innumerable small moving units which step up their speed when the wood is oxidized, and thus release energy. According to the interpretations of modern science, any given kind of energy can be transformed into another kind of energy. We can extend this concept so that, for example, we see water not as inert matter, but as potential energy. It can become steam when it is heated, and when the steam is appropriately channelled, it can drive a locomotive. The steamship and the train have shortened the distances between different parts of the world; and the factory, with its powerdriven machinery, brought about the industrial revolution. These are but representative instances of man's power to harness nature to his service.

Gradually the dynamo is being substituted for the steam engine, and now we have the telegraph, the telephone, and the electric light—still further instances of man's having harnessed nature to serve his needs. The invention of mechanical power was not accidental, nor is it something that we just happened to have discovered; it is the result of the application of human intelligence to the materials and laws of nature. In the early days of the industrial revolution governments legislated against machinery, religious leaders inveighed against it, and mobs sometimes burned factories and destroyed machines—but uncounted inventors have, nevertheless, continued to find improvements and to build new devices. The most important thing about this development, though, is not the production of engines and machinery, but rather that these devices are evidence of a new attitude and a new orientation toward the pursuit of knowledge.

Everybody knows that the steam engine and the dynamo have contributed to the development of industry, trade, and transportation; but still some people complain that these inventions have induced disorder in European society, and they enter this conclusion on the debit side of the ledger. But those who argue this way aren't necessarily correct. The development of modern science has had far more positive effects than negative. For one thing, this development has made people recognize that the welfare of society should be the concern of all people, not of just a few—and this is a great step forward. This recognition that social welfare involves everyone has brought into existence all sorts of institutions which have contributed to social progress and have ameliorated human suffering—quarantine stations, hospitals, departments of public health, settlement houses, and a host of others. Actuarial tables show us that, on the average, people in Western countries nowadays live ten years longer than they did fifty years ago—another result of the development of science.

I conclude this lecture by commenting on the influence which the development of modern science has had on politics. According to classical political theory, it was impossible to have a republic in a land as large as the United States, because it was too difficult to communicate between and among all parts of the country. But with the development of modern science these difficulties in communication have been overcome—we have the telegraph, the telephone, the newspaper, and railroads and steamships —so it is quite possible for us to have large republics. This is one example of the influence of the development of modern science on political life.

If our new education is to take the present social situation into account —and I certainly think it should—teachers must be aware of the real significance of the development of modern science. They must also know the fundamental changes in methods of thinking, and the characteristics of the new methods. They must understand the influence of the development of modern science on social development, on human life in general, on politics, and on religion. Only by developing such insight can we prevent our educational enterprise from becoming imitative and mechanistic.

SCIENCE AND THE MORAL LIFE

Ⅰn the lecture before this one I pointed out that the rapid development of science in the last few centuries has brought about a change in methods of thinking in general, and new concepts of science in particular. These new methods and new concepts have exercised their influence on both content and method in education. With the development of modern science the relative amount of attention devoted to the humanities has been reduced, and greater emphasis is devoted to the objective world in which we live. The tendency has been to abandon dogmatic methods of instruction, such as indoctrination in old beliefs and traditions and memorization of the Chinese classics. The method of direct observation and experimentation has been gradually introduced into schools. For the sake of convenience we may look at the influence of science under two aspects: first, the material influence of the development of science; second, its moral influence. Elevation of living standards and improvement of transportation are examples of the material aspect of the influence of the development of science. The creation of new hope, the evolution of new beliefs, and the broadening of moral concepts are the moral aspects of its influence.

Since the development of science has exercised such tremendous influence upon both moral concepts and material progress, it becomes the essential factor which accounts for the difference between Western culture and Eastern culture. Science developed in the West two or three hundred years before it did in the East. And as I have just pointed out, the development of science in the West has had tremendous influence both on material progress and on moral concepts.

To repeat something I have mentioned several times in earlier lectures in this series, people of the West understand the real meaning of the development of modern science better than people of the East do. The West has developed a material civilization and, at the same time, a scientific attitude which enables people to control and direct the development of their material civilization for the promotion of human welfare. Granted that they they still have not fully achieved this direction and control, they have, nevertheless, made enough progress in this direction to keep the development of their material civilization by and large within the bounds of manageability, and to profit from it without paying too high a price for the benefits it brings. Oriental people, on the other hand, do not really grasp the significance of the development of science; they confuse the results of science—the development of technology—with science itself, and consequently fail to develop a scientific attitude. Naturally, then, the people of the East are frequently unable to adjust effectively to the innovations which development of their material civilization has brought about—a failure which can be very dangerous indeed.

Because this danger is so manifest in the East, I should like to talk today about the influence of the development of science on man's moral life. We have already made significant advances in material civilization; we have railroads, the telegraph, roads and trucks and buses. But as long as we fail to understand how we have made this progress, we will remain ignorant of the real significance of the development of modern science for man's moral life. When this happens we find ourselves having to separate civilization into two parts, each isolated from the other—the material and the spiritual. We have already donned the trappings of material civilization, but our moral outlook remains unchanged. Japan is a case in point: she has modern military weapons, a newly developed commerce, and efficient transportation; but she still has not changed her old concepts, her old morals, her old habits. As a result of this failure, Japan is paying the price both of the old civilization and of the new, without being able to reap a full measure of profit from either.

I am going to talk today about the influence of the development of modern science upon man's moral life. The point I want to establish is that the development of material civilization and of moral ideals and ways of thinking should go hand in hand, so that we can control material developments and direct them toward promotion of human welfare, instead of having mankind suffer unnecessarily drastic dislocations, as has sometimes been the case. Since I arrived in China many people have asked me how China can import Western material civilization to develop her economy, and at the same time forestall the difficulties which material developments have brought in their wake in the West. It is true that in the Western world the development of material civilization has been accompanied by negative outcomes such as acquisitiveness and cruelty, contention between capital and labor, and strikes and lockouts. Today, however, we will explore the positive influences of the development of modern science, and identify those aspects of this development which can help us overcome the difficulties with which we are confronted. What I am going to say is a sort of prediction of things to come, a description of a state of affairs which not even the Western world has yet achieved. I hope you will recognize that when these predictions become actualities, many of the troubles which material civilization has brought in its wake will have been obviated.

The development of modern science has had two sorts of influence on man's moral life. The first is that modern science has introduced new hope into life, and has provided the basis for new courage in living. As is the case with a man, when a state or a nation grows old it becomes less active and more conservative; it loses the resilience of youth, and begins to disintegrate. There is need for hope and courage if we are to recover the strength and resilience and adaptability of youth.

Whence comes this new hope and courage? It springs from man's confidence in his own intelligence. The development of modern science has opened ways in which man can employ his intelligence to get rid of ignorance, wrong and disorder; knowledge that this is so is the basis for a new attitude toward life. Man can now confront ignorance and wrong and disorder without panic, because he is confident that his intelligence assures him ultimate victory.

Before science was developed man looked at nature in one of two ways. On the one hand he looked on it as being utterly without order, and therefore not susceptible to any sort of control; or on the other, noting that the sun, the moon, and the planets moved in fixed orbits and that the seasons came in predictable sequence, he concluded that the universe was so completely ordered that nothing he could do could possibly make any difference to it. The influence of either of these two outlooks was oppressive to the social life of man, because whether men conceive nature to be so irregular as not to be susceptible to any control, or so completely ordered that human intervention is unthinkable, they become pessimistic and abandon any concern with nature. This pessimism has manifested itself in three ways:

1. Men disparage the subject matter of the natural sciences. Most men partake of a universal disposition to derogate those things which they cannot have. There is an old Greek fable about a fox who found a bunch of grapes hanging just out of his reach. When his highest jumps still fell short of the grapes, he stalked off, remarking that the grapes were sour anyway, and that he really hadn't wanted them. Men do the same thing. Can we really deny that men want to subject nature to their service? Who would not want to use electricity to propel his trolley cars, or to light his streets, factories, stores, and homes? But when men can't have this control, they console themselves with the pretense that nature isn't worth controlling.

2. Men adopt a pessimistic fatalism. When people think that everything moves exactly according to preordained law and that all is therefore beyond any possibility of human control, they become pessimistic and passively acquiescent to the world in which they live. This tendency has given rise to the hurtful attitude of trying to transcend the material world, of seeking to live a life of utter resignation. But the development of scientific method has brought new hope to mankind, for with it, man can penetrate the secrets of nature and make her work in the service of his welfare; his attitude of passive acquiescence changes to one of active participation, and his fatalism is superseded by confidence that he can conquer and control a significant number of the forces of nature.

3. Men, convinced that there is no point to the search for truth, resign themselves to following traditional ways of doing things, to behaving according to traditional customs, to accepting traditional wisdom. They accept the assertion that the ancients were not subject to error, especially the wise men of the past, and they feel obliged to accept their pronouncements at face value. The real reason they behave in this fashion is, of course, their conviction that they lack the power and the methods of seeking truth for themselves.

Let us contrast the three ill effects we have just talked about with the opposite attitudes that the development of modern science and the growth of scientific method has made possible: instead of disparaging the study of natural phenomena, man now regards the study of nature as interesting, challenging, and worthwhile; instead of being pessimistic and fatalistic, he has begun to conquer nature and to subject it to the service of mankind; and instead of blindly following traditional custom and blindly accepting ancient wisdom, man cultivates a spirit of inquiry, becomes creative, discovers new truth, and invents new instrumentalities for better living.

Let me explain how the development of science can eliminate traditional superstitions. When, in the past, people believed that everything possessed a given nature, that the universe was composed of innumerable discrete entities (among which were human beings), that all of these were manipulated by God, or by a divine spirit, and that each moved toward a preordained destiny, naturally the vicissitudes of life were presumed to be beyond man's control. Man could be nothing more than a mere spectator in such a universe; its control was obviously beyond his power. The development of science brought the knowledge that the universe is not composed of innumerable discrete entities, each possessing its own mysterious nature, but that instead it is composed of a known number of chemical elements; and that the universe is not manipulated by some transcendent power, but rather that it operates in terms of ascertainable laws. Since the development of science has brought this knowledge to men, they have proceeded to investigate nature with confidence.

The structure of the universe has been greatly simplified by the chemists who have discovered that the whole universe is composed of sixty or seventy chemical elements rather than of uncounted entities of mysterious and unknowable nature. Further, they have also discovered that each element has its regular valence, and that certain compounds can be produced by the combination of given elements, while other elements cannot be combined with each other. A scientific study of the universe is now possible, because men have discovered its structure and the regular patterns of behavior of the elements. On the basis of this discovery of chemical elements and the laws of their operation, man can make further inquiry into new problems; the fact that some of these are complex and have thus far defied solution does not lessen our interest in conducting research. With the discoveries he has made, and with the experience of constantly making new discoveries about nature and the laws according to which it operates, man will never lose his courage nor become despondent. Hence, where there was formerly acquiescence and resignation, there is now positive involvement in the discovery of the secrets of nature.

To sum up, the first way that the progress of science has changed man's moral life is that he no longer suffers disappointment and discouragement in the face of the difficulties that nature has imposed upon him. Men have developed the power to seek the sources of their troubles, and to devise ways of dealing with them with intelligence and confidence. The ancients were superstitious about the law of cause and effect, seeing it as a monstrous revolving wheel to which all men, except a few favored of the gods, were lashed. But now science tells us that the universe operates in terms of relatively few laws, and that it is within man's ability to determine the causes of events which earlier were matters of mystery.

So far we have been talking about the first influence on the moral life of the development of modern science, namely the creation of new hope and new courage. The second influence is that modern science has produced a new honesty. I do not mean that honesty, as such, is a result of the development of modern science; all of us know quite well that honesty is one of the most important of the traditional virtues. But we must recognize that it is not easy for us always to be honest, because in order to be honest we must have some truth to tell. All too often something appears to be true, but later experience proves it to have been false. The development of modern science enables men to pursue truth, to discover what things actually are true, so that they can be fully honest in talking about them. Before modern science developed, the universe seemed to be full of irregularities, and this circumstance often made the pursuit of truth impossible. Even when it was possible, men still encountered many difficulties. Consequently there were many handicaps to honesty, even when men wanted to be honest. When nature was presumed to lack systematic order—an assumption which made man's study of nature impossible—the desire to tell the truth was stifled under the pressures of selfishness, prejudice, partisanship, and other external forces. Men tend to share the view that the immediate peace and welfare of society is more important than facts and truths about nature; and when they think there is a conflict, they generally prefer to sacrifice the latter for the former. Much of the time people are so loathe to offend public opinion or to create unrest that they hide or neglect the truths which scientific investigation can reveal—oblivious to the fact that in so acting they are laying the groundwork for more serious and more consequential disorder at a later time. The sacrifice of truth and the nullification of the search for truth are always sooner or later followed by sacrifice of the social welfare.

The progress of science has created a new honesty which is assured by the efficacy of scientific method and the confidence of mankind. This is to say that men have become confident of the power of their intelligence to pursue truth and to solve the problems with which they are confronted. Science has enabled men to discover facts, and to identify the real problems of life, and then to seek for solutions to these problems. It is not nearly so important to tell the truth as it is to be able to distinguish truth from falsity. Characteristics of this method of science include publicity, investigation, observation, and public discussion, all of which are ways of making people capable of telling, and of being disposed to tell, the truth.

Plato held that 'being' should precede 'seeming', and that the former is more important than the latter. This is a value both in metaphysics and in morality. Often 'seeming' appears to be real at first glance, but actually is not; many social "facts" are this sort of thing. It is difficult for us to identify the real problems of our society; many obstacles lie in the way of our doing this, the chief of which is the preoccupation of the public mind. Too many people are preoccupied with their own interests and their own advantage, a circumstance which keeps them from being really honest. Some people not only refuse to tell the truth, but exert pressure to keep others from doing so. Some people fail to tell the truth because of personal feelings, or through fear of offending others. Under such circumstances they embrace 'being' within 'seeming', and in so doing, give rise to all sorts of confusion.

I am not saying that men intentionally refuse to tell the truth, or that they are consciously the enemies of truth. But they unconsciously become the enemies of truth because their inability to control their emotions and their fear of offending others makes them unable to tell the truth when they should do so. The progress of science is changing people's attitude, though; they are beginning to know the value of truth, and to know how to apply the methods of science and the scientific attitude. As they learn these things, they are progressively better able to apply the methods and attitudes of science to social problems. This is why we say that science has introduced a new dimension of honesty.

I am going to talk about the application of this new concept to education in a later lecture in this series; but here I will give you a preview of what I am going to say—in one sentence, and without going into details and applications. It is true that the development of science has increased our fund of knowledge about education; but it is much more important that it has been responsible for new methods and a new attitude, that it has made it possible for us to move out from under the cloud of pessimism, passivity, conservatism, dishonesty, and disregard for facts, into the sunlight of new hope and new courage and a new dimension of honesty, where men are capable of discovering the truth, of discerning the causes of events, and of mastering methods for remedying deficiencies and overcoming difficulties.

I n the three preceding lectures of this series, we have dealt with the influence of modern science upon man's intellectual and social development. Of these three lectures, the first two were devoted to science's general influence, and the last one to its influence upon moral life. Today we will concentrate on the influence which science has exerted upon man's intellectual development.

We must first deal with the nature of the scientific method in the pursuit of knowledge. It goes without saying that both learning and teaching are involved in the pursuit of knowledge, and therefore the most significant influence of modern science upon man's intellectual development consists of the modification of methods of learning and teaching. I must remind you once more of the fact that science is not a mere accumulation of knowledge; it is not what is found in books. Chemistry, physics, and astronomy are merely the results of scientific endeavor, not science itself. The basic significance of science lies in its method, in the way in which scientific knowledge is obtained—not in its results. The person who knows only the outcome of science, such as the subject matter of chemistry or physics, and who ignores the method of science, does not really perceive the meaning of science.

Let us imagine a cataclysm which would destroy all the methods of pursuing knowledge, but which would leave extant all the knowledge which men had accumulated. We could not then say that any scientific knowledge still existed; we could say only that we had an accumulation of strange knowledge that was without life. The importance of science is that it introduces a method of pursuing knowledge which enables man to predict and control the future on the basis of his past experience. This is what we mean by science in the truest sense of the term. I repeat that accumulations of knowledge represent only the outcomes of scientific endeavor; they do not constitute science. This may seem a strange thing to say; but when we begin to wonder why so little result has been achieved from the teaching in our schools of the various fields of science, such as biology, mineralogy, chemistry, and physics, we may infer that the "science" which the school has been teaching is merely the results of scientific investigation, and that the real significance of scientific method has not been brought home to the students to a degree that would enable them to pursue truth for themselves. What the students get under such circumstances is only an accumulation of dead knowledge, not an ability to do independent research, to invent, to observe, and to control the powers of nature.

I will not take time today to deal separately with teaching methods for the several sciences. There would be small profit in doing this. Instead, I am going to talk about what the scientific method is, and what its implications for education are. Once we understand the meaning of science, we can apply it to the teaching of all the scientific disciplines.

What is the scientific method? In brief it is the method of experimentation; a method for applying human action to creating a connection between the functions of the mind on the one hand and the facts of nature on the other. Suppose that our problem is to determine whether a given piece of metal is gold. There are a number of ways to go about doing this. In prescientific times, people gauged the color of the metal, found out what polish the surface would take and estimated the refraction of light from the polished surface, or checked on its weight. These methods were crude, and likely to be inaccurate. Now science tells us that we can apply a certain acid to the metal and observe the reaction; then add another acid, and repeat our observation. If we still are not completely sure, we can heat the metal and determine the temperature at which it melts. All these are methods of bringing human action to bear upon a natural object, so that by its reaction we can determine its nature and function. This is an instance of the scientific method—the method of applying human action to connect the function of the mind with the facts of nature in such a way that both mind and nature undergo a sort of change.

The same thing can be said in greater detail. The function of mind is to draw a plan of action in order to predict what results will occur when nature is acted upon in this way or in that. If the actual occurrence is what was predicted in the plan, the hypothesis is verified; if not, the investigator must draw up another plan and make another prediction. This experimental process continues until the plan or hypothesis is finally verified by the actual occurrence of natural phenomena, so that the investigator is sure of his facts. Then from these new facts he derives new ideas and constructs new hypotheses. The whole process is a purposeful one.

I have been told that there is a Chinese proverb to the effect that "to know is easy, to act is difficult." This is just the opposite of the experimental method, for in this method it is only after we have acted upon a theory that we really understand it. There can be no true knowledge without doing. It is only doing that enables us to revise our outlook, to organize our facts in a systematic way, and to discover new facts. The conclusion is that we cannot expect to gain true knowledge without acting upon our ideas.

The whole matter becomes clearer when we compare scientific knowledge with knowledge which is not scientific. Some knowledge cannot be regarded as scientific because it is not systematized. Scientific knowledge is systematic knowledge, knowledge that has been systematized by the arrangement of natural phenomena through human action. Some traditional philosophers have held that truth can be sought by the mind quite independently of external phenomena; but this is a far-fetched assumption. There is no warrant for supposing that a theory devised purely within the mind could ever be reliably descriptive of nature. Mere ideas are not science; science is those ideas which can be empirically verified and which produce predicted results. This is science in the truest sense of the term.

We may compare experiment and experience. Normally we think of experience as being passive, with its order not controlled by human action; it exists only in a chronological sequence. But this is not the case with experiment; experiment is intentionally directed and controlled by human action and directed toward a foreseen purpose. Or we may say, if we wish, that there are three kinds of experience. The first is trial and error, blind effort without anticipation of results. It takes time and energy, but gets significant results only by accident. A second type of experience is withdrawal—a pulling back from experiencing. The less one tries to do something, the better. The third type of experience is experiment. This type is different from the first one in that it is guided by intentional anticipation instead of being blind trial and error. It is also different from the second one in that it is a positive attitude; it is experience marked by the intent to act upon the idea, rather than by withdrawing from the situation. This is experience by experiment.

A chemist cannot perform his experiments without a plan. He must have a plan at hand, and a purpose in mind. He must first draw up a plan, and then subject it to experiment, with the truth to be determined by the observable result. Although his plan represents a prediction of the future, this prediction must be made on the basis of his observation of existing facts. The experimental method always has two phases: an experiment is the search for new facts, but it is always conducted according to a plan which is drawn up with reference to existing facts. The experiment is to be distinguished from blind trial and error, and it is the opposite of withdrawal.

The method of trial and error can, it is true, be spoken of as a kind of experimentation, but it is not scientific because it lacks the element of anticipation, and seeks success by chance alone. The distinguishing characteristic of scientific method is its anticipation of the result, step by step, and the systematic organization of the step-by-step procedures. This attitude toward learning has been developed along with scientific method. Here I must point out that the most important thing in scientific method is the hypothesis, which is something quite different from mere speculation or arbitrary supposition. A hypothesis is devised to control and give direction to experimentation. The concept of hypothesis is extremely important in science, because scientific experiment cannot take place arbitrarily or according to a fixed law which is not subject to change. The usefulness of a hypothesis lies in its function as a guide for experimentation. Thus, all experiments are hypothetical in the sense that when the hypothesis is confirmed by the occurrence of the anticipated result, the experiment is a success; otherwise, a failure. Science does not recognize eternal truths, but only the temporary truths of its hypotheses. An idea is also a hypothesis to be verified by the anticipated result it implies; once it is verified, it becomes truth for the time being, but always subject to further testing and further verification.

Traditionally, when a proposal was set forth, people reacted in one of two ways: if it looked like a good idea, they would adopt it; if it didn't look good, they would reject it. But the development of the attitude of scientific experimentation has introduced a third mode of reacting, which is to look upon the proposal as a hypothesis, the worth of which is to be determined by the result of experimentation—if, of course, there is adequate indication that the proposal is worthy of experiment. Prior to the development of modern science people tended to be either dogmatic or skeptical. The dogmatist thought that he could determine truth by the action of pure reason; the skeptic doubted all truths and thus lived in a state of uncertainty or indifference. Today we recognize the inadequacy of these two types of thinking, but both have made their contribution. Dogmatism clings without doubting to whatever it regards as truth, while skepticism refuses to recognize any so-called eternal truths. There are advantages to both; but both need constructive revision. The experimental method incorporates into its theoretical construct both the dogmatic's confidence in truth and the skeptic's insistence upon subjecting so-called eternal truths to rigorous examination. Thus it incorporates the strengths of both positions while avoiding their weaknesses.

The strength of the experimental method is that it is at the same time real conservatism and real radicalism. It neither rejects the idea of truth nor clings tenaciously to the "truths" of tradition. It insists upon subjecting traditional theories and established truths to examination by experiment. It is real conservatism in that it promotes the conservation of those aspects of the culture which have been verified by experiment, and it is real radicalism in that it does not hesitate to reject those aspects of traditional culture which do not stand up under experiment.

The experimental method is progressive, in that it does not oppose change, but rather encourages it. It recognizes the fact that everything is subject to change in relation to time and circumstance. The experimental method intentionally introduces new elements to produce changes in the situation, and in this sense it is planned, confident adventure. But the worth of the new elements introduced into the situation is also to be determined by experiment.

The development of the experimental method has resulted in many new discoveries and inventions, and as a consequence, the range of new machinery available to industry has been rapidly extended. Since the conception of progress is universally recognized as being implicit in the experimental method, those who use it do not look to the ancient past as a golden age. They rather look to a golden age in the future, because progress is made whenever new elements are added to the present situation. This shift in viewpoint is one of the major contributions of science to our contemporary culture.

The ancient Greeks, a vibrant and alert people, developed intricate philosophies and magnificent literature, but their philosophy failed to achieve the idea of evolution. Profound as were some of their philosophical constructs, Greek philosophers tended to eulogize their past, to disparage their present, and even to retreat from reality into utopian fantasy. The idea of evolution, even though it was the object of speculation for some of them, was alien to their philosophical outlook. It was not until the development of the scientific method in Europe that the conception of continuous progress emerged—the product of a method which determines all truth by experiment.

In one sense the experimental method is progressive, while in another it is conservative in that it seeks to conserve all aspects of traditional culture which have been, or can be, proved to be true. It looks ahead to the future from the vantage point of existing fact, but at the same time it refuses to indulge in wholesale rejection of the past. Like the wind which blows away chaff and cullage while leaving the rice on the threshing floor, the experimental method eliminates only those parts of the traditional culture which are proved worthless by experiment, while conserving all those which are proved worthwhile. The experimental method has increased rather than decreased man's interest in the study of traditional culture, because it puts present and past on a par, and subjects both to the test of experiment.

We do not have enough time today to deal in detail with the influence of this experimental method on education, but there are a few general remarks I should like to make. The application of the experimental method is not limited to this or that subject, but should characterize everything the school does, so that the school becomes pervaded with the spirit of experiment and pupils breathe in an atmosphere of experiment. The traditional attitude of dogmatism sees school regulations promulgated once and for all, and expects pupils to comply with them all the time. The other side of the coin, traditional skepticism, deprecates planning as unnecessary, since people can live only for today, and tomorrow is unpredictable. The weakness of both positions as a source of educational thought is so obvious as to require no further comment. The experimental method requires that we have a plan, the validity of which is to be determined in experiment.

There are indications that today school people are caught up in a quest for uniformity, so that they tend to set forth prescriptions first, and then put them into practice in the school. The results of such a quest are only ostensible and superficial uniformity, not real uniformity of spirit. A good school must have a plan for experimentation; administrators and teachers ought to be caught up in the excitement of genuine experimentation that comes from testing their theories of education, modifying them when the need becomes evident, and communicating among themselves the results of their experiments. When educational practices are judged on the results of teachers' experimentation, we get a flexibility in education which is not just a superficial uniformity of procedure, but a genuine uniformity of spirit.

oday I will continue talking about the place of science in education. In the preceding lecture we discussed the influence of scientific method; today we will deal with the subject matter of science and the way it functions in the educative process.

By way of introduction we may note that for nearly three hundred years there has been a continuing argument in European education, with one group contending that the humanities, such as language, literature, history, and philosophy should be the major subjects of school instruction, and another group insisting that the subject matter of the natural sciences was more important. After the Renaissance, when people rediscovered the value of literature, history, and the arts, they wanted to preserve them, and so made them the major subjects of education; ever since they have opposed the invasion of the natural sciences into the curriculum. We can still find examples of this contention today.

In this perennial argument both sides have set forth their advocacies and have mustered arguments to justify them. Those who favored making the humanities the major studies of education argued that such subjects as language, history, literature, and philosophy deal with things which concern man, and therefore called them humanistic studies or the humanities. They viewed such mundane things as chemicals, air, force, matter, insects, and plants as less relevant to man's spiritual concerns, and as being therefore of inferior importance. They put a higher value on language and literature because these were concerned with, and reflected, human affairs. They attributed aesthetic value to the humanities, because they could cultivate noble attitudes, good behavior, proper manners and bearing, while such results could not be expected to eventuate from the study of force, matter, space, animal life, or other content of the natural sciences.

They went on to argue that the highest human ideals and hopes are embodied in literature, which is thus a means to moral instruction and offers ancient wisdom that can inspire men to undertake great tasks. The same thing is true of history, they said; it records events which should stimulate men to aspire to higher things in life. In their view, science was concerned with things inferior to man—with insects, lower animals, plants, minerals, crystals, atoms, molecules—which were not so greatly to be valued as were the human concerns with which literature and history deal.

Those who favored humanistic studies did grudgingly grant a certain utilitarian value to the natural sciences, admitting that science might be useful in the enhancement of material enjoyment, or in the production of food, clothing, housing, and transportation. But these concerns they rated as inferior to the spiritual life of man; for if science did have anything whatever to do with man's spiritual life, it was limited to the training of the mind. One example was mathematics, which was valued for its disciplinary function. But even granting this, they insisted that the sciences could not be compared to the humanistic studies which could enrich the moral and spiritual life of man.

Those who argued the superiority of naturalism over humanism claimed that science led to the discovery of truth which was real and practical, not mere speculation. Knowledge of nature was the highest purpose of man, they insisted, because it made the practical truths of reality accessible to man. They often deprecated the humanities as being not dependable because they were man-made, artificial, contrived, and speculative in nature. Consequently, they concluded, the scientific disciplines were of greater moral worth than were humanistic studies. Moreover, they observed that literary education too often concentrated on a superficial, formal kind of training, with the result's being pure formalism devoid of significant content. Originally, language was a system of symbols representing facts, but literary education was often diverted from its original purpose to such an extent that people became preoccupied with the symbols apart from the meanings which the symbols were supposed to designate. In this respect, the naturalists argued, instruction in science could rescue education from empty formalism. Further, they argued that there were no dependable standards for teaching literature, and that therefore, while literature might teach virtue, it could also teach vice. This was not the case with science; science had publicly recognized standards which admitted of no contradiction. Those in this camp made a strong case for the superiority of science over literature as the appropriate subject matter for education.

I have mentioned this perennial quarrel in history not for the purpose of taking sides with one party or the other, but rather to set the stage for our consideration of a problem in philosophy, namely, what is the relationship between man and nature? Both sides in this quarrel fell into identical error; both separated man from nature; both made the one independent of the other. A major problem in the philosophy of education is that of establishing the fact that man is not separated from nature; that man and nature are not separate and opposing forces, but on the contrary, that each is dependent on and connected with the other.

If man could live divorced from nature, then the superiority of humanistic studies would have to be granted. But in actual fact, man cannot live without nature. Nature is the medium in which man lives, the stage on which he acts. How could man be separated from nature when his whole existence is carried on in the medium of nature? The common mistake made by both sides involved in the quarrel was to assume that man could be separated from nature, and nature from man.

Look at this coin: it remains the same whether I lay it on the table or put it in my pocket, because the coin is not dependent for its existence upon its environment. But the relationship between man and his environment is not the same as that between the coin and its environment. The relationship between man and nature is more nearly comparable to the relationship between a plant and the soil in which it grows. The growth of the plant is a function of the soil in which it grows, and also of sunlight and water. By the same token, man's past and future are closely related to nature.

Nature provides man with at least three things: first, the materials without which he can not live—his food, water, and air; second, the instrumentalities which are indispensable to his living, such as coal, iron, and other materials from which he fabricates his tools; and third, energy —light, heat, electricity. Even man's muscular energy is supplied by nature. Thus we see that it is impossible even to imagine what man would be like if he could be separated from nature. Moral and spiritual values are important, but they are unthinkable without the foundation of materials, tools, and energy. The development of man's moral and spiritual values would be impossible if he were to be separated from nature.

True, we do have instances in which men have been cultivated to a state of greatness by a literary education, but this is exceptional and accidental, and not by any means a common phenomenon. The few great men cultivated by a literary education may claim to devote themselves to the welfare of mankind, even to be representative of all men; but in most cases they are from the aristocratic class. As a matter of fact—and this is true virtually all over the world—a literary education is for the most part a prerogative of the aristocracy, of those who have leisure. The majority of the common people simply aren't interested in noble, inspiring, humanistic studies, and will have little to do with them; as a consequence, the few who have the privilege of education tend in one way or another to oppress those who do not enjoy such a privilege. Of course, there is also the danger of overemphasis on education in science, but yet there is the redeeming feature that even when it is overemphasized it does enable people to make their livings more effectively. In this it is more democratic than a preponderantly literary education.

Education in science, however, is profitless when it is separated from human concerns. It is strong when it connects with and reflects human concerns, and when its function is to enable men to control their materials, their tools, and their supply of energy. Advocates of education in science sometimes go to the extreme of regarding all education in science as training for professional scientists; and, of course, when they do this, they make education in science as irrelevant to the needs and interests of the common man as is education which is exclusively classical and literary. They end up by teaching terminology, and a miscellaneous collection of facts which have little bearing on actual human affairs. When they do this they are making the same mistake that the classical humanists made —trying to have education take place apart from the natural environment of man.

The cultivation of expert scientists is an important task of education, since without such specialists the further development of science would not be possible. But the subject matter of science cannot be taught in schools from the elementary to the upper levels in the same way in which the outcome of scientific endeavor and the sophisticated techniques of scientific investigation are taught to graduate students. In schools, both education in science and the teaching of humanistic studies must be connected with nature and related to daily human affairs. The quarrel between the two camps disappears when men are closely connected with nature. But if education in science takes place apart from the everyday concerns of human life, the most that it can achieve is memorization of terminology and acquisition of a smattering of unrelated information.

So much by way of introduction—now let us talk about practical applications to education. If the teaching of science in school is not to become empty of significant content, it must begin with the practical problems of human affairs, and end in practical application to human affairs. We are saying that both the starting point and the termination of science teaching are in human affairs. Unfortunately however, the traditional way of teaching science in the West has become fixed in a mold that is almost the exact opposite of what we are saying. Two methods of teaching science dominate the Western scene, and neither of them takes account of the principles we have just set forth.

The first method is that of teaching the natural sciences as separate subjects. Zoology, botany, mineralogy, chemistry, and physics are separately taught—separated not only from each other, but also from human concerns and human life. They are separated from each other just as the rooms of a house are (and it often appears that the teachers are determined to keep the doors between the rooms locked)—a division which makes communication all but impossible. But when we get right down to it, the aspects of our natural environment cannot be cut off from each other. Let us look at a plant, for example. It is true that a plant is the subject matter of botany, but it is equally true that it absorbs water and fertilizer from the soil—and these are the subject matters of chemistry, physics, and geology; the connection can even be extended to astronomy and meteorology. Since the phases of the natural environment are so closely interrelated, it should be natural that the teaching of natural sciences must take these interconnections into account. Ideally, the teaching of science should start with those human affairs in which the pupils are already interested, and should reveal factual connections between phases of the natural environment to the learners.

The second method which prevails in the West is to drill the students on the results which scientists have achieved in their investigations. Actually this method of teaching science is identical with the methods of teaching literary subjects that science educators so deplore. Sterile teaching is sterile teaching, no matter what the subject matter; and just as formal instruction in the humanities results in pupils' learning meaningless rules and a few isolated facts, so instruction in science, when it is divorced from human concerns, can result only in memorization of bits of terminology and unrelated items of information. The mistake common to both fields is that teachers ignore the concept of historical evolution, and adopt the method of covering the ground.

We must remember that the science we now have is the combined achievement of unnumbered scientists who have labored for hundreds of years. Small results can be expected if we thrust this whole body of knowledge at students and ask them to take it at a wholesale rate, without knowing anything about the methods by which the knowledge was originally gained. And since it is impossible for students to take in wholesale the outcome of scientific endeavor that scientists have accumulated little by little over hundreds of years, the only alternative is to encourage the students to learn the procedures by which scientists have discovered scientific truths. If we could teach students the spirit and the method of scientific investigation, our education in science would be immeasurably improved.

If we were to plan our teaching of science within the framework of our daily activities, we should not encounter nearly so much difficulty as we might think. Things we might start with could include planting a tree, growing flowers, milling a small amount of rice, preparing a meal, or making clothes—all activities closely related to the living experience of children, and therefore things easy for them to understand. After this preliminary teaching, we can introduce more advanced knowledge of science, step by step. I'm sure that this method is better than our traditional practice. I wish that those who advocate the teaching of science as a major part of the curriculum would start with the daily activities of life which are within the experience of the child, and not with generalizations and abstractions that are transcendent to it.

Let us take the teaching of electricity for example. If we start out in the customary classroom procedure, having the children learn abstract definitions and formulae, even older children find the material difficult to grasp. But if we begin with an electric light, a telegraph key, a telephone, or the battery of a car, all of which are within the daily experience of the child, it will be much easier for him to understand what we are talking about than the abstract definition of electricity in his textbook will be.

Naturally, children cannot understand the subject matter of science very well when it is presented to them in the traditional manner, for after all, they are still children. But our method is different. We begin with the daily activities of the children, and then proceed to something more advanced—a continuing process without any sharp breaks. The process can be compared to the growth of a plant—first the sprouting of the seed, the growth of the roots, the gradual spreading of the branches. This method is equally applicable to the teaching of zoology, mineralogy, physics, and chemistry; the experienced teacher can start in any of these areas with the daily experience of children, and then go on to the more theoretical aspects of the subject. Under traditional methods, children are expected to learn about the outcome and products of science, regardless of their ability to understand and get meaning from what they are learning. Consequently, the purpose in such learning is all too often nothing more than that of passing an examination; once this is done children are likely to forget most of what they have learned. They may retain a smattering of the scientific terminology that they have committed to memory, though probably not much else. But the method we are advocating is one in which the teaching is so planned that children can proceed naturally from the easy to the difficult, from the simple to the complex, from the concrete to the abstract—recreating in their own experience, as it were, the development of human experience and knowledge. They grow as a tree grows, step by step, day by day, year by year. This method enables children to understand the subject matter of science, and lays down the foundation upon which they can eventually develop a systematic body of knowledge.

We have been talking about the first rule of our method of teaching, namely that we must start with the daily activities of life. The second rule is just as important: the teaching of science should also have its end in the daily activities of living. Every human being, of course, lives in an environment of nature; but we think of farmers and laborers as being closer to nature than executives and intellectuals. The methods which farmers and laborers use, for the most part, are those handed down to them by their fathers and grandfathers, and which remain unchanged from generation to generation. They know how to apply these methods to their farming or other work, but they do not know why these methods, rather than others, are used; nor do they know how to improve them. But social progress requires that there be progress in every segment of society. The end of school education is not to make scientists of the students, but rather to promote generalized application of scientific knowledge. Production of a few scientists and technologists is far less important than broadening the application of scientific knowledge. This is what we mean when we say that education in science must end, as well as begin, in the daily activities of man's living.

The method we are advocating can accelerate the development of agriculture and industry on the one hand, and promote the welfare of people through the broadened application of scientific knowledge to everyday problems on the other. The trouble with the majority of farmers and laborers is that they really do not know what they are doing, so they go about their work mechanically. The only interest they have in their work is that it enables them to make a living. Their work is drudgery; it causes them pain to carry it on. But the generalized application of scientific knowledge can infuse new interest into their work, because such application reveals the interrelationship of the tasks they perform, and makes it possible for them to see meaning in their work. There are, of course, a number of reasons for labor unrest in the West, but one of the chief causes of such unrest is the ineffectiveness of so much education in science. Because scientific knowledge has not permeated these segments of society, mining, road building, and factory production are largely mechanical activities, devoid of any interest for those who work at them. Effective and widespread education in science would, I am sure, obviate a great deal of labor unrest and thus improve the situation; for workers are much more likely to be interested in their work if they understand and see meaning in what they do. I foresee wide application in China of the method we are advocating. It goes without saying that the next fifty years will see an extremely rapid development of China's material civilization; and as she develops this material civilization, China will go this way or that, depending upon what the Chinese people do about education in science.

One way in which things could develop would be to produce a minority of experts who understand the functioning of machines and who know how to apply scientific knowledge, but to leave the vast majority of people ignorant of the application of science to the affairs of their lives. This procedure would keep control of the advantages science can bring in the hands of a small minority. It is true, of course, that all people would benefit from the application of science to the production of material goods; but the fact that control would be by a small minority would certainly conduce to inequality.

The other way would be for the Chinese people to start now to prepare themselves to cope with the situation which is going to emerge in the next fifty years. The Chinese can popularize education in science, and

260 | *A Philosophy of Education*

make scientific knowledge and scientific method available to all people, so that everybody can benefit equally from the development of science. Such a procedure would obviate marked inequality, and forestall much of the trouble which comes about when social inequalities are pronounced.

If the peoples of the West had been aware of what could have been accomplished by popularizing education in science, and by promoting the development of scientific knowledge and attitude in the majority of people, instead of withholding such knowledge from the masses and concentrating on the production of specialists, the Western world would now be in immeasurably better shape than it is.

ELEMENTARY

AND SECONDARY EDUCATION

n the early lectures in this series we showed that education must be based on the natural development of children and on their activities and abilities. We then went on to talk about the social function of education; after this we discussed the influence of the development of modern science on history, culture, and ways of thinking. In the lecture just before this one we looked into the application of scientific method to the subject matter of the school.

In the eleven earlier lectures in this series we have discussed the elements of education one by one. We said that the innate drives and interests of the child should be the basis of education; we talked about the subject matter which introduces the child into his society; and we examined the social life which furnishes the aims of education. Even though all of these are aspects of a single process, and are therefore inseparable, we had to deal with them individually and separately for the sake of clarity. But beginning with today's lecture we will bring them together again, and see how our viewpoint can be applied in the construction of an educational system which starts with elementary education and moves step by step through secondary education to higher education. As we investigate the application of our theory to the building of a school system, we will have to pay particular attention to the question of which aspects of our theory are applicable to each stage of the educational process.

In virtually every country of the world we find that there are three levels in the educational system: first, the elementary school which enrolls children; second, the high school, which enrolls adolescents who are in the transitional stage between childhood and maturity; and third, higher education, which is for adults—normally, though not invariably, young adults. What we are going to discuss today is the theories of education which should be applied to the different levels of the educational system, taking into account in each case the maturity of the educands. We will talk first, of course, about elementary education, and in doing so will take account of two important facts. The first of these is that this is normally the child's first experience with formal instruction; it comes at a time of maximum plasticity, when the child is impressionable, eager for new experiences, and capable of learning. The second is that what the child learns in elementary school, his habits, his dispositions, his attitudes toward himself, toward his fellows, and toward the process of learning, will in large degree determine his response to high school, to college, and even to his entire career.

As we formulate policy for elementary education we must keep ourselves reminded of these facts. It is true that traditionally we have looked upon elementary education as of relatively small importance, and have often been impatient with the long duration of this period. We have regarded it as something to be got over with as rapidly as possible, so that the child could really get down to business and learn something important. While it is true that the amount of actual knowledge which the child acquires during this period is relatively small, we must recognize the significance of this stage to his subsequent development. Because we have thought of the period of childhood as one of marking time, we have assumed that practically anybody who could read and write was qualified to teach in the elementary school. Nothing, of course, could be further from the truth; the period when education is the most crucial should have the ablest and best prepared teachers. Some people know this; the Roman Catholic teaching order, the Jesuits, know that by the time a child is nine his future is pretty well determined—if up to that age he has learned under the direction of skilled teachers, he will continue to learn even if some of his teachers are not very good. Many educational reformers, too—men such as Rousseau, Pestalozzi and Froebel—have emphasized the importance of the education of young children, for they were convinced that what happens when a child is young provides the basis on which all future education must be built, and that it is even a determining factor in the child's whole future development.

It seems strange that elementary education, to which the great educational reformers of history ascribe such tremendous importance, should be held of such little account by people in general. I suppose this is the case because of the common tendency to equate education with the amount of information or knowledge acquired, and because people think of children as though they were small receptacles—little ricebowls or tiny teapots—into which only a limited amount of knowledge can be poured. But as a matter of fact, and as we have already indicated, the things that happen to children during their childhood, the attitudes they develop, the behavior which becomes part of the pattern of their being, the ways in which they learn to think and to feel, the quality of relationships which they form with other people—all these are of crucial importance to their later development. Either a child's innate curiosity is cultivated and encouraged, and transmuted into a disposition to question and to experiment, or else he becomes repressed and insensitive. His natural inclination to ask questions and his love of adventure can be developed into a love of learning and the stance of courage. His pleasure in playing with other children can be made the foundation of habits of cooperation and association—or it can be suppressed so that the child grows up to be an isolated and lonely person. The amount of knowledge (as adults measure knowledge) acquired during childhood may indeed be small; but the importance of laying the foundation stones for the system of habits that will guide a life, for the better or for the worse, is incalculable. Thus, if we must make comparisons, we can say that elementary education is more critical and of greater ultimate importance, than either high school or college.

What I have just said indicates that the main purpose of elementary education is not so much the inculcation of knowledge as it is the cultivation of basic abilities, techniques, and habits which will affect the course of subsequent development. There really isn't anything new or startling about this concept; the curriculum of the elementary school in past ages suggests that educators were at least intuitively aware of it. The curriculum of the old elementary school consisted of just three subjects—reading, writing, and arithmetic—a fact which suggests that elementary education was not so much intended to convey knowledge as such as to cultivate basic practical skills and abilities, techniques, and habits.

While the old-fashioned elementary school recognized the function of subject matter in the cultivation of abilities, techniques and habits, its method was quite different from that of modern education. And, of course, different methods produce different results. Under the old method, pupils were taught to do things in one definite way, and only in that way; they did the same things in the same way day after day. This was an inflexible and largely profitless method; pupils could recite what they had committed to memory, but they could not apply what they had learned. Thus, although the old education did recognize the function of reading, writing, and arithmetic in the cultivation of habits, the habits it cultivated were isolated, mechanical, and inflexible, and with extremely limited application.

We still believe that reading, writing, and arithmetic are important for the cultivation of abilities, techniques, and habits. Our ultimate purpose, though, is far broader than the abilities and habits involved in reading, writing, and arithmetic as such; it is the cultivation of habits and abilities that have a broad application in many areas of life; of habits that are flexible and adaptable; of habits which will assist pupils in selecting worthwhile reading matter and appropriate historical material, which will enable them to distinguish the good from the meretricious, the true from the false, the valid from the spurious—in short, it is the cultivation of habits that will serve to relate subject matter to the living experience of the learner.

We have already said so much about relating subject matter to the living experience of the child that it shouldn't be necessary to say much more. But even at the risk of repeating myself, I want once more to emphasize the point that pupils must be able to apply reading, writing, and arithmetic in their daily living, not just learn each skill for its own sake, or for the pupils' amusement. Reading is more than being able to call the words; writing is more than being able to combine brush strokes to make characters. The pupil must know what the word he reads or writes means; he must see it not as an isolated entity, but as a symbol representing something in his experience. Mere computation is not arithmetic; arithmetic must represent relationships among things the child knows about and lives with. An essay is not just something in a book, or something to be studied, but a record of someone's thoughts about real experiences. School subjects must represent and extend the child's experience in living, not be just something to occupy his time and keep him busy.

We have said that the purpose of elementary education is the cultivation of basic abilities, techniques, and habits; but this should not be taken to mean that knowledge as such is irrelevant to this period of education. Knowledge is important, but it cannot be imparted directly. A child gets knowledge only by the exercise of his abilities, the utilization of his techniques, the operation of his habits. The operation of this fundamental principle can be observed when we watch a young baby. He moves his hands and feet constantly; give him a piece of paper and he tries to crumple it, and then tears it up; he touches whatever he sees, to find out whether it is smooth or rough. These are the ways by which he comes to know things. Perhaps they sound rudimentary, but they are the ways children get knowledge. The same fundamental principle operates in the lives of growing children; the cultivation of techniques and habits will enable children the more effectively to gain knowledge from the observation and manipulation of their environment. The techniques and habits are the starting points; knowledge is the result. Thus, education starts by cultivating techniques and habits, and these naturally lead to the fruits of knowledge; this is always the order, and it cannot be reversed.

In many cases the method by which we adults acquire knowledge is the same as that in which the child comes to know things. How do farmers come to know about the fertility of the soil, the use of fertilizer, or the amount of rain to expect in a given season of the year? They do not set these things out as items of knowledge to be acquired, but learn them because they are involved in the things that farmers do as they earn their living. A farmer's knowledge about farming is the natural outcome of his activities as a farmer. And a stonemason or a carpenter gets his knowledge in the same way. Did these men get knowledge about using a file or a saw or a scale by learning about them and then start using them? Or did they use them, and thus grow in knowledge about them? The same thing that happens in man's occupational life happens in the child's experience at school—the cultivation of abilities and habits naturally results in the attainment of knowledge.

Now let us look at high-school education. This level is somewhat different from elementary education; it enrolls youth who are in the transitional stage between childhood and adulthood. The emphasis in elementary education is on the cultivation of techniques and habits; but in high school the emphasis is on knowledge and understanding. The two broad divisions of knowledge which the high school seeks to develop in its students are the environment of nature, and the social environment, or human society. The high school builds on the techniques and habits developed in the elementary school, and extends the student's interest in and understanding of his natural and social environment. An adolescent is ready to participate actively in the events of both his natural and his social environment; he must gain knowledge about both in order to participate satisfyingly and effectively, and in order that he may avoid needless frustration and failure.

The knowledge which is indispensable to the youth who are going to participate in the activities of their natural and social environments can be classified under two headings: history and geography in their broadest senses. The former represents the activities of human soicety; the latter, those of the natural environment. We will talk about history and geography next week. Today we raise the important problem of high-school education which has to do with the question of the amount of material about specialized technology in agriculture and industry that should be included in the curriculum of the high school.

Since the high school stands in between the elementary school and the college, many people have looked upon it as being an institution whose chief purpose is to prepare students for higher education. But the trouble is that many of the high-school graduates—in some places most of them—do not go on to college, but enter the labor market upon their graduation from high school. If they concentrate too much on courses which are preparatory for college work, they do not learn the things they can apply to their work and to their lives when they take jobs. Colleges can enroll only a fraction of those who graduate from high school; the other students terminate their formal education with high-school graduation. This problem is particularly pronounced in Japan, where only one, or at the most two, out of every ten high-school graduates can continue on into higher education. And not only this, but when preparation is too exclusively in a specialized field of study, the result is that we have students in engineering who cannot write acceptably, and students of the arts who know nothing whatever about engineering. And these are only some of the troubles that stem from overspecialization. Consequently, I am convinced that the high school should be independent and should plan its program to meet the common needs of adolescents, so that its graduates can either take jobs or continue on into higher education.

The experience of America may be instructive in this regard. In the United States there are many college preparatory schools—schools which serve the high-school age-group and which put their exclusive emphasis upon preparation for college. Teachers in these schools are all college graduates; curricular choices and teaching methods are geared to college-entrance examinations. But there is growing dissatisfaction with this type of school; more and more people object to having all youth study only those things which are needed by the minority who will go to college.

There is a strong movement to make the four-year high school an institution which will meet the needs of all youth. An increasing number of educators contend that the high school should ignore college entrance requirements and concern itself with the actual needs of society. Some of the more progressive state universities have indicated their willingness to enroll any high-school graduate who has good grades, regardless of the pattern of courses taken in the high school. Thus we seem to be moving toward a time when higher education will adjust to secondary education, instead of the reverse, which has been the case up to now.

We have been talking about specialization in preparation for higher education, but there is also the question of specialization in preparation for work. In this respect the German system and the American system are two extremes. In Germany there are many kinds of vocational schools—agricultural schools, commercial schools, mining schools, industrial schools, engineering schools, normal schools to train elementary school teachers, schools for training law clerks, and so on. The obvious strength of the German system is its systematic and economical arrangement of an educational hierarchy. In the United States, on the other hand, there are relatively few vocational high schools as such. The typical institution is the comprehensive high school which tries to do everything, and its weakness is that there are simply too many subjects for it to deal with all of them effectively. But the danger in the German system lies in the fact that children of thirteen or fourteen years of age are ordinarily not ready to choose their occupational careers. Agriculture, industry, mining, commerce—all these are lifetime careers. When a person has prepared himself for one of these careers, it is difficult if not impossible for him to change to another one. The looseness of the American system may well be compensated for by the fact that it avoids the difficulty of forcing youth into premature choice of occupations.

There are three arguments against the German system of routing children into rigid occupational specializations as soon as they complete their elementary schooling.

1. It is unfair to youth to force them into a choice of a single career at a time when they cannot have developed independent judgment. This may well be less of a question in Germany than in America, since Germany still has a fairly well defined class system in which most people's stations in life are predetermined, and in which it is customary for a boy to follow the occupation of his father. But in a democratic society the

ideal is that each person should choose his own vocation, so that he can expect to develop his own potentialities fully. We can hardly expect a youth of thirteen or fourteen to make such a decision.

2. Youth at this age cannot make wise vocational choices. They do not know either their own capabilities or the requirements of the occupations. If a boy chooses engineering, only to find out later that he does not have the requisite abilities, or that his interests run in other directions, he can change only at a tremendous cost in time, energy, and money; and consequently, he may be doomed to a lifetime of unproductive, unsuccessful, and unsatisfying drudgery.

3. The world is undergoing change at an increasingly rapid rate. At the same time, the school curriculum is by its nature comparatively conservative. Thus there is more and more danger that a student will spend four or five years preparing himself for a job that may not even exist by the time he graduates. Rapid advances in technology make anything like full-scale preparation for an occupation during the school years more and more a matter of wishful thinking.

I have been criticizing two extremes, neither of which appears to me to be necessary or even desirable. I am sure that it should be possible for the high school to put certain emphases on certain subjects in such a way that they would not lose their general nature, and that this could be done without high-school education's forfeiting its independence. Most subject matter is susceptible to degrees of specialization in one direction or another, or in several. In some subjects, for example, practical application to agriculture might be emphasized, while in others the application to industry might be the focus of attention. Students who gain a degree of applied knowledge in a number of areas have an advantage, whether they go on to college or get jobs upon graduation. While it is true that at the time he graduates from high school a youth who has had this sort of education will not have mastered all the specialized skills required for whatever job he takes, he can learn these skills quickly and economically because he can base them in the applied knowledge he got in school.

Let us take an example: The curriculum of a village high school may put emphasis on the sorts of knowledge which are useful in the development of local agriculture because most of the students are from farm families. It may even emphasize certain aspects and special problems, such as increasing yields of common crops of the neighborhood, the use of fertilizer in relation to different types of soils, and so on. But what the students learn is still knowledge of fairly general application to many phases of agriculture. It seems to me that there really isn't a need for an agricultural school as such, because the graduates of this general high school can become farmers within a short time; and they can become good farmers with an adequate knowledge of agriculture. But their knowledge of agriculture is still independent in the sense that they can use it not only on their farms but also in their pursuit of more advanced knowledge.

We have used up all our time talking about the high school, so I can do no more today than mention higher education. The function of higher education is the cultivation of specialized abilities, not the production of specialized machines. The end of higher education is the cultivation of specialists in industry, in business, in politics, and in literature; the production of men who, by pioneering in the formulation of methods in their fields of specialization may pave the road for others to make progress in the same fields. And the man who can do this will be both a leader in his field of endeavor and a contributor to the body of knowledge about his specialization. There is no nobler goal at which higher education can aim.

I n the lecture just before this one we talked about the aims of education on the levels of the elementary school, the high school, and college. We went into detail about elementary education, and also said quite a bit about the aim of high-school teaching's being that of getting students acquainted with their natural environment and with human society. Today we will have more to say about the aims of high-school education; but before we go into that, we must look at the reasons that high-school students should learn about natural environment and human society.

There are two justifications for this emphasis, the first being that knowledge of nature and society makes youth better able to know what they are likely to do with their lives, and provides them with criteria by which they can choose their lifework. Since high-school education takes place at a time when young people are undergoing the transition into maturity, knowledge of nature and society can supply them with criteria for choosing jobs—criteria which they would never get by mere internal reflection. High-school graduates can perform more effectively as adults if they are familiar with what is included in nature and what is happening in society.

We are all familiar with the personal suffering and the social wastage which result from unsuitable vocational choices. When a person chooses a vocation that is not consonant with his abilities and his interests, on the one hand he gets no enjoyment from the work he does, and on the other, society is not likely to profit from his contribution; thus both he and his society are the losers. There is a Western proverb to the effect that you can't fit a square peg into a round hole, which has reference to a person poorly suited to his job. When a person chooses a job to which he is not suited, he usually does so because he doesn't know enough about himself and about the requirements of the job. Suppose that a person with good potential ability as an engineer is born in a remote farming village. His immediate environment does not include mills and factories, and the social activities which surround him do not coincide with his natural bent. A potential natural scientist born in the city is surrounded with modern buildings which separate him from the environment which would stimulate his natural interests. These and many other factors stand in the way of a person's getting enough knowledge of nature and society, and make it impossible for him to choose a suitable vocation, with resultant human suffering and social wastage.

The mistake that most people make in choosing a vocation is that they either just pick a job at random, or perhaps they have no real choice in the matter. And not infrequently, parents or other persons make the choice for a young man or woman. Most choices are no more than blind trials, which bring all manner of suffering and waste of human potential in their wake. Thus, it is of the utmost importance that one must have sufficient knowledge of and sound judgments about nature and society, so that he can make a wise choice, one that will give scope to his interests and abilities. When we have a piece of unidentified metal, we test its hardness by scratching it with another metal that we do know, or we heat it to determine its fusing point, or apply an acid and observe the reaction. We keep on experimenting until we find out what metal it is. What is true about metals is also true about men. We give a person a broad education so that we—and he—can observe his abilities in different fields. High-school education cultivates individual attitudes and preferences which become influential in later life. For this reason it is important that we make the scope of high-school education as broad as possible, so that students can find out how they react to different things in nature and in society, and thus be in better position to make wise vocational choices.

The discovery of one's interests is not exclusively a matter for the student; the teacher also has a responsibility in this regard. The teacher should guide students into those subject areas in which the students' interests lie. One of the serious troubles with traditional school instruction is that students are required to pass every course, regardless of their abilities and interests. But if the school is to be truly educative, the teacher should inquire into the reasons why a given student makes good progress in some subjects and does failing work in others. The matter at issue should be not so much achievement in general as identification of the student's real interests and abilities. The practical achievement which a student makes in certain courses may well determine his choice of a vocation.

The second justification for our insistence that a high-school student should know as much as possible about nature and society is the need to avoid premature overspecialization. As we have already said, high-school education is a period of transition either to higher education or to employment. If the student has a broad knowledge of nature and society, he may escape the dangers of overspecialization, which we discussed earlier in this series of lectures.

Now that we have elaborated on the reasons that high-school students should learn as much as possible about the nature which surrounds them and about the society in which they live, let us go on to discuss some of the principles which apply to secondary education. First, let us consider some of the relationships between nature and man. Unfortunately, we do not have a word which adequately expresses the fact that the world of nature is not just mountains and rivers and oceans, but is the very home of man. Since we do not have an adequately expressive term, we must press "geography" into use, remembering that we employ it in the widest possible connotation.

Ordinarily geography is taught in such a way that students are asked to memorize the location in which a given river rises, the direction in which it flows, the names of the places it passes through, the names of other rivers which flow into it, and the name of the ocean into which it finally empties. Or, students must remember where a given range of mountains is located, how long it is, the elevation of the highest peaks, and the nature of the forest cover. It is difficult to memorize such things as these; and not only difficult, but useless. If the occasion should occur when we need such information, we can look it up in a few minutes. With so many really important things to learn, why should we spend time and energy on committing mechanical facts to memory? What real difference does it make whether we memorize such trivial facts, or memorize the length of the cracks in the ceiling and the floor? Facts about rivers and mountains are useful only when they are related to men's living, as when we learn why the capital city was located where it is, or how topography determines what commodities are produced and how they are distributed.

The basic reason we must deal with nature is that man is closely related to nature and must deal with nature in order to live. History is the story of man's struggle to subject nature to his ends. In the negative sense, man has to contend with the power of nature which threatens his very life by drought, flood, typhoon, and infestation of pests; in the positive sense, man must take advantage of nature to construct his civilization, and so make constructive use of forces which might otherwise destroy life. It is only as nature is related to man's life that we can make the study of nature interesting to children. In astronomy books we are usually told that the axis of the earth is oblique, and that the degree of its obliquity contributes to the different amounts of sunlight which the north pole and the south pole receive. In the traditional method of teaching the students are asked to memorize the degree of obliquity which accounts for the existence of frigid zones and a torrid zone, and to remember which are the winter months and which the summer months in each hemisphere. I doubt that it does anybody much good to memorize these items of information. A much more profitable approach would be to relate these facts to the development of human culture. The fact that it is very cold in the Arctic region can be taken as a starting point for inquiry about the people who live in that area. Facts about the climate can be related to the fact that these people have not developed civilizations comparable to those in other regions because of the rigors with which they have to contend. Further inquiry can show that in spite of their handicaps, people in this region have the courage to contend with nature, and to overcome it by producing a culture suited to this sort of environment. The problems of getting fire in a region where there is no wood, of making clothing where there is no fiber, of catching fish when the ocean is covered with ice, provide a fascinating impetus to the study of geography, and can make students interested in more general questions about the influence of natural environment on man's life, and the influence of man's ingenuity on his natural environment.

The fact that the portions of the earth south of the Arctic Circle receive more sunlight and are therefore warmer can be related to other aspects of human culture. Students can learn that the elevation of the land, the existence of mountain ranges and their relationship to the plains, the fertility of the soil, and the amount of rainfall, may be responsible for differences in temperament, customs, and habits of people who live in various areas. For example, the geographical characteristics of Mongolia make it suitable for raising livestock; hence the development of a nomadic herdsman culture among the Mongols, and the development of their courage and love of adventure. Because the geography of the region is adapted to stock raising, the products are butter, cheese, milk, hides, and so on. The manner of life of the people has fostered a certain temperament and produced a distinctive culture, one aspect of which is the joy of combat—a characteristic that has certainly had its effects on their Chinese neighbors to the south. As a matter of fact we have many instances in Western history, as well as in Eastern, of wars having been started by northern peoples who invade their neighbors to the south, where more advanced civilizations have developed.

Where the land is fertile it is easier for people to live and make a living; it is not just accident that the great civilizations of the world have had their beginnings in fertile river valleys, where a bounteous nature made it possible for men to live in permanent cities, instead of following the flocks about in search of new pastures. It is natural for people who live near the sea to sail ships, to develop commerce, and to become adventurous. These are only a few examples which illustrate the relationship between climate and human culture. Relating nature to human culture should certainly make the study of geography easier and more interesting; it also makes it possible for students to recognize the fact that geography is not merely a matter of locating mountains and rivers and cities but is also a guiding factor in human affairs, as these occur in a context of nature.

The way of teaching geography that we are advocating is one which will help students gain insight into both nature and society, and which will help them apply what they learn in geography to their study of social and political problems. They will understand, for example, why a country such as the United Kingdom, which is composed of a few relatively small islands off the northeastern coast of Europe, has developed her commerce to such an extent that the sun never sets on the British flag; they will understand how Britain has become the world's greatest colonial power, and why her fleet is preeminent on all the oceans of the world. The student will understand that these things happened because Great Britain is surrounded by the ocean and because she possesses great natural resources—the coal, the iron, and the lime which are indispensable to the development of industry. The same problem can be approached through both history and geography, with geography covering such things as location, natural resources, climate, and other factors which influence the events that make up a nation's history. Starting here, we can go forward with our investigation even as far as social and political problems.

We must not overlook one extremely important consideration, which is that we need to give particular stress to especially important areas in our studies, rather than paying equal attention to every area. For example, we may at the beginning introduce students to a number of general ideas and concepts in geography; but before long we should concentrate on the study of an area—perhaps the high plains—devoting attention to the people, their culture, their habits, their occupations, their art, and their contributions to the development of culture in general. Investigation of this single area may continue for a number of weeks, or even for several months, until the students are thoroughly familiar with it. Then they can apply the same questions and similar methods of investigation to a seacoast region. Our point is that the students profit more from a thorough study of a few regions than they would by rapid and superficial coverage of a vast range of material, because in making a thorough study they master the techniques of investigation, learn how to ask questions, and how to interpret information to give them answers to their questions.

We have been talking about nature, which is closely related to man's life. Now we will turn to something else which has an even more direct relationship with human life: history, in its broadest sense. The traditional teaching of history is marked by two major flaws, the first of which is preoccupation with dates. Students are asked to memorize the date on which a given dynasty began, and the date on which it came to an end; or the date on which a given emperor ascended the throne and the date on which he died. Dates such as these can scarcely mean anything to the students who are asked to memorize them. A date is something by which we can indicate the temporal order of some historical development of our culture; it has no meaning at all when it is isolated. If in our study of history we fail to develop a sense of time sequence in the development of our culture, and of causal relationships among events, we have wasted our time, no matter how many dates our students have committed to memory and are able to recite.

The second flaw in the traditional approach to history is that it puts too exclusive an emphasis on politics. The date on which a given emperor ascended the throne or a given president was inaugurated is stressed; his influence on the developing culture of his country is scarcely mentioned. Wars loom large, as though they were the major part of the content of history, when as a matter of fact they are for the most part relatively unimportant in comparison with other developments. Certainly we do not deny the importance of politics, but there are many other matters which are more important than politics. The discovery of fire, the invention of the wheel, the appearance of machines, the development of industry, commerce, and religion—these are certainly far more important than the date of an emperor's death. When political history is too greatly emphasized students form perverted impressions. The exclusive emphasis on political history is a heritage from the time when education was a prerogative of aristocrats. Political history is probably quite appropriate in aristocratic education; but we are talking about education in a democracy, in which industry, commerce, agriculture, religion, and the fine arts, are at least as important as politics. In a democracy there is no justification for exclusive emphasis on politics in the teaching of history.

Industrial history, for example, is more instructive in many regards than is political history, but unfortunately many of the important facts of industrial history have not even been recorded. There is some hope, though, that the concept of evolution may enable us to reconstruct the history of industry from paleolithic times to the present. We know that in the Stone Age axes and knives were made of stone, and that after iron was discovered, people used fire to heat the iron so that they could transform cast iron into wrought iron. Centuries later someone invented the loom, which has played such an important role in the development of civilization. The discovery that silk could be got from silkworms and the invention of machines to spin and weave the silk must have played a tremendously important part in the development of Chinese culture and social organization.

The basic weakness of the traditional approach to history is that it has ignored those aspects of history which are the very foundations of our culture. The new approach will help students develop their imaginations to enable them to see history in the long perspective, and to know that human culture is not built by a few emperors or a few dynasties, but is the product of all sorts and conditions of men who pooled their efforts over the centuries.

The history of cultural and intellectual developments is as important as is the history of industry. A mistake common to most historians is that they have devoted most of their effort to extolling the fortitude of a few heroes, while they have virtually ignored thinkers, scientists, and philosophers. In Western histories the wars won by Alexander of Macedon are described in the greatest detail, while the great geometrician, Euclid, is usually not mentioned at all, though he is certainly a far more important historical figure than Alexander. And Aristotle, who was a contemporary of Alexander, is usually referred to as the tutor of Alexander the Great, despite the fact that the thought of Aristotle has dominated European thinking for a thousand years.* This is, of course, gross imbalance.

A fundamental error into which teachers of history are wont to fall is that of looking upon history as being no more than the record of the dead past. But history is alive; it is the interpretation of events the effects of which can still be observed; it is a living prelude to the present and to the future. The process of human evolution is continuous; the present state of any given nation is a combination of many elements, all of them having their origins and earlier operations in the past. By the study of a nation's past, we can foresee much of its future development in politics, culture, thought, industry, and commerce. History is not the story of heroes, but an account of social development; it provides us with knowledge of the past which contributes to the solution of social problems of the present and the future.

If someone were to ask me how I would go about arranging the history curriculum of the high school and upper elementary grades, I would suggest that before starting with history as such it would be a good idea to identify the important problems of present-day society—problems in politics, social problems, economic problems, problems in diplomacy, and others. Then explore each of these problems in its historical setting; try to determine the origin of the problem; examine past efforts to deal with the problem; find out what sort of situation caused it to become a problem. Such inquiries would throw light on the significance of the problem in its present context. This approach is more flexible than the traditional one; it makes more sense; and it certainly contributes more to the solution of present problems. We will know more about the background of our problems, and therefore understand them better, if we take the approach to history that we have been advocating.

To sum up: in teaching history or geography, we must cease treating

* At this point, Hu Shih, who was interpreting the lecture into Chinese, interjected the remark that the eminent Chinese historian, Ts'ien Se-ma, had devoted ten thousand words to a biographical account of the great general, Shiang Yu, but had dismissed the outstanding philosopher and scientist, Mo-tze, with only twenty-four words—an illustration of the fact that Eastern historians fall into the same trap as the Western ones.

each trivial event or fact separately. We must stop worrying about the height of mountains and the length of rivers, about dynasties and heroes. When we do give consideration to these things, it must be in the context of cultural development. The approach which concentrates on a few special problems or areas is much more effective educationally than the one which tries to cover everything—and which succeeds only in being superficial and meaningless. When students concentrate on the study of an identifiable problem, they will acquire a great deal of knowledge applying to the problem, and in doing so will develop the ability to think critically and to judge independently. It is only by employing this new approach that we can hope to relate history and geography to human life.

VOCATIONAL EDUCATION

For the past several years the problem of vocational education has been the subject of vigorous debate in the United States, and now I find that the people of China are keenly interested in the same problem. This fact suggests the conclusion that vocational education may be the problem of an era rather than of any particular areas of the world; in any case the people of the East are as much concerned with it as are we in the West. So today we will discuss the practical application to the problem of vocational education of the basic educational outlook propounded in this series of lectures.

As we discuss vocational education we must keep ourselves reminded of the dual aspect of vocation—working, manufacturing, producing on the one hand, and consuming the products of industry on the other—and recognize that vocational education must be concerned as much with the one as with the other. Even industry in the narrow sense involves both production and consumption, to say nothing of industry considered in its broader sense. The ability to produce and the ability to consume can both be improved by, and only by, education. Through education the cultivation of competent workers and informed consumers is possible.

Let us take a case in point: not too many years ago the typical working day for factory workers was twelve hours. Then came the ten-hour day, and now, in most industries, the working day is eight hours. Not everybody is happy about this reduction; there are some people who find themselves distressed, because after workers finish their eight-hour stint in the factories, some of them spend their time drinking, or gambling, or in other unpraiseworthy amusements; these people argue that the working classes would really be better off if they had to stay on the job for longer hours. Of course these people are wrong. When workers do engage in reprehensible activities in their leisure time, it is because they have not been educated in the wise use of leisure. It thus becomes obvious that vocational education must be as much concerned with the worthy use of leisure as with the ability to perform a job.

I introduce this thought into the discussion to draw attention to the fact that traditionally, from antiquity right down to some cases in the present, education was of two sorts, education for the rulers, and training for the ruled. The rulers were a leisured class, their role in society being one of management, while the ruled were the workers whose labors produced the material goods of life. A great deal of attention was devoted to the education of the leisured class, with their schools offering literature, history, geography, and the arts, to the end of cultivating an elite whose task was the management of affairs, and who were not expected to engage in manual labor of any sort. Even though educators often spoke of the ideal of the well-rounded man as the goal toward which their efforts were directed, the education of the leisured class wasn't well-rounded at all, but distinctly one-sided.

Since formal education was devised for the leisured class, most workers naturally did not have access to it. They had to work for a living, and if they were in a skilled trade they acquired their skills in an apprenticeship; when they had completed the apprenticeship no further training was available. But even the apprenticeship was for the relatively few in the skilled trades; the vast majority of workers went to work in the factories while they were still children, and grew up without any formal training, without even an apprenticeship. But although these workers did not have any formal education in school, they did receive vocational education in the rudimentary and restricted sense that they were drilled by their foremen in the tasks they had to perform in the factories. Thus, vocational training is not a new concept; people have always been given the basic minimum of training to enable them to do particular jobs. What we are driving at is that before we begin to discuss vocational education, we must dispense with the dichotomy between education for an elite who will manage affairs on the one hand, and training for the workers or the producers in our society on the other.

It is easy enough to discern the historical origins of this dichotomy.

Before man harnessed the power of steam and electricity, society was made up chiefly of two classes, workers who did not have leisure, and the leisured class who did not have to work. As long as this state of affairs prevailed it was both inevitable and appropriate that members of these two classes received different sorts of education. A member of the leisured class had to use his mind, the worker his muscles. Education, in the sense in which we think of it, was concerned with members of the upper classes; it was intended to cultivate their powers of thought, memory, and imagination; the development of physical skills was irrelevant; education was predominantly literary in character. At the other end of the scale, the worker used his muscle power, and the development of his intellect was irrelevant. His was a training in skills. So long as the vast majority of the populace had to labor from dawn until dusk just to produce the material necessities of life, and so long as it was necessary to have a small elite responsible for the management of affairs, nothing could be more natural than for each to be educated (or trained) for the station in life that he was to occupy.

We have referred several times to the tremendous influence which Aristotle has exerted on Western thought. More than two thousand years ago Aristotle created an educational design which is still very much alive in some quarters. He designated education for the leisured class as liberal education, or education fit for free men; and education for the working class as mechanical or servile education, or education fit for slaves. Liberal education emphasized spiritual values and the power of imagination, and employed as its subject matter literature, philosophy, rhetoric, logic, grammar, and music. On the other hand, the mechanical education for the laboring class consisted of development through work of physical capacity and some rudimentary skills. Aristotle's scheme of education, designed for ancient Greece, has been a dominant influence in Europe for more than two thousand years. The dichotomy, which was appropriate enough in Aristotle's time, and for centuries thereafter, has been rendered obsolete by the development of science and technology in the past two centuries, and by changing social conditions and modern social movements. These developments call for the abandonment of the ancient dichotomy and the integration of education, but the deep-rooted influence of Aristotle has prevented the achievement of such integration.

Even though it has been almost two centuries since the first stages of the industrial revolution, it is only within the last fifty years that we have made any significant reform in the one-sided literary education designed for the elite and have begun to give thought to the sort of vocational education appropriate to an industrial age. China may differ from Western nations in many respects, but in her education based on a class system, and in her emphasis on literary education, she is remarkably close to where we were in the West only a few decades ago.

The development of modern science has changed our view of education; in science both the mind and the body must be employed in many cases—especially in the applied sciences. In the laboratory one uses physical energy in performing experiments, and naturalists collecting specimens in the field often have to walk great distances, climb mountains, and work their way through swamps. As we have grown in our understanding and appreciation of democracy, we have gradually come to recognize the important role that labor plays, and have developed a new sense of the dignity of labor. The development of commerce has made us aware of the fact that economics is the very foundation of our social life. All these factors have combined to cause man to have a new outlook; more and more we recognize some of the mistakes embodied in our attitudes in the past, and learn to respect that which we formerly deprecated. We are finally admitting that the concept of two classes—an elite who manage, workers who produce—is an anachronism in a democratic industrial society; and this admission allows us to see vocational education in its proper perspective—not as education for the working class, but as the vocational education of a single associated society.

Vocational education is not trade education; nor is it education for any particular trade, or for that matter, for trades in general. Training for a special trade is mechanical because it does not usually require thought and learning, but only a specific group of skills. This is not what we mean by vocational education. Vocational education provides training in the scientific method, and thus enables people to appreciate the significance of the various processes utilized in industrial enterprise. Workers who have had good vocational education can make effective use of their physical energy on the one hand, and can have scientific knowledge about their work on the other. Formerly factory workers had little or no interest in their work, but a worker who knows what he is doing gets involved in his work and looks for ways in which the processes in which he is engaged can be improved. He is more effective, both as a producer and as a consumer, than the man who finds no meaning in his work and does it only to make a living.

We need to be on guard against two dangers where vocational education is concerned. First of all, we must not fall into the trap of thinking that certain people are born for certain jobs. If we entertain this misconception, we are likely to decide when a boy is still young that we will train him for a particular kind of work; then, when he grows up, it will be all but impossible for him to switch to another sort of work. This has happened millions of times in the past, of course, and it has made it impossible for countless persons to realize their potentialities. The alternative approach, and one which avoids this danger, is to give each person a broad education which can be the foundation upon which he can erect any structure of particular skills required by a given trade, and do it expeditiously and economically.

Second, we must never, under any circumstances, accept present conditions in business and industry as our standard. Social conditions change, and technological progress is so rapid that it simply does not make sense to try to prepare boys while they are in school to perform certain specified jobs. When a student who has spent his time in school preparing to do a certain job graduates, only to find that the job no longer exists, he is in a bad way. Recognizing the rapidity of change, education must look to the future for its standard. We can't afford to spend precious time imparting skills which may be obsolete by the time the student graduates. This is of particular importance in China at the present time. The task of education is to cultivate fundamental methods and techniques, and thus to make students sensitive and disposed to improve conditions. This is far more effective than a narrowly oriented vocational education.

I have been emphasizing the importance of knowledge and thought, but I have no intention of slighting the importance of work. Even in general education I believe that the use of physical strength in work is important. Science teaches us that knowledge and thought are incomplete without experiment. The English word *laboratory* comes from the word *labor*, and names the place where the scientist works. This is something worth thinking about. It reminds us that even in pure science, let alone in vocational education, work is indispensable. Mere work, in and of itself, is not knowledge, any more than literature divorced from life is knowledge. All thought and knowledge must be tested in the laboratory of experience. This is the education we have been advocating, and I repeat, it is as true of general education as it is of vocational education.

Both those who are going to be workers and those who are going to be managers need to work, and to learn through work. A man who has not had practical experience in work cannot be a good manager; those who shy away from work because they are afraid of getting their clothes dirty will never make good managers. We can observe that managers who make the greatest contributions are those who have been workers themselves, and have gained their skill and knowledge through practical experience.

We have been talking about professional workers and managers. What about the ordinary people in a democratic society? First of all, every one who makes a contribution to his society must work; those who do not work, but reap the advantage of others' work, we call drones. Second, money is not the only reward for work; there is also the sense of accomplishment, and improvement in one's competence. Work ought to be so planned that the intellect of the person who does it is always kept active. Methods should be flexible, and the work should be characterized by an intellectual component, so that the worker is always on the alert for ways in which to improve his own performance as well as to modify for the better the conditions under which he works. I do not claim that it is simple or easy to devise the kind of vocational education that will achieve these purposes, but I believe that if these are what we want, we can find ways to get them.

The problem of labor unrest is a serious one throughout the world; I'm sure you are all aware of this. The problem is not by any means solely one of hours and wages; a fundamental source of trouble is that so many workers have no interest in their work, and this is true because they have no opportunity to make use of their knowledge and their intelligence. Workers will not be satisfied with material rewards alone. This is a particularly important problem in present-day China, as she enters into a period of rapid industrial development. The intellectuals in the universities understand the importance of the problem; they must plan for social reconstruction in such a way that workers in the future will have full opportunity for intellectual development. If you can do this, China may not have to contend with the labor problems which trouble European countries and the United States. Lawyers, teachers, and other professionals are interested in their work because they have the opportunity for intellectual development. It is only the workers—and not even all of them—who have no interest in their work. The new leaders of China must direct their attention to this problem.

To conclude: both work and the development of the intellectual capacities of the individual must be stressed in vocational education. We have said enough about the social importance of both aspects in earlier lectures, so that there really isn't any need to press the matter further here. We also indicated earlier that secondary education must provide students with the opportunity and the means to test their own vocational interests and aptitudes, and that acquaintance with nature and with society are necessary to this end. We also noted that on the elementary school level we should identify the sorts of work and play which can provide a background of experience upon which vocational education can draw. Both in work and in play children must employ their thinking and their physical energy; we can even say that this is a kind of preliminary vocational training.

The four primary concerns of daily living are food, clothing, housing, and transportation—all the complexities of farming, building, industrial production, and traffic can be subsumed under one or the other of these headings. A major interest of elementary school children is in imitating adults; this interest can be utilized to provide experience with all four primary concerns. Children in school can prepare food, make clothing, weave cloth, and engage in other simple industrial production, and they are inevitably involved in traffic, so the curriculum of the school can introduce them to the basic techniques and fundamental understanding which will later be part of their vocational education. Such instruction offers opportunity to create a beginning awareness of the social implications of all these activities. This isn't vocational education in a technical sense, of course, but it is good preliminary preparation for vocational education.

There is also a vocational aspect to higher education, but we must not let this crowd out general studies. Certainly, specialists in medicine, law, and engineering play important roles in our society, but their effectiveness depends upon their having a broad general education as a context within which to understand the meaning and significance of their specialties, and to make them fully contributing members of the total society of which they are parts. One of the functions of the specialist is to interpret his specialty to his fellow citizens, and to this end we see that the enterprise of journalism involves not just reporters and interviewers, but specialists in many fields who contribute this sort of interpretation for the benefit of the general public. But specialists cannot properly interpret their own specialties and create public appreciation for them if they themselves are not broadly educated.

MORAL EDUCATION /

THE INDIVIDUAL ASPECT

We are going to devote the last two lectures in this series to moral education, which is universally recognized as the ultimate and final end of the educative process. But even though morality is universally recognized as this ultimate and final end, the realization of this goal is a problem which causes concern in every quarter. The subjects of instruction in school—reading, writing, arithmetic—are ostensibly irrelevant to moral education; in fact, in some ways our preoccupation with subject matter seems to run counter to our professed concern with morality as the end of education, since reading, writing, and arithmetic are obviously taught as a means through which pupils can seek and gain knowledge. How can we explain this paradox?

The problem becomes one of examining the relationship between knowledge and morality. If such examination were to show that there is no relationship between knowledege and morality, we should have to stop talking about morality's being the ultimate end of education, and admit frankly that the final and ultimate aim of education is the pursuit of knowledge. On the other hand, if we can discern a valid relationship between the two, the problem which becomes of concern to us is that of achieving the aim of morality through the development of knowledge.

The commonest approach by the school to the problem of moral education is the direct, frontal attack—direct instruction in morals or ethics as a discrete segment of the curriculum, separate classes in which pupils are

286

told how they should behave and are instructed in the rationale for right conduct. This approach, of course, presupposes absence of relationship between the knowledge subjects and morality, and accepts the dichotomy between knowing and doing. But the hard, cold fact is that direct instruction in morals or ethics in separate blocks of time is profitless. All the evidence points to the conclusion that even the most earnest direct and theoretical moral instruction in ethics classes, which are like history or geography classes, fails to have an appreciable effect in conduct.

In many cases knowledge can influence human conduct. For example, when we know that something is too hot or too cold, we don't touch it; we eat what we know is edible, and refrain from eating what we know is poison. In such instances knowledge does influence our conduct; but in many other cases knowledge, such as the recall of terminology in geography, seems to have no effect on behavior in relation to geography. A person must know trigonometry in order to make certain kinds of measurements; but there are many people who have memorized the formulae of trigonometry but who cannot make trigonometric measurements. A metallurgist must know chemistry; but many people who can recite the relevant chemical formulae still cannot work with metals. We could multiply indefinitely instances of knowledge that does not influence human conduct. Our present problem is one of finding a way to pursue knowledge so that it does influence our conduct.

To the list of cases in which knowledge does not affect human behavior we can add the theoretical knowledge about morals which students derive from courses in morals or ethics in school. Such courses can hardly be expected to influence behavior because their content is too abstract, too far removed from immediate, day-by-day experience. There are two possible explanations of the fact that abstract knowledge seldom influences conduct in any significant degree: one is that abstractions lack the power to inspire men to act; the second is that even when abstractions do stir up emotions and a disposition to take action, they do not provide sufficiently concrete suggestions for actual behaving.

We said a moment ago that people do not touch things that are too hot or too cold; this is because we are aware of the practical value of knowing about heat and cold, and want the knowledge so that it can direct our conduct. But knowledge that is removed from the ordinary desires and concerns of man is not likely to result in involvement, no matter how well it is learned; men may have knowledge of morality, but they do not know what sort of action this knowledge requires of them. This being the case, how can we expect knowledge as such to have a significant effect on conduct?

Still another difficulty lies in the fact that separate instruction in morals or ethics implies a differentiation of morality from other subjects of instruction; when, as a matter of fact, morals are not isolated from other subjects, but are closely related to them. Thus, when we deny this relationship by setting up separate instruction in morals, we compound the difficulty of having our teaching significantly affect the practical behavior of men.

Of course I do not mean to say that morality itself cannot be made the subject of inquiry; it can, and there are circumstances in which it should be. But when our aim is to influence behavior, the study of morality in isolation from other subjects is about the poorest method that we can adopt. And instruction which does not influence conduct does not really result in any improvement in children's moral ideas and ideals. It thus becomes obvious that the thing for us to do is to forego this sort of frontal attack on the problem of moral education, and devote our attention to teaching those subjects which are directly concerned with life. Ostensibly there are many things that have a direct relationship to human behavior, such as the cultivation of the desirable habits of concentration, perseverance, accuracy, and loyalty. These are matters of knowledge as well as moral habits of behaving. But the relationship between these habits and morality depends upon the quality of the teaching employed; good methods result in good habits, poor methods produce bad ones. For example, we may aim to produce the habit of concentration, by which we mean the cultivation of a sense of responsibility, but if the methods we employ are inappropriate we may end up with habits of pretense and slovenliness. This is just one example of the fact that good habits can be cultivated only by proper methods.

Another thing to keep in mind is that the desirable habits that are cultivated in school must be practiced not only in the presence of the teacher, but in his absence as well. Many habits are superficial and insubstantial—things which students practice when they are in school and forget about when they go home. The important point here is that, if habits are to be cultivated substantially rather than superficially, they must develop with relation to the students' reflection and desires, for only those habits which are formed on the basis of reflection and desire are indications of truly moral behavior. The intellectual habits involving reflection and desires fall into three categories: open-mindedness, intellectual honesty, and responsibility.

We can approach the first of these, open-mindedness, by considering for a moment its opposite, closed-mindedness. People have closed minds for one of three reasons—or some combination of them. The first of these is prejudice, or the state of commitment to the first idea on a subject that one encounters, the acceptance of this idea as final and absolute, and the rejection of any idea or opinion that conflicts with or runs counter to the position originally taken. The second is pride, which makes a man refuse to consider an idea or a theory which runs counter to his preconceptions. The third is selfishness, a willingness to consider or accept only those ideas which work to one's personal advantage, and to reject everything that doesn't.

Open-mindedness is the antithesis of prejudice, pride, and selfishness; it means accepting all truth even when this means that one's own ideas and preconceptions must be altered or abandoned, or even when this requires that one forego some personal advantage. At first glance it would appear that this sort of open-mindedness is a matter of knowledge; but when we think about it, we can see that it is also a matter of moral behavior, or of morality. All of us know, for example, that justice is a moral problem, but how can one be just without being open-minded? It is only when one is willing to give respectful consideration to others' opinions that he can be sure that he is being just. Generosity, too, is a moral value; but how can one be truly generous if he is prejudiced? These two examples are enough to make our case that open-mindedness is not merely a matter of knowledge, but is also a matter of morality, since one must be open-minded if he is to accord respect to others' opinions and viewpoints.

I have commented in another connection that one of the most serious shortcomings of the kind of teaching that goes on in most of our schools is that it inhibits the development of open-mindedness, and nourishes habits of prejudice and dogmatism. One of the commonest examples of this bad teaching is its requirement of conformity and uniformity, its insistence that all students must comply in the same way with fixed regulations and all must complete the same assignments. This procedure conduces to habits of dogmatism, since students are taught to regard the teacher as the final authority and to parrot his opinions, both in recitation and on examination. This is certainly no way to cultivate the habit of open-mindedness. Whether reliance is on the teacher or on uncritical acceptance of what is in the textbook, the result is almost inevitably going to be habits of dogmatism and prejudice rather than of open-mindedness.

In other words, open-mindedness means being reasonable. And what do we mean by being reasonable? One is reasonable when he decides what to do by rationally thinking about the situation, instead of being swayed by his own advantage or his own preconceptions. In traditional teaching the teacher requires students to memorize what he has said, or what is in the textbook, and the result is blind acceptance and inflexibility, behavior that is irrational rather than open-minded.

Now let us talk about the second value on our list, intellectual honesty. This is something more than the ordinary, everyday honesty with which we are all familiar and which we all recognize as a moral quality. This is the idea that we are honest if we don't tell lies, cheat, or steal. But intellectual honesty means more than this; it means recognizing the value of facts, no matter where they point or lead; it means freely admitting that you are wrong when you have made a mistake; it means giving proper credit, even to an enemy, when he has done something right. Attempting to cover up or to discount facts, surrendering to one's own prejudices and preconceptions, confusing right and wrong, twisting facts around in order to save face, concealing or denying one's faults and mistakes—all these are examples of intellectual dishonesty.

Since intellectual honesty recognizes only facts, without reference to one's advantage or disadvantage, traditional teaching procedures in many cases produce subterfuge, deceit, and double-dealing. Perhaps you wonder what I mean by double-dealing in school; I refer simply to students who sit at their desks and think about whatever pops into their heads, whether or not it has anything to do with their lessons. It is double-dealing because they pretend to be paying attention to the teacher when in actuality their minds are off woolgathering. On examination the students write only what the teacher has said, or what they have read in their textbooks, without any modification or application; and, in order to get good grades, they pretend that this is what they believe, whether it is so or not. Is it any wonder that we fail to cultivate the habit of intellectual honesty when we employ teaching procedures that virtually require the students to engage in double-dealing?

The third value on our list is responsibility. What do we mean by responsibility? Actually we mean two sorts of things: sometimes we refer to being reliable and prompt; at other times we are talking about making every effort to overcome difficulties, about being willing to accept the consequences of what we do, and about finishing whatever we undertake, without giving up or backing out. The habit of responsibility is both moral and intellectual. A little child, for example, cannot know what responsibility is; and we do not expect him to be responsible. But as the child grows, he learns to look ahead and to anticipate the possible consequences of his behavior; eventually he learns to calculate the possible consequences accurately, and then to put forth real effort to complete the job at hand. If his calculations go awry because he was misinformed or deceived about the facts of the case, there is no question of his responsibility or lack of it. Responsibility means finishing a course of action of which the consequences are foreseen, whether these consequences be advantageous or otherwise, pleasurable or painful. Because this calculation of possible consequences is an intellectual activity, responsibility is a matter of knowledge; because it is the acceptance of the obligation to carry a task through, it is also a matter of morality.

These two kinds of responsibility—being reliable, and carrying through, at whatever cost all that one undertakes after calculating the probable consequences—are not as common in the ordinary behavior of the people around us as we should like them to be. But people have to learn to be responsible, just as they learn other behavior. Students can practice this habit of being responsible while they are in school; they can be encouraged and helped to anticipate the probable consequences of what they decide to do and to see the act through to completion, once they have undertaken it, without reference to their own personal advantage or disadvantage; and as they learn, they are developing a sense of morality. School offers many opportunities for the cultivation of effective personality, and such cultivation should be its primary concern.

How does it happen that a relatively small number of men have control over the behavior and destinies of the vast majority of the people of the world? It is because the majority have not known how, or have refused, to accept responsibility. The great mass of people have failed to anticipate the consequences of their decision to turn over to a small military clique the management of the affairs of the world. This is why so many people all over the world are at the beck and call of the few who are in positions of power. It has been this same failure to accept responsibility that has delayed the development of democracy. One would suppose that nobody really wants to be controlled by others; but the fact is that most of mankind has been under the control of a small elite for tens of thousands of years. Most people think that they value freedom, but the achievement of freedom requires more effort than they are willing to put forth. They have said that they wanted freedom, but they have been unwilling to pay what it costs, and consequently they have had to forego freedom. Thus, we can say that actually they have preferred to be controlled by the few rather than to put forth the effort and make the sacrifices entailed in being free.

Our present problem is that our schools do so little to cultivate a sense of responsibility. And I have shown you that the methods and procedures which now prevail in our schools cannot be expected to cultivate habits of responsibility based on independent judgment. In a school situation in which responsibility resides solely in the teacher and the textbook, and the students are allowed only to recite or write what their teachers and textbooks tell them, there is no opportunity for them, in any realistic sense, to anticipate the consequences of freely chosen courses of behavior; there is no opportunity for practice in the exercise of independent judgment; and with no opportunity to practice, they cannot develop the ability to do these things. Harsh as it may sound, irresponsibility is the logical outcome of the kinds of experience the traditional school provides for its students; the school, by denying opportunity for practice and development of the ability to be responsible, actually teaches irresponsibility.

As I indicated a few moments ago, one aspect of responsibility is being reliable and being able to get things done promptly. The traditional school fails here, too. With the textbook as the only recognized source of knowledge, and with no opportunity or encouragement being offered to apply what is learned in meaningful situations, how can we expect that students will learn to be reliable? And if school cannot cultivate even this small facet of responsibility, it certainly isn't going to succeed in developing responsibility in the wider sense. School could do a much better job if it reduced the number and range of facts and information it asks the students to memorize, and paid more attention to doing a few things thoroughly and in such a way that students would have the opportunity and encouragement to cultivate habits of responsibility, and to learn to get things done, regardless of whatever difficulties they might encounter.

I hope that we have established the fact that mere superficial knowledge of facts cannot be expected to have any significant influence upon conduct. If we really do agree that morality is the final and ultimate end of education, then we must devise effective methods of integrating knowledge and morality, so that he who knows what is right will also do what is right. When we have done this we will have shown that we mean what we say when we set up morality as the final and ultimate end of education.

This is the very basic problem of modern education. We must decide whether school will cultivate the habits of mind which make up morality —such qualities as open-mindedness, intellectual honesty, and responsibility—or whether it will continue to concentrate on reading and showing off the achievements of its students in school exhibitions. If our choice is the former, we must recognize that knowledge is not an end in itself, but a means to the end of cultivating open-mindedness, intellectual honesty, and responsibility; that is to say, a means to the end of producing effective personalities. This is the most profoundly important problem of education.

At the beginning of this series of lectures, I noted that we would deal with education under three headings or aspects: first, the drives, the emotions, and the daily activities of the child, since these are the raw materials with which we work; second, the society into which education is to introduce the child in such a way that he can become a creatively contributing member of it; and third, the subject matter by the use of which the natural interests and drives of the child are to be transformed and developed to the end of realizing the aims of his society. All three of these aspects are equally relevant when we consider moral education, so today we will try to see them as aspects of one integrated process rather than looking at each as though it were an entity in itself.

In the lecture before this one, dealing with the individual aspects of moral education, we gave attention to three moral qualities which we said should be cultivated in each person: first, open-mindedness, which involves elimination of personal prejudices, dogmatism, and selfishness, taking account of facts, and being just in our judgments; second, intellectual honesty; and third, responsibility, or being accountable for what one does, and accepting the consequences of one's actions. We also called attention to the fact that morality, and more particularly, the moral qualities with which we dealt specifically, require cultivation on both the intellectual and the spiritual level. Today we are going to deal with the same problem, but from the standpoint of society; that is to say, we will look into the problem of identifying and integrating the moral aims and the social aims of education.

We have frequently insisted in this series of lectures that the aim of education is social; now we are saying that it is moral. But there isn't any contradiction; the moral aim of education is identical with the social aim. When we talk about the social aim we have reference to our hope that education will enable the individual to be a useful, contributing member of his society, but we can use exactly the same terms to sum up what we mean by moral education. Effective morality is a tripartite matter, involving knowledge, emotion, and ability. Without knowledge, which enables him to anticipate the consequences of his action within the framework of his society, the individual cannot effectuate his ideas into action. But knowledge itself, in the absence of supporting emotion, does not provide the dynamics of action. Knowledge, conjoined with emotion, can enhance the desire for action, and produce strong social sympathy and loyalty. But action involves effort, so the conjoined knowledge and emotion must be activated by effort if we are to do those things that we think should be done.

The practical aspect of our problem is to devise methods by which the school subjects of language, literature, arithmetic, history, geography, physics, chemistry, and so on, can be taught so that students, instead of merely memorizing them mechanically, can appreciate the social and moral significance of what they learn. Knowledge must enhance social sympathy; training must increase ability to live effectively and constructively in society. All school subjects should serve all three parts of morality—knowledge, emotion, and effort, all of which are social.

Let us look for a moment at language as one of the subjects to which school devotes a great deal of time. Language is a means of communication; human behavior is related and unified through language. It should not be difficult to get students to appreciate this social function of language, and to recognize that without language there would be no communication of behavior and opinions—that, indeed, the very existence of society itself is dependent upon the communication that language makes possible. In the past when the effective social unit was confined to a limited locality, oral communication was a sufficient means to social integration. In such comparatively simple societies there was no need for schools to teach language, for, as we all know, children learn to speak their language by imitating those around them, and do so long before they go to school. But when people began to leave their own small communities, when commerce and the business of government called them into other places, and when the need arose to communicate with people who could not be physically present within earshot, they found that oral communication was not sufficient, and the written word assumed increasing importance. One of the chief reasons it took so long to get around to planning for universal schooling is that transportation was so inadequate that local communities remained isolated from each other, and that people in these isolated local communities managed fairly well, on the whole, without having to know how to read and write.

But today, social life is less and less focused in the limited local unit; the boundaries of people's interests and involvement become broader and broader, and social life, both here and elsewhere in the world, is being transformed—a fact which makes a common written language a matter not only of importance, but of necessity. This isn't hard to understand: the very existence of a national consciousness depends upon a community of tradition and concern; upon the study by all the people, through the medium of a common language, of the history and traditions of the land; and upon a common concern with her future and with her relationships with other countries. The problem of a common written language takes on even greater importance in China when we consider what a huge country she is, when we note that she is only beginning to develop an adequate system of transportation, and when we observe the persistence of such a wide variety of dialects. The age has passed when oral communication was a sufficient condition of social integration; the problem before us is one of formulating a common written language as an essential means for building a democratic nation.

I have heard many foreigners—and quite a few Chinese, as well—say that China will never be able to build a unified republic, because the Chinese people do not feel any patriotism and do not share common life habits. But the people who say this forget one thing: a hundred years ago, virtually all the nations of the world faced the same situation that China now faces. Common habits of associated living are impossible in a country which does not have popular education; for in the absence of popular education there is no effective concept of nationhood, because the majority of the people, unable to read books or newspapers, communicate with each other only through spoken dialects. But people can be unified into a nation as soon as there is universal education, so that they can read books, newspapers, and magazines, and so that they can share in a common appreciation of their heritage, a common concern with their future, and a common understanding of the bearing on their own lives of their nation's relationships with other nations. Therefore a real republic on a stable basis must be built through the use of a common written and spoken language, since this is a *sine qua non* of associated living.

I do not know as much as I should like to know about the Chinese language, so I cannot propose a solution to the problem. But I do offer two suggestions which have both social and moral implications.

1. The first of these is that in correspondence, and in the publication of books, newspapers, and magazines, as well as in the conduct of transportation and commercial activities, the written language that is closest to the language spoken by the majority of the people should be used. As long as the written language used in these activities is far removed from the language spoken by the majority of the people, any attempt to achieve associated living is doomed to failure. I have an idea that the reason that the move to adopt *Paihua** has been so phenomenally successful in such a short time is that people have come to recognize the need for a common daily language.

2. The second suggestion has to do with the use of phonetic symbols. It has been amply demonstrated that with the use of Chinese phonetic symbols illiterate adults can be taught to read within the incredibly short time of one month. These are people who missed the opportunity of learning to read when they were young; but now, using Chinese phonetic symbols, they can learn to read Chinese more quickly than their counterparts in the West can learn to read English—a task that takes at least a year. I can imagine how much more effective these Chinese phonetic symbols must be than the extremely difficult Chinese characters. But it is not enough to teach the phonetic symbols to a few people; you must also make their use practical by using them in the publication of books, magazines, and newspapers.

All school subjects must have a social function; we have mentioned spoken and written language as examples. The purpose of learning spoken and written language is not to improve one's social status, or to show off the fact that one is educated, or to have something to boast about; it is not even just to be a means for further self-study. The main purpose of language is to promote common ideals of associated living which will obviate the provincialism that results when local communities are isolated

---

* *See* note 60 to the Introduction for discussion of *Paihua*, *kuo-yü*, and *kuo-wen*.

from each other. Correspondence and expository writing are among the most effective means of producing the community of thinking which is the basis of associated living. We can take the matter further and say that it is language which produces the common knowledge and builds the common traditions and habits which are requisite for associated living. Thus, the function of language is both emotional and intellectual. Morality is to be cultivated both directly and indirectly. Whatever education facilitates the formation of social habits, effort, and emotion is moral education.

There is no need for me to delineate the social function of each of the school subjects such as arithmetic, history, geography, physics, chemistry, and so on, or to show how each of them can be utilized as means to realize the moral aims of education. I am sure that you can deduce these things without my having to spell them out. I will sum the whole matter up in one sentence: the social and moral aim of education can be achieved only through the integration of teaching methods, the guidance program, and school administration. We can put this concept of integration to the test, and determine experimentally whether it cultivates the sort of character that is needed in society. I am confident that the results will be good if we keep our attention focused on the outcome we want, and gradually improve our procedures as we evaluate the results that occur. The most important thing for us to remember about moral education is that it takes place everywhere, and that it is not something to be sought by having separate classes in morals and ethics one or two hours a week. The moral aim of education can be realized only when the social function of all school subjects is recognized.

Moral education has deep and pervasive implications, especially when we look at it from the point of view of the philosophical problem of the relationship of the individual and society. The difference between education that is moral and that which is not lies in the fact that in the former the knowledge, the ability, and the emotion of the individual are emphasized at the same time that they are directed to the development of social sympathy. Thus the main problem of moral education is to develop individuality in such ways as will enhance the individual's social sympathy, as will dispose him to subordinate his own advantage to the interests of social welfare, and as will develop a feeling of identification with and loyalty to the society of which he is a member.

We create difficulties for ourselves when we assume that the individual and society are entities opposed the one to the other. When we make this assumption, we are likely to overemphasize either individuality or society; and either overemphasis introduces a fatal weakness into the educative process. When we overemphasize individuality we produce persons who are self-centered, or who feel superior to their fellow men, or who are selfish, or insensitive, and who have only tenuous and unsatisfactory relationships with others. On the other hand, when we overemphasize the social aspects of education, we produce individuals who have no sense of personal responsibility and who conform too readily to the demands of others, or who follow blindly the traditions that have been handed down to them. When we assume an opposition between the individual and his society, we create the necessity for different educational approaches for the one and the other, and the problem of moral education becomes all but impossible of solution.

But we need not assume such an opposition. When we look into the matter we can see that the problem of moral education is essentially the same as that of democracy. Let us see what this means. We know that there are two aspects to democracy: on the one hand each individual must have the opportunity to develop his potentialities to the fullest, regardless of the status he occupies; and on the other hand, the common will of the society must be realized. Another way of saying the same thing is that each person must develop his individuality to the end that he can be a useful member of his society and make his contribution to the realization of the aims of the society of which he is a part. The common will of the society takes precedence over individual preference; but at the same time, this society is composed of individual persons who recognize their responsibility and who are willing to subordinate their individual interests to the common good. Thus, just as the individual and society are two aspects of a single process in democracy, they are also two aspects of a single process in moral education.

How can school contribute to the solution of this problem, which is common to moral education and to the democratic process? School is not merely preparation for social life; school life *is* social life. When we regard the school as a society, then, as in the larger society, the problem of the individual in relation to his society becomes of direct and immediate concern. School can gradually develop the potentialities and the interests of the individual students, and do it in such a way that the individual, in the process of realizing his own potentialities, develops social knowledge and becomes aware of the needs of his society and of the many interrelationships between and among the different segments of that society. He learns, also, that associated living requires that at times the individual must sacrifice his own interests, or subordinate them to broader social interests, to make possible the achievement of the greater social good. Thus it is possible for school to promote the achievement of a social life which gives due regard to and makes optimum use of each person's individuality.

In both the democracy of the school and in the larger democracy outside, each person must be both a leader and a follower. The greatest handicap under which democracy operates is that there are a few leaders who cannot be followers, and a vast majority of followers who cannot be leaders. The ideal of democracy is that one is a leader when he has the ability to lead and when the occasion demands it, and a follower when it is appropriate for him to be one. A given individual may be a leader in a certain enterprise where his special abilities are relevant; and the same person should be a follower in other enterprises in which his particular abilities do not warrant his being a leader. In a real democracy everyone is a leader at times, a follower at other times.

A group, to be a group, must have a leader; but the man who can only lead and never follow, who can only command but never obey, will in time find his relationships with his fellow men so attenuated that he will ultimately lose touch with the majority of his group and eventually forfeit his eligibility for membership in the group. At the other end of the scale we find the man who has not developed any capacity for leadership. This is a problem for education: how can one develop ability to lead if he never has the opportunity to practice leadership; if, during the formative years of his youth, he must always obey his teacher, or follow his textbooks, and imitate and conform to his fellow students? Such a person not only is prevented from contributing to his society, but he, too, like the man who can lead but never follow, ultimately forfeits effective membership in his group. To forestall these difficulties the school should give every student the widest possible opportunity to practice being both leader and follower.

And the activity that offers the richest store of opportunities is discussion. The school should give major attention to perfecting the art of discussion, for it is in discussion that common purposes are evolved, and through discussion that means are selected for giving effect to these purposes. When engaged in a discussion, a person is a leader at the moment he offers a suggestion that contributes to the progress of the discussion, a follower when he accepts appreciatively the contributions of other members of his group. It is in the practice of this art that almost everyone can achieve the sense of real membership and contribute meaningfully to the solution of the problems of democracy. Education in the art of discussion is thus a fundamental aspect of moral education.

During the whole period while I have been delivering this series of sixteen lectures one thought has kept coming back to my mind. I arrived in China on the first of May; only three days later here in Peking occurred the May Fourth uprising, an incident which gave birth to the Chinese student movement. This movement has made a marked impression on me. Even though I have not said anything about it in my lectures, it has been much in my mind. The significance of the student movement lies in the fact that it is an indication of a new consciousness on the part of the people, a demonstration of their recognition that school education must be social in character, an assertion that education must serve not just the interests of a local community or a small segment of society, but that it must be dedicated to the good of the whole society and to the welfare of the state. These ideas were only incipient and vague in the earlier phases of the movement, but as it has grown they have been developed, formulated, and adopted as guiding principles. In the past several months people have become conscious of their involvement in social and national affairs—an involvement of which they earlier seemed to be almost totally unaware. I am sure that this consciousness, once aroused, will not wane; and to me this seems to be the most significant import of the student movement.

There were, to be true, certain negative aspects of the Chinese student movement, and these were so pronounced as to be obvious even to the casual observer. In the first place, the movement was accidental; it was touched off by an incident. In the second place, it was sentimental; the students were stimulated by indignation to act against the government. And in the third place, it was negative in character; the mob tried only to forestall a particular diplomatic step which the government was about to take. Everyone, including those of us who now give enthusiastic support to the movement, must admit that in the initial stages it was marked by these three negative characteristics.

Fortunately, however, by the time the movement was in full swing, it manifested a new consciousness that the aim of education is social, and that social reconstruction is a function of education. I hope that this new consciousness will continue to characterize the movement, and that it will give rise to action that will be wise; that the negative orientation of a

302 | *A Philosophy of Education*

movement born of an accident will be permanently redirected toward more fundamental concerns; that the sentimentalism will be transmuted into an abiding dedication to the rational reconstruction of society; and that the stance of opposition can be replaced by one of constructive endeavor.

I do not deprecate emotion; emotion is essential, but it must be under the control of intelligence if it is to contribute to the solution of fundamental problems. The student movement now has this characteristic of controlled emotion; it is a conscious movement which hopes, with reason, that it can help build a new China. Using emotion merely for destructive ends, or reacting irrationally and emotionally to an accidental event is obvious foolishness. We have a proverb in the West to the effect that Rome was not built in a day. The problems facing China are complex and many faceted. The popularization of a national language, and the use in education of written characters which everyone can read, will contribute much. In economics, the problems are even more complex. The planned development of natural resources must be undertaken, so that China may not fall into the errors that have plagued the West, that have allowed great discrepancies to develop between the rich and the poor, and that have made the class struggle wastefully expensive. These are tremendous tasks, but China looks to you who have the privilege of higher education to exercise the leadership that will enable her to accomplish them.*

---

* The Chinese text contains a recorder's footnote which reads, "This series of lectures by Professor Dewey was sponsored by the following four institutions and organizations: National Peking University, the Ministry of Education, the Shan-Chi Society, and the New Learning Society. At the conclusion of the last lecture in the series, Mr. Pei-chiang Liang, representing the four institutions and organizations, made an address of thanks to Professor Dewey in Chinese, and Dr. Hu Shih interpreted it into English. After the address, Professor Dewey responded: 'In order to avoid misunderstanding, I should like to add one word. In what I have said, I have had reference not only to the successful experience of the West, but in many instances what I have said has referred to our failures in the West. I have mentioned these in the hope that China will be able to avoid many of the mistakes we have made in the West, and find success where we have experienced failure. I want to see China make full use of the opportunity she now has to rebuild her educational system from the ground up. I am convinced that if she will do this, China can make achievements far greater than those we have made in the West.' "

APPENDIXES

APPENDIX A

DEWEY'S "MESSAGE TO THE CHINESE PEOPLE"
(*Original text*)

*Dr. Dewey, great American philosopher and educator, is the revered teacher of Dr. Hu Shih, our ambassador to the United States. He visited China some twenty years ago, and spoke extensively to university audiences all over the country. Dr. Dewey's theories have had considerable influence over modern Chinese education.**

Your country and my country, China and the United States, are alike in being countries that love peace and have no designs on other nations. We are alike in having been attacked without reason and without warning by a rapacious and treacherous enemy. We are alike, your country and mine, in having a common end in this war we have been forced to enter in order to preserve our independence and freedom. We both want to see a world in which nations can devote themselves to the constructive tasks of industry, education, science, and art without fear of molestation by nations that think they can build themselves up by destroying the lives and the work of the men, women, and children of other peoples. We are alike, your country and mine, in being resolved to see this fight through to the end.

In one important respect we are unlike. You have borne the burden, heat, and tragedy of the struggle much longer than we have. We are deeply indebted to you for the enduring and heroic struggle you have put up. Our task is severe but it is much easier than it would have been were it not for what you have done in holding a powerful enemy at bay through these long years

* The writer of this introductory paragraph cannot be identified.

of suffering. We are now comrades in a common fight and in defending ourselves; all our energies are pledged to your defense and your triumph.

The United Nations will win the whole war, and the United States and China will win against Japan. Of that there can be no more doubt than that the sun will rise tomorrow. Because we are a peaceful nation, we, like you, were taken at a disadvantage at the outset. I assure you that the early disaster has been a stimulus that has evoked the united energies and the unalterable resolve of the people of this country. We are in it with you and with the other peoples near you, and we shall carry on till complete victory is ours, and till you and they are forever relieved of the menace under which you have lived for so many years. For the twenty-one demands Japan made upon you a quarter of a century ago is an enduring memorial of how many years you have lived under a threat from which you shall not suffer in future years, and you are able to return to the peaceable task of building up your own culture in peaceful cooperation with other nations of goodwill.

You have assumed by your heroic struggle a new position in the family of nations. You have won the undying respect and admiration of all nations that care for freedom. As the result of the victorious outcome of the war all inequalities to which you have been subject will be completely swept away. Our gratitude to you, our respect for you, our common struggle and sacrifice in the common cause, guarantee to China an equal place in the comity of nations when the light of victory dawns. Both of our nations, even in the midst of the sufferings we undergo and the sacrifices we make, can be of good cheer as we make a reality out of our vision of a world in which we can live without constant dread, and where we have taken a step forward toward a world of friendship and goodwill. In this new world you are assured the position of spiritual leadership, of Eastern Asia to which your enduring tradition of culture as well as your present heroic struggle so richly entitle you. We cannot forget that as Japan got her technical and mechanical resources, industry, and war from Western nations, so she got her literature, her art, and all that is best in her religion from you. The coming victory will restore to China her old and proper leadership in all that makes for the development of the human spirit.

John Dewey

DEWEY'S MESSAGE TO THE CHINESE PEOPLE

(*as retranslated into English by the authors*
from the Chinese text of a propaganda leaflet distributed over
Chinese cities by the U.S. Army Air Force, 1942)

AN OPEN LETTER TO THE CHINESE PEOPLE BY DR. DEWEY

Dr. Dewey is now over eighty years old. When he taught at Columbia University, he had many students from China, among them Dr. Hu Shih, who is currently the Chinese Ambassador to the United States of America. Dr. Dewey has traveled extensively in China, where he lectured on his well-known theories of education which have exercised such a tremendous influence on modern Chinese education.

The [Chinese] Translator

China and the United States of America are two of the great nations of the world. We are both peace-loving countries. We have no intention of invading other lands; at the same time we are both determined that we shall not be invaded. Nevertheless we are now both at war against an aggressive enemy. Both your country and mine have been forced into this war. Our joint involvement in the war unites us in a common purpose—preservation of our independence and freedom.

The world which both the American people and the Chinese people desire is one in which, unhampered by aggression by any nation which seeks to exploit us, we can concentrate our efforts on the development of our industry, our economics, our education, and in which we can cultivate the sciences and the arts. China and the United States of America are united in their determination to win this war, and to have this kind of world.

There is one very important respect in which we—China and the U.S.A.—differ: you have endured a great deal more suffering in this war than has fallen to our lot. The courage and determination demonstrated by the people of China have impressed us in America. Even our present strenuous involvement in our war effort almost seems slight in comparison to the struggle you have engaged in and the sacrifice of life and property you have made in your conflict with a powerful enemy over the past several years.

Now the American people and the Chinese people are comrades-in-arms. We both fight on the front lines of the same war. We are both defending our countries; and we are both putting forth supreme effort to guarantee final victory.

The Allied Nations will prosecute the war until victory is theirs. The United States of America and China can, and will, defeat Japan. The outcome of the war is as inevitable as the orbits of the planets are immutable. We are both peace-loving peoples; neither of us seeks unwarranted advantages. It seems to me that the very sacrifices we have been called to make have brought us—and other nations as well—into unity and harmony. We must perpetuate this unity and harmony until we have won our victory, and until you have been released from the suppression and exploitation to which you have been subjected in recent years.

The twenty-one demands which Japan imposed on China 25 years ago are examples of the sort of coercion which China will no longer endure. You will resume the development of your own culture, and will cooperate in peace with other peace-loving nations.

Your courageous struggle has already earned for you a new international status. China is now, more than ever before, admired by other freedom-loving nations. The unequal treatment to which you have been subjected in the past will end when the war is won. The same goodwill and respect which we in America feel toward you, and which now unite us in a common struggle and in common sacrifice, will be extended to all peoples, and once again you will be treated equally and fairly by all nations.

Our common struggle and sacrifice have united our two great nations in their determination to bring into being a new world—a world in which there will be no ruthless coercion, but an embracing society characterized by love and friendship and sympathy. In this new world, China will exercise leadership in recreating the spiritual civilization of East Asia. Your ancient and imperishable culture, as well as your fortitude under adversity, entitle you to this leadership. Japan took its technology, its engineering, the pattern of its economic and industrial life, and its military strategy from the West. But Japan's nonmaterial civilization—its literature, its arts, its religion—came originally from China. When we have brought the war to a victorious close, China will assuredly regain its spiritual leadership and thus promote the development of culture and welfare for all of mankind.

APPENDIX B

JOHN DEWEY, ADDITIONAL LECTURES

IN CHINA, 1919–1921

An annotated table of contents of a typescript copy in the Gregg M. Sinclair Library, University of Hawaii, Honolulu, Hawaii 96822, of additional lectures delivered in China by John Dewey, retranslated into English and edited by Robert W. Clopton and Tsuin-chen Ou. These lectures have not been printed; copies may be ordered from the Reprography Department of the Thomas Hale Hamilton Library, University of Hawaii.

THE DEVELOPMENT OF DEMOCRACY IN AMERICA

This series of three lectures, delivered in Peking, June 8, 10, and 12 or 13, 1919, designed to acquaint Chinese audiences with the salient features of American democracy is an excellent example of Dewey's ability to organize and condense a great deal of material into brief compass.

1. BACKGROUND AND GENERAL CHARACTERISTICS OF AMERICAN DEMOCRACY/*page 1*
   Historical and geographic factors; political democracy; democracy of rights; social democracy; economic democracy. Immigrants to America forsook much of their European heritage, for example, social stratification. Extension of the franchise; necessity for and growth of federalism. Universal schooling under local control. American practicality activated by imaginative ideals.

2. FREEDOM, EQUALITY, INDIVIDUALISM, AND EDUCATION IN AMERICAN DEMOCRACY/*page 13*
   Liberty the individual aspect of democracy; fraternity the social. Compari-

sons with Britain and France. Equality of opportunity an ideal not yet fully realized. Democratic as distinguished from rugged individualism. American enterprise. The state as instrument of collective action. Democracy is itself educative. Democracy requires full communication; education therefore essential to democracy, and designed to serve it.

3. THE SOCIAL ASPECTS OF AMERICAN DEMOCRACY/*page 23*

Democracy emphasizes not only individual development but also associated living; social emphasis appears in education, religion, politics. Need for adequate systems of transportation and communication. A national consciousness extends the conception of the public interest. Voluntary associations serve to initiate social and political reforms. Public schools serve integration of society, promote equality, reflect the culture. Democracy never completely realized, always in process.

NEW PROBLEMS OF KNOWLEDGE/*page 34*

Increasing complexity of the world highlights the need to substitute scientific thinking for trial and error. Rigid ideological commitments may be fatal, as witness the recent Versailles conference. China's traditional concern with moral and ethical problems may contribute richly to an emerging world culture. (Delivered at the New Learning Association, Peking, August 15, 1919)

THE UNIVERSITY AND PUBLIC OPINION IN A DEMOCRACY/*page 46*

Public opinion is the ultimate power in democratic government; the function of the university is to provide the basic knowledge necessary for informed and enlightened public opinion, to be an effective agent for developing an informed public conscience and a vigorous public consciousness. (Delivered at National Peking University on the twenty-second anniversary of its founding, December 1919)

THE CONCEPT OF 'RIGHT' IN WESTERN THOUGHT/*page 50*

Right not susceptible to interference or abrogation, not related to social status, economic standing, age, sex, religion, or ethnic origin. Rights to life, to one's good name, to property, and to due process evolved in Britain, were made secure by the Glorious Revolution. Right first specified in law; then universal acquiescence is sought, so that right applies to all men. Equality before the law compensates for inequalities in natural endowment. Western political individualism based in individual political right, buttressed by law, and exercised by individual initiative. Government primarily safeguard of individual rights. Anglo-American and French emphases differ from the German. Suffrage the most important political right; the guarantee of other rights. (Delivered at Chinese University, Peking, January 20, 1920)

VOCATIONAL EDUCATION AND THE LABOR PROBLEM/*page 59*

The labor problem a heritage of the industrial revolution and a consequence of the factory system. Demand increases with increased production. Labor unrest an expression of man's upward drive. The West had no precedent for dealing with rising expectations resulting from increase of goods; China has opportunity to utilize the experience and mistakes of Europe and America to forestall labor-capital conflict. Capitalists are part of the labor problem, and must be educated along with laborers. The culture of China is characterized by enough democratic elements to give ground for hope that she can effect the transition to industrialism more creatively and effectively than the West has done. (April 30, 1920)

IMPRESSIONS OF SOUTH CHINA/*page 65*

Lack of effective transportation systems a major factor in backwardness of China; ocean shipping in hands of foreigners; railroad construction hampered. Geographical isolation leads to parochialism, inhibits intellectual interchange, results in multiplicity of mutually unintelligible dialects, retards development of education. Public school systems actually deteriorating; plans for educational reform often exist merely on paper. Excessive expenditures on military inhibit both educational and industrial development. Inauguration of Sun Yat-sen in Kwangchow on May 1. (Given before the Student Self-Government Club at an unidentified institution in Peking, June 1921)

THE SCIENTIFIC SPIRIT AND MORALITY/*page 74*

Rapid developments all over the world give rise to a range of problems. Uncritical adoption of superficial and external aspects of Western culture a grave peril. Western material progress an effect, not a cause; it rests on a foundation of scientific outlook and method. Modern science encountered opposition as it developed in Europe, as it now does in China. China should profit by experience of the West and thus escape some of the penalties which followed the development of Western science. Though first developed in the West, science is a common possession of all mankind. (Delivered at the Kwangtung Provincial Education Association, July 1921)

THE MEANING OF DEMOCRACY/*page 83*

Democracy is not abstruse; the works of philanthropy, public health, and education carried on by this club are democracy in action. Friendly and intimate association the foundation of fruitful human relationships. China's backwardness results from failure of Chinese people to learn importance of cooperation. Democracy starts with individual effort. Even a benevolent government cannot know everyone's needs; only we can know our real needs and wants. Too much help from others actually harmful, saps initiative, weakens the power to act, as witness present state of the Chinese people. (Delivered at the Fukien Shang-yu Club, July 1921)

ESSENTIALS OF DEMOCRATIC POLITICS/*page 87*

The power of privilege must not be confused with the power of right; the former disappears in a democracy, in which all men are equal and none possess rights which do not extend to all their countrymen. Britain was the first nation to develop democratic politics after centuries of struggle. The three fundamental rights are due process, the right to own and dispose of property, and freedom of thought; the latter including freedom of speech, freedom of assembly, and freedom to publish. China now has suffrage, supposedly the guarantee of these rights; but rights can be abdicated as well as abrogated. The Chinese must learn that rights are not granted, but are constantly earned by unremitting struggle. Democratic politics not fully developed, even in the West. Securing basic rights is achieved by willingness to start with tasks immediately before us. (Delivered at the Private Fukien College of Law and Administration, Spring 1921)

THE RELATIONSHIP BETWEEN DEMOCRACY AND EDUCATION

Two lectures given before the Chiang-su Educational Association, Shanghai, May 3 and 4, 1919. Recorder's Introductory Note/page 91

1. THEORETICAL CONSIDERATIONS/*page 93*

Even when, in fairly recent decades, schooling became universal, and often compulsory, what happened was that education designed to meet the needs of gentlemen was made available to the common man; an education designed for the needs of working men is still in the future. Since China is only now concerning herself with universal education, she can profit by the mistakes we have made and devise an education truly suited to the needs it is to serve. The long delay in development of Western science stems from the Greeks' exaltation of the intellect over the hand; doing something an indispensable first step in scientific investigation. Democratic education has two fundamental aims: the fullest possible development of the potentials of each individual person, and the cultivation of the disposition toward and habits of cooperation. Both require consistent and deliberate planning.

2. PRACTICAL APPLICATIONS/*page 103*

As we try to devise education for the common people we must find ways to encourage them to recognize their interest in, and to discover the significance of, their day-by-day occupations so that these become the focus of their involvement in a wider world. Democratic education concerns itself as much with profitable use of leisure as with vocations. When education fails to help men to see problems in perspective, they fall prey to superficially plausible arguments and engage in revolutions which make matters worse instead of better. Vocational education is more than imparting skills, or guiding young people into more lucrative occupations; it must enable men to recognize interrelationships and interdependence of all occupations. School subjects must be related to the practical affairs of society; must promote and enhance social morality. It may be fortunate that China delayed so long in providing universal schooling, since this delay enables her to avoid the mistakes of the West.

THE REAL MEANING OF EDUCATION IN A DEMOCRACY/*page 111*

China need not be discouraged at making a late start in developing universal education—for one thing, the idea is relatively new (having been achieved in America only about 70 years ago); for another, by studying the experience of the West, China can avoid mistakes made there, and develop better schemes more rapidly. Universal education is a governmental function, but a responsibility of the total society. Efficient organization a necessary, but not sufficient, precondition to democratic education, which is ultimately a matter of the spirit. Germany and Japan as examples. Class education inappropriate in a democracy. Democratic education requires attention to each person's strengths, weaknesses, unique qualities; aiming at the fullest development of individual potentials. Criterion of success is students' ability to make sound judgments, to think imaginatively and independently, to adjust creatively to associated living. Artificial boundaries between school subjects must be breached. The effective teacher must continually learn. The teacher's obligation is great; the scope of his opportunity is to be envied. (June 1919)

TRENDS IN CONTEMPORARY EDUCATION
Three lectures given at the Peking National Academy of Fine Arts, May 1919.

1. THE NATURAL FOUNDATIONS OF EDUCATION/*page 124*

Traditional education saw the child as passive, viewed the mind as a receptacle to be filled or as a blank tablet on which knowledge was to be inscribed. In contrast, contemporary education views the child as active, recognizes that effective learning results from the guidance of innate drives and dispositions—instincts. Instincts, which are internal and unlearned, must be brought into consonance with the external environment. The school is not only an embryonic society; it is a model for what the larger society may become. Learning, to be effective, must bring satisfaction to the learner. Contrast of language learning at home, ineffective instruction in school. Instinct has a wide range and potentially incompatible developments are possible. Conservative societies develop the inherent tendencies of fear of the new and unfamiliar, fear of criticism, of difficulty, of responsibility; progressive societies develop dispositions to like and seek out the novel, to enjoy risk, to assume leadership, to accept responsibility. Where there is no learning, there has been no teaching.

2. THE NEW ATTITUDE TOWARD KNOWLEDGE/*page 138*

Traditionally knowledge was viewed as preexistent, its acquisition an end in itself; but today knowledge is seen as an indispensable instrument for right action. The old view of knowledge caused education to try to force ready-made history, geography, and other subjects into the child's mind, and was not concerned with the usefulness of such knowledge or its effect on the child's behavior. It resulted in methods largely limited to memorization, recitation, examination. It bred an aristocracy of learning, and developed an exaggerated regard for antiquity. It isolated the academic discplines. The new view of knowledge, on the other hand, sees it as an instrument for guiding man's life and conduct, as created anew for each situation. It causes the school to identify questions and problems which children encounter in actual life situations. It seeks not only to develop individual abilities, but to guide them in directions which will benefit society. The fact that China is only now developing a system of public education should enable her to escape some of the handicaps and mistakes of the West. She should not try to copy, but study other systems and make appropriate adaptations.

3. THE SOCIALIZATION OF EDUCATION/*page 149*

In a democracy people must be able to judge independently and to think freely; it takes democratic education to produce citizens for a democracy. Innumerable activities afford opportunities to develop desired qualities; even such an apparently minor thing as planting may help develop the child's innate drives toward experimentation, adventure, trial, aesthetic response, personal involvement. The development of science comes from nurture of these dispositions. Such activity may lead the child to seek further knowledge—with advancing maturity the technical sciences of botany, chemistry, meteorology, and so on. It also carries within itself the spirit of a democratic society. The spirit of self-government inheres in everyone; it developed only in recent years because schools failed to develop the skills and insights essential to its practice. The outstanding characteristic of Western culture is not its materialism, but its effort to control natural forces. Science cannot be divorced from ethics; education must teach man to relate the two. The question which faces China is "How can we utilize Western scientific education and enjoy material progress while at the same time we avoid the ill effects of extreme materialism?"

INDUSTRIAL EDUCATION/*page 160*

Industrial education in the past has been preoccupied with short-range job efficiency. In a democracy, however, industrial education would train bus drivers and handcraftsmen who would combine the skill of their hands with the development of their minds, who would approach their work in a creative and inventive spirit. Workers are consumers as well as producers; technology will increase their leisure. Education which ignores these facts is not education for democracy. In a democracy men must be free to make their own choices, not be subservient to their superiors. A good workman understands principles and their applications. (September 1919)

STUDENT GOVERNMENT/*page 165*

Student government is a means through which pupils learn through experience what is involved in organizing a group, and in progressively taking responsibility for the conduct of their own affairs. Wise teachers will help their pupils learn how to govern themselves, recognizing that such ability is not instantaneous, but must be developed step by step. Authoritarian schools have a place in authoritarian states, but are an anachronism in a democratic state in which the end of education is cooperative, creative citizens with a sense of involvement in common enterprise. The task of bringing a democratic state into existence is a difficult one; the maintenance of democracy, once achieved, just as difficult. Much of the necessary experience in democracy must be gained in school. Even very young children can assume simple responsibilities; sensitive teachers will delegate increasing responsibilities to pupils. Through student government pupils develop skills and insight which are necessary for effective participation in the wider community. Law always a means, never an end in itself; overelaboration often impedes functioning; better results are achieved by simpler governmental design. Government of law is based on consensus; when this is recognized, government becomes the means of giving effect to the shared ideals of the people. If we can employ freedom as an instrument of responsibility, there is real hope of achieving effective self-government, and of bringing into being a truly democratic Republic of China. (July 1920)

CULTIVATION OF CHARACTER AS THE ULTIMATE AIM OF EDUCATION/*page 174*

The cultivation of character is the moral aspect of education; but treating moral education as though it were a separate phase of the curriculum is a fatal pedagogical error. Moral education takes place only when it pervades the entire school experience. Moral principles cannot be taught by precept; they can be grasped only when encountered in practice in ways which have meaning. Effective morality is developed only through cultivating a spirit of cooperation, feelings of fellowship, and awareness of involvement in associated endeavors and activities. Overemphasis on grades and examinations constitute a major impediment to the development of effective social morality. Student government can be a rich resource for moral education. Ability to judge between or among alternatives is a fascinating aspect of the human intellect; standards which are the bases for the judgments we render derive from our total experience. Experience is the process by which we learn from the mistakes we make. Knowledge cannot be imparted by one person to another; nor can morality, for knowledge is at the core of responsible morality. The importance of knowledge lies in its application; whatever one knows, that he should be able to do. (Delivered at Shan-Shi University October 10, 1919)

SCHOOL AND VILLAGE/*page 185*

The teacher's responsibility extends beyond his classroom and embraces his community. Each teacher should join forces with other members of the community who are interested in social reform and community improvement. The school must be the community center for dissemination of knowledge of sanitation; pupils must be encouraged to influence their families and their neighborhoods to take preventive measures against common diseases. School playgrounds should be recreational resources for the entire community. The teacher should be the liaison between the provincial health department and his village. He should also promote interest in wholesome recreation. Bands, choruses, and orchestras made up of pupils should stimulate formation of musical groups of adults. Teachers should harness talent for dramatics and present social drama which can be understood by villagers. School auditoriums should be utilized for public lectures, as well as for showing films and slides. Teachers should pressure provincial departments of education to establish traveling libraries. The school should be the scene of political rallies; and on election day, the polling place for the village. China has always shown great respect for education; now teachers have the opportunity to bring education back into a fruitful relationship with the society which it serves. (Delivered before the students of the Normal School at the Headquarters of the Tenth Regiment of the Infantry of the Shan-si Army, on October 12, 1919)

THE REAL MEANING OF DEMOCRATIC EDUCATION/*page 198*

In a democracy the public welfare is the objective of government; public opinion is the foundation on which political institutions are erected; and the legislative, executive, and judicial functions of government are tools for accomplishing the objective. A benevolent despot may have the well-being of his subjects at heart, but his concern is limited to physical matters; nothing he can do will liberate their characters and broaden their ideas. In a democracy, all are equal; laws are enacted by elected representatives with the welfare of the people as their objective. The school can promote the spirit of democracy and help students develop the ability to govern themselves. Liberty and responsibility are equal and complementary aspects of democracy. Only when student organizations possess direction and goals, only when they exemplify democratic methods and exhibit democratic spirit, do they afford opportunity for the students to put to the test their ability to live democratically. Even when we have an ideal, and a clear view of the objective we want to attain, we must traverse a long road of experience. Students can directly stimulate public opinion, work for the establishment of compulsory education, and show concern for the public welfare; such activities contribute to their mastery of methods and development of public spirit. Those who are now students will eventually lead the people of China in the realization of true democracy. (June 1920)

EDUCATION FOR CITIZENSHIP/*page 206*

By giving attention to matters of organization and administration of a school we can transcend mere classroom instruction and make the school into a society of which the students are citizens, and thus give primary attention to their education for citizenship. School may be an opportunity to serve an apprenticeship in citizenship. Students must unite and form the habit of working for the public good; they must be aware of their membership in the group. In classwork students must cooperate, with the abler assisting and teaching the less able. Curricula must be restated in terms which bear identifiable relationship with social reality. Practical education must direct the learner's attention to the social relevance and social value of what he is learning. (Delivered at P'u-tung High School [near Shanghai] June 1920)

STUDENT SELF-GOVERNMENT/*page 214*

Self-government expands the rights of the individual person, but it also increases his responsibility. An essential of self-government is the increasing responsibility of each man to think for himself. Some people endure autocratic regimes because they think that it would be more difficult to think for themselves than to be dictated to. Open-mindedness is essential to self-government. History shows us that full discussion by the general populace, even when many are uneducated, leads to decisions better than those reached in the unchallenged reasoning of a few wise men. No plan or decision will please everybody; but the minority must subordinate its opinions and desires to those of the majority, while retaining the right to persuade others to its point of view, and thus to become a majority. The experience you will gain from governing yourselves here in this college will prepare you to deal with the more complex problems you will encounter in your larger society. (Delivered at Peking Teachers College on the eleventh anniversary of its founding, on the inauguration of student government, October 1919)

ON THE CHINESE FINE ARTS/*page 220*

Chinese art is preeminent in at least three fields: architecture, drawing and painting, and the decorative arts, especially in fabric designs and porcelain. You who are interested in the arts must use every possible means of persuasion and influence to halt the neglect and destruction through which so many works of art have already been irretrievably lost. Teachers must assume responsibility for creating interest in and appreciation for art objects in their localities; where numbers of examples exist they should agitate for construction of museums. Teachers must also engage in continual study to cultivate their own taste, both so that they can enjoy and profit themselves, and so that they can influence the development of taste and appreciation in their students and in the general population. Contemporary fine arts must be more than a continuation of the classical; traditions must be conserved; but the Chinese people must also utilize new materials and processes, new dyes, new pigments, new media. Classic Chinese fine arts have an extrinsic as well as intrinsic value, particularly in attracting tourists. China must offer goods that are authentic and distinctive, or lose some of her rightful share in the international market. The practicality which attaches to the fine arts is secondary to their primary function, which is to speak to the human spirit. You must continue to explore the relevance of classic art to our own times as well as to its own, and you will discover in classic art a resource that can feed richly into contemporary art. (Given before the Fine Arts Club of Peking Teachers College, March 1921)

EDUCATORS AS LEADERS IN SOCIETY/*page 225*

The educator who is to be a leader in his society must have clearly defined objectives; he must be master of method appropriate to the achievement of his goals; and he must have unflagging endurance. Leaders are people who keep ahead of others and lead them along step by step. A republic has greater need for leaders than does any other form of government. The educator who aspires to leadership must acquaint his students with living knowledge; he must guide the development of his students' character; and he must accept responsibility for helping to bring about social change. China is an ancient civilization, but she possesses a fresh and vigorous culture. If the educators of China will assume the burden of leadership, today's aspirations can become tomorrow's realities. (Given at the First Normal School, Fukien, April 1921)

SELF-ACTIVITY AND SELF-GOVERNMENT
Three lectures, printed as though they constituted one./page 231

The raison d'être of self-government in school is its contribution toward the achievement of democracy in the larger society. Earlier the aim of education was to cultivate leaders for an authoritarian state; now it is to produce citizens for a democracy. Chinese students are either too radical or too conservative. China's low prestige in international affairs is, in part, a reflection of two major weaknesses in Chinese morality—untrustworthiness, and a tendency toward unbridled competition. This situation can be remedied only in the schools. Students may forget what they read; but they will never forget the experience they have in self-government activities in the school.

In many schools in China the management of practical affairs has been delegated to students. These activities are truly educational. They require cooperation and unity of purpose, two characteristics sadly lacking and sorely needed in China. The Chinese people are afraid of defeat, ashamed to fail. School games can counteract this, and help people learn that losing or winning is not the point, but that playing the game is what counts. Student government helps people combine theory with practice; and the effective union of knowledge and practice is one of China's crying needs. A third justification for student government is that it involves activities which are immediately relevant to students' participation in the larger society. Schooling was originally for the leisured class, and methods were speculative rather than practical. Some of this attitude still persists in China, as witness the opposition to the use of *Paihua* in the schools, and the argument that if everyone should learn to read, there would no longer be any advantage in being learned. Classical education encourages passivity; it might be all right for puppets, but not appropriate for children capable of spontaneity and initiative; it served very well for the time when it evolved, but it cannot meet today's needs. The only way that the problems which now beset China will ever be solved is by the spontaneous efforts of the Chinese people themselves. (Delivered at Fukien First High School, Foochow, May 1921)

THE ORGANIZATION OF EDUCATIONAL ASSOCIATIONS IN AMERICA AND THEIR INFLUENCE ON SOCIETY/*page 245*

To understand the topic for today it is necessary to sketch in a few salient facts about the organization and administration of American education. In America there is no ministry of education. Each state has its own scheme of educational administration, but none wields very much power. In America, school systems are subject to local control, and support is largely from local property taxes. Each school district has an elected board; school personnel are responsible to this board. Local support and control is traditional in America. The first educational associations sprang up spontaneously on the local level; soon these local associations federated. They are voluntary groupings of people concerned with educational matters. Such associations, on the national, state, and local level have annual meetings. There are also associations based on common interests, for mathematics teachers, for example. The aggregate membership is large, and the associations do much to influence legislation. American associations might do well to emulate Chinese educational associations, which are more effectively organized, which own their own headquarters buildings, and which show more interest than their American counterparts in educational matters which transcend national boundaries. (Delivered at the Educational Association of Fukien Province, May 1921)

THE RELATIONSHIP BETWEEN EDUCATION AND THE STATE/*page 252*

The spiritual and intellectual irrigation of education is needed to make the Chinese desert bloom, to develop the most important of her natural resources, her people. In the recent war, Russia, with a wealth of resources and a huge military establishment was the first nation to go down in defeat, because her masses were ignorant; the United States, on the other hand, with virtually no military establishment, but with an educated citizenry, was able to mobilize quickly and achieve victory. China's underdevelopment results from her people's inability to unite their interests and efforts, a weakness which will be overcome only when she has universal compulsory elementary education. The United States has had compulsory education for only about 80 years; the states did not take action until pressured into it by public opinion. The same thing must happen in China. (Delivered at the Fukien YMCA, May 1921)

EDUCATIONAL PRINCIPLES FOR TEACHING THE YOUTH/*page 258*

Children learn more out of school than in; they learn when the learning helps them get something they want; but often the lessons in school have no discernible relevance to children's wants, and they learn these only imperfectly and with difficulty. The proper subject matter of instruction is the children's own experience. To coordinate the learning which goes on in school with that which goes on at home and on the playground, we must make use of the things at hand. The teacher must be alert and resourceful, and must continually increase his own store of commonsense knowledge. (Delivered at Peking Women's Teachers College, May 1921)

EDUCATION AND INDUSTRY/*page 265*

Education and industry must undergo complementary development, industry providing the school with problems and materials for investigation, the school producing responsible talent which can promote industrial development. Science teaching must emphasize experimental observation; direct experience is the matrix from which theoretical principles are later derived. Only a few years ago foreign scientists helped China increase her silk production five-fold merely by selective breeding of silkworms. Industrial education is often thought of as training in imitative techniques; but what China needs is industrial education which cultivates creativity, which has a moral as well as a technical dimension. China should study, but not blindly imitate, the West; her educational system must be built to operate in specific conditions and to meet specific needs. (Delivered at the Foochow YMCA, May 1921)

THE RELATIONSHIP BETWEEN ELEMENTARY EDUCATION AND THE STATE/*page 272*

China must accord to elementary education a place of fundamental importance. It is the foundation upon which the entire educational system is built. It is essential to the nation's stability, and for the development of its tremendous potentials for leadership. China, one of the two largest democratic countries in the world—if she will get down to business and develop a sound educational system—may equal, or even surpass, the United States. China does have the resources to support an educational system if the Chinese people will only unite in demanding it. This they must do if China is to take her rightful place in the world. (Delivered at the Fukien YMCA, June 1921)

SPONTANEITY IN LEARNING/*page 278*

Other nations in the past have suffered, as China now suffers, from bookish education based on an untenable faculty psychology. We must foster spontaneity if education is to be effective. Spontaneity is not primarily physical or emotional, but rather mental. Traditional education discredits and inhibits spontaneity; often people who are unschooled achieve a better quality of spontaneity than does the scholar. The man who acts spontaneously has a purpose in mind, and is willing to experiment in order to effect his purpose. Glib repetition tells us nothing about students' grasp of moral principles; we can tell only by observing their actions. Theory is meaningless until it is given effect in practice. One of China's most urgent needs is that for a vastly increased number of playgrounds and trained recreational leaders who can encourage children of all ages to develop their creative ability by formulating purposes and giving them effect through games. (Delivered at the Foochow YMCA, June 1921)

THE RELATIONSHIP OF THE NATURAL AND SOCIAL ENVIRONMENTS WITH HUMAN LIFE/*page 283*

It is unreasonable to expect children to respond positively to school lessons which are foreign to the natural and social environment in which they live. Overemphasis on literary education has in the past been characteristic of Western education as it is today in China, with the same result—neglect of subject matter which calls for experimentation. One of China's greatest needs is language reform; without this there can be no universal education. Another factor which impedes educational progress is the inappropriate insistence on complete centralization of educational administration—possibly all right for Japan, but not for a nation as large as China. All subjects lend themselves to methods which begin with the child's experience—geography, history, sciences. The teacher who uses such methods must be confident, be willing to experiment with the unknown, have a thorough knowledge of local natural and social environments, and be able to teach what he really knows to his students. It is difficult, but it can be done. (Delivered at the Foochow YMCA, June 1921)

HABIT AND THINKING/*page 292*

Human behavior, like other aspects of the world, may be static or dynamic; when static, we call it habit, when dynamic, thinking. Social habit we call tradition or custom. The Chinese people thought that the revolution which overthrew the Manchu dynasty would bring social reform, but things are still pretty much as they were because the attitudes and modes of thinking of the people were not changed. New trends call for new methods of examining and judging; new goals require new methods of thinking; decisions must be made on the basis of outcome, and not be unduly influenced by tradition. Now China is in flux; she will either move forward or slide backward. The three observable reactions are obstinate devotion to tradition, blind and uncritical acceptance of new ideas merely because they are new, and the method of thinking, which analyzes problems and evaluates possible courses of action in terms of their probable outcome. The first two are fatal; only the third has any hope of success. Fundamental social reform must therefore be approached through the education of the young; education which is spontaneous and creative, which undertakes more than transmission of the cultural heritage. (Delivered at the Foochow YMCA, June 1921)

THE IMPORTANCE OF DYNAMIC MORALITY/*page 300*

The static and passive morality which is characteristic of the Chinese people may produce strong and enduring character, but it stresses obedience and filial piety; dynamic morality, on the other hand, stresses creativity, venturesomeness, willingness to assume responsibility. When China was an authoritarian state, static and passive morality was appropriate; but in a democratic state where the maintenance of social equilibrium and progress of social reconstruction are functions of individual responsibility, dynamic morality must be cultivated. The static morality of China has impeded progress. The people of China who are already educated must assume responsibility for remedying the weaknesses which beset their country. Intellectual and moral education must be supplemented by physical education. Teachers must recognize that children are individuals, each one unique, and that their education must be planned so that each realizes his own potentials. Such well-rounded education is essential to China's survival as a democratic nation. (Delivered at the Kwantung Teachers College, July 1921)

EDUCATION FOR INTERACTION/*page 309*

The education which one gains from interaction with his fellows is better preparation for citizenship than the lessons learned from teachers and books. School as it is now does not cultivate interaction in learning. China's underdevelopment is not because of population or lack of resources; it results from the absence of social unity and cooperation directed by a common purpose. The school must be a miniature nation, providing experience in associated living. Students must be meaningfully and responsibly involved in as many phases of school life as possible. If you cannot manage the small problems of the school, you cannot deal successfully with national affairs. China's most urgent problem is not the political, the economic, nor the legal one, but the moral one—the fact that the Chinese people suspect and distrust one another, and cannot cooperate. (Delivered before the Kwantung Provincial Educational Association, July 1921)

SOCIAL FACTORS

Three lectures concerning society and education, given as part of a longer series in Tsi-nan, spring 1921.

1. THE SOCIAL FACTOR IN EDUCATION/*page 317*

Educational reconstruction requires understanding of the social milieu. Three dominant trends can be discerned, not only in the West, but throughout the world. The first of these is the industrial revolution which brought drastic changes in production, distribution, and communication, and which made the world smaller. This poses three problems for education: (a) the absolute necessity that science become a major curriculum concern; (b) the need for history and geography to be taught in ways that result in reliable knowledge about one's own and other nations; and (c) development of industrial education which will increase students' understanding of industry and commerce, and their relation to society's current needs. The second trend is the growing participation of the common people in politics—a development which would not have occurred had it not been for the industrial revolution. This trend has resulted in a tremendous emphasis among all the great powers on elementary education. The ability to read and write is now a precondition to public consensus. The third trend is the increasing importance attached to individual judgment, creativity, and choice. There is danger that individualism may lead to harmful selfishness, but education can forestall this danger.

2. THE RELATIONSHIP BETWEEN SCHOOL SUBJECTS AND SOCIETY/*page 327*

In a democratic society the individual is free; but to be free, he has to think, to judge his beliefs by experimentation, by application of the scientific method. This means that schools must teach science, not as a separate subject, but as something which pervades the whole of life. Machine production increases the quantity of material goods, decreases time spent in work, raises the standard of living. Men have more time for recreation, more energy to devote to social reform. Science must be taught in ways appropriate to development of children, always beginning with experiences close at hand and familiar, and only then proceeding to laws and abstractions. If schools in silk-producing regions make the silkworm the subject matter of instruction, production would be increased and the economy benefited. By the time they graduate, students should have much practical knowledge concerning their society and its operation. Morality cannot be taught by precept; it can be taught by scientific analysis of relevant case histories. If Chinese politics is to be improved, students must be involved in actual problems. China is undergoing rapid change; the people who must deal with these changes must be educated in the methods of science, and must have first-hand experience in social and political processes.

3. THE RELATIONSHIP BETWEEN THE ORGANIZATION AND ADMINISTRATION OF THE SCHOOLS AND SOCIETY/*page 337*

If there is to be a viable Republic of China, attention which for centuries has been focused on higher education must be transmuted into determination that elementary education must become universal. Only when people can read can they become conscious of their membership in a nation and be concerned about the national welfare. An educated populace can protect itself against exploitation by self-seeking officials. Universal elementary education is a necessary condition to the expansion of higher education. But elementary education must not be conceived as preparation for middle school; nor middle school as preparation for the university. Each must make its own peculiar contribution to individual development and social consciousness. In a nation as large as China, education cannot be centralized in its organization and control; the government must provide incentives for people to establish and improve their local schools, and to make them responsive to local needs. The curriculum of China's schools is crowded with too many subjects, leaving students no time for investigation and reflection. Education must result in ability and willingness to serve one's society and one's country.

PSYCHOLOGICAL FACTORS IN EDUCATION/*page 347*

Teaching methods must be adjusted to children's individual dispositions and suited to their stage of psychological development, all to the end of developing individuality. This idea is a recent and revolutionary development in the history of education. Traditional education stands condemned on three counts. First, it regarded children as receptacles into which to pour knowledge which the teacher regarded as important. Second, it encouraged habits of dependence and acquiescence. Third, it insisted on a great deal of subject matter which had neither present nor future utility, but which was treasured because it was ornamental, valued because it was intricate and difficult and useless. When students are aware of possible relationships between school subjects and out-of-school life, they develop and maintain interest. It is necessary for teachers to study psychology, not by abstruse theorizing, but by careful observation of children as they learn. The school must direct existing impulses and tendencies, extend children's interests, help them direct their activities toward achievement of goals. Construction and play activities cultivate creative abilities and power to think. A childhood filled with directed and constructive activities, creative and spontaneous, is the best possible preparation for adult life. The learning of more mature students must have relevance to the privileges and obligations of citizenship. No teacher succeeds completely, but each one can improve his performance by continuing to learn through observation and analysis. (Delivered in Tsi-nan, spring 1921)

THE RELATIONSHIP BETWEEN SCHOOL AND SOCIETY/*page 358*

The school must work toward two objectives, simultaneously seeking to satisfy both the demands of society and the natural tendencies of the child. To perform this dual task the school must be a miniature society, a society so simplified that the child's school experience can constitute real social living. This can be done in all subjects—history, geography, the basic sciences. These must be means to the development of the child's creative and inventive power to the point where it can serve social progress. It is easier for the Chinese school to be a miniature society because the students live at the school. China's underdevelopment is not the result of her people's stupidity, nor to scarcity of material resources, but to the lack of unity of purpose among her people, their inability to organize themselves, and their unwillingness to cooperate. The Chinese people stand sorely in need of a national identity, and this can be produced only through education. The future of society does, in truth, depend on the education of the young. (Delivered in Tsi-nan, spring 1921)

FAREWELL ADDRESS/*page 366*

The most essential single element in the profession of teaching is an esprit de corps which will enable teachers to devote themselves to a common ideal, to identify themselves with a common purpose, and to make sacrifices for the sake of its realization. Members of any profession must equip themselves with the most advanced professional knowledge, and use it for the advancement of the group. Not all teachers are professional; some teach while seeking other employment, others to supplement their income. Sometimes competition precludes development of authentic professional spirit. Professionally minded teachers seek development of the entire educational enterprise as well as the improvement of their own schools. Educational associations encourage teachers to continue to study and engage in research after they have graduated from college, with each contributing his discoveries to the improvement of the entire profession. Economic goals are important, but only where there is also selfless spirit and purpose. The experience of teachers is the foundation upon which educational reform in China will be based. The rebuilding of a nation is a tremendous undertaking, but the rewards will more than match the effort, because your nation will again have become great and will stand as an equal and independent member of the family of nations. (Delivered at Peking Teachers College, June 1921)

THE HISTORY OF PHILOSOPHY

A series of nineteen lectures delivered at Nanking Teachers College, April–June 1920. These lectures give a brief but comprehensive account of the development of Greek philosophy from prehistory through Aristotle. For a reader with only a general interest these lectures constitute a sufficient coverage of the subject, one probably not equaled in similar compass elsewhere; even for the professional, they may suggest new relationships and interpretations. The fact that the translations average only a bit more than three pages per lecture (as contrasted with lengths of nine to fourteen pages for other lectures) suggests that the recorder summarized rather than taking down Dewey's every sentence. The titles of the individual lectures, furnished by the translator-editors (the lectures do not bear individual titles in the Chinese text) are sufficiently indicative of the content; hence no annotations are offered.

TYPES OF THINKING

A series of eight lectures at National Peking University; the first lecture delivered November 12, 1919. Through the device of choosing four philosophers, each of whom is associated with a major philosophical outlook or development, Dewey develops a fascinating capsule history of Western philosophic thought. The titles of individual lectures (supplied by the translator-editors) are sufficiently explicit not to call for annotation.

THREE CONTEMPORARY PHILOSOPHERS

A series of six lectures delivered in Peking, March 1920. These lectures introduced Chinese audiences to three of Dewey's most important contempories. Russell was also lecturing in China at this time.

ETHICS

A series of fifteen lectures delivered in Peking, at intervals between October 1919 and March 1920. In this series Dewey covered, in greatly simplified and abbreviated form, the material he had used in his classes for three decades. In a way, it is almost a synopsis of the great work, Ethics, on which he had collaborated with James H. Tufts, some twelve years befor these lectures. In this series, as was not true of the others, the individual lectures were titled in the Chinese text; the titles used here are literal translations.

EXPERIMENTAL LOGIC

A series of eighteen lectures delivered at Nanking Teachers College, April to June, 1920. Again in very elementary and simplified form, Dewey develops for his Chinese audiences much of the material he had worked with in Studies in Logical Theory *(1903),* How We Think *(1910), and* Essays in Experimental Logic *(1916). The titles of the individual lectures were supplied by the translator-editors.*

from society, 187; *is* social life, 299; links child and society, 198; regulations, purpose of, 220; subjects, 226, 298
School and Society, 38
schooling: formal, 185; ineffective, 195
Schools of Tomorrow, 38
science: applied, 58, 259; authority of, 168; influence on intellectual development, 245; influence on material life, 237; influence on moral life, 238; meaning of, 245; medical, 60; methods of, 54; moral influence of, 237; new concepts of, 237; not mere accumulation of knowledge, 245; and publicity, 170; pure, 58; rapid development of, 237; subject matter of, 252; teaching of, 256
scientific attitude, 54, 238
scientific disciplines, 253
scientific journals, 170
scientific laws and theories, 55
scientific methods, 54, 169, 240, 246, 282
scientists, publication the source of success of, 170
'seeming' and 'being', 243
selfishness, rational or enlightened, 104
self-seeking, 104, 107
servility, 96
Shan-Chi Society, 302
Shen Chen-sheng, 8
Shiang Yu, 277
Shih-hsueh, 37
Shu Hsin-cheng, 38
silkworms in kindergarten, 202
Sino-Japanese War, 15
social and political philosophy, 99
social chaos, 110
social conflict, 72f.
social contract theory of government, 143
social environment and school, 215–217
social equality in China, 154
social institutions, customs, and habits, 85, 99, 131
social interest, 78
social knowledge and experience, acquisition of, 221

social life: furnishes aim of education, 261; improvement of, 87, 223
social philosopher and philosophy, 55, 64
social problems and economic problems, 100
social progress, dependent on educational progress, 185
social reconstruction, 80; the basic instruments of, 213
social sciences and scientists, 54, 55
social theory, 57
socialism, 72, 154; difficulty in defining, 118; of knowledge, 178; moral and ethical, 119; national, Marx's concept of, 122; opposed by privileged classes, 178
socialists, 118
socializing students, 217
society: authoritarian, 93; caste-oriented, 96; one of three reference points of education, 191; democratic, 93; reconstruction of, depends upon the school, 213; reform movements and, 78; rights of, 115
Socrates, 46
sorcery, 60
Sources of the Science of Education, 38
sovereignty, concept of, 158
Spain, as nation-state, 157
Spencer, Herbert, 5, 103, 226
Spinoza, Baruch, 138
spiritual life, 140, 253
state: authoritarian, 91; exercise of authority by, 141; problem of, 125, 133; responsibility of, 140; traditional concept of, 233
static substance, concept of, 232
statesman, 97
status: idea of, 108; systems, 108; women's, 109
Stuarts, 143
student movement, Chinese, 301
students' real interest and abilities, identification of, 272
"*Sturm und Drang,*" 49
subservience, 96
subject matter: exaltation of, 197; ill effects of misuse of, 192; introduces child to his society, 261; significance